श्रीकालिदासविरचितं

विक्रमोर्वशीयं

VIKRAMORVAŚĪYAM

OF KĀLIDĀSA

Critically edited with Introduction, Notes,
Translation and Appendices by

C.R. DEVADHAR

MOTILAL BANARSIDASS PUBLISHERS
PRIVATE LIMITED • DELHI

Reprint: Delhi, 1977, 1979, 1982, 2002, 2006, ***2008***
Third Edition: Delhi, 1966

ISBN: 978-81-208-1922-1

MOTILAL BANARSIDASS

41 U.A. Bungalow Road, Jawahar Nagar, Delhi 110 007
8 Mahalaxmi Chamber, 22 Bhulabhai Desai Road, Mumbai 400 026
236, 9th Main III Block, Jayanagar, Bangalore 560 011
203 Royapettah High Road, Mylapore, Chennai 600 004
Sanas Plaza, 1302 Baji Rao Road, Pune 411 002
8 Camac Street, Kolkata 700 017
Ashok Rajpath, Patna 800 004
Chowk, Varanasi 221 001

Printed in India
BY JAINENDRA PRAKASH JAIN AT SHRI JAINENDRA PRESS,
A-45 NARAINA, PHASE-I, NEW DELHI 110 028
AND PUBLISHED BY NARENDRA PRAKASH JAIN FOR
MOTILAL BANARSIDASS PUBLISHERS PRIVATE LIMITED,
BUNGALOW ROAD, DELHI 110 007.

VIKRAMORVAŚĪYAM

CONTENTS

PREFACE

The text of the present edition of the Vikramorvashiya is in the main the same as that of Mr. S. P. Pandit's with but a few variations of readings, obvious corrections and the substitution of a correct orthographic representation of Prakrit words. Of the two main recensions, we have followed the Southern recension, but the peculiarites of the Northern recension are not unrepresented; for while all additional stanzas to be found in the first three acts and the fifth are given in the introduction, the fourth act is given in full in an appendix with the additional Apabhramsha passages carefully collated from Pandit's and Pishel's texts.

There is a growing tendency among sanskrit Scholars to make a literal translation their main object, despite the fact that such a translation not only loses the spirit of the original, but degenerates into a word-for-word rendering into a language which no one who has a proper sense of English, will dare to name English. We give a typical instance in illustration.

" मूर्ध्नि तेषां कृतः पादः......स्वेन कर्मणा ।

By his feat, has been placed a foot on the head of his enemies etc." There is considerable truth in the dictum that " A translation to be literary ought not to be too literal." Of course, in a book like this, high literary ambition,-creative effort-is out of question. And while care should be taken to keep as close to the original as possible, that does not warrant the kind of jargon, such as we have given above, which fails to convey either the meaning or the spirit of the original and offends most egregiously against a living language.

The notes are copious enough and give everything that is essential not only to a student reading for an

Arts course but also to a general reader. The introduction deals exhaustively with all essential questions. We have drawn upon all available editions and other sources for information in the preparation of our work aud we cannot but express our deep obligation to all these, but principally to the following among several authorities consulted:—

Wilson, Hindu Theatre, his free but graceful rendering is, in many places where it happens to be literal, followed; S. P. Pandit, the text is practically wholly derived from his edition; Sten Konow, Das Indische Drama; M. Winternitz, Geschichte der Indischen Litteratur, Band III; Pischel, Materialien Zur Kenntnis der Apabharamsa; Ryder, Shakuntala and other poems of Kalidasa.

It is with particular pleasure that we express our thanks to Prof. K. V. Abhyanakar M. A. of Gujarat College, Ahmedabad, at whose suggestion we ventured upon the publication of this edition of the play, and who has all along evinced such interest in our work. Our best thanks are due to Mr. R. P. Kothari, the manager of Messrs. C. M. Parikh & Co. for his readiness to undertake the publication on behalf of the firm and for the uniform courtesy and kindness he has shown us during its progress.

We regret we could not use diacritical marks, owing to the inability of the press to supply them, and therfore 's' does duty for स श् ष्.

Willingdon College
SANGLI.
23 May 1932

C. R. Devadhar
M. V, Patwardhan

INTRODUCTION

Kalidasa, His Date, Life and Works.

Howsoever overlaid with fantasies or encrusted with a mass of isolated events separated in time and place, a widely circulated literary tradition contains within itself a germ of historical truth and can be set aside on pain of doing serious harm to that truth. Thus it is with king Vikramaditya of Ujjain, the liberal patron of learning and arts, of whom the great poet Kalidasa was a contemporary. This tradition forms the starting point and the basis of the numerous theories regarding the age of Kalidasa. Of these two rival theories may here be stated as those deserving of consideration. According to one held by most European scholars, the Vikramaditya of the tradition is no other than the Gupta king Candragupta II who assumed the title of Vikramaditya and succeeded his father Samudragupta 375 A. D. and made Ujjain his capital. Vincent Smith in his early history of India (P. 304, foot-note) expresses the view that the earlier works of Kalidasa were composed before 413 A. D. during the regime of Candragupta and his later works were written under Kumaragupta I (413 A. D. to 455 A.D.) and that possibly his literary career extended even into the reign of Skandagupta (453 A. D. 480 A. D.).

Some are inclined to suggest from the reference to the conquest of the Huns by Raghu in his Digvijaya, that Kalidasa must have lived after the victory of Skandagupta over the Huns half a century later than the date suggested. But the evidence has no probative value. "There is nothing to indicate any reference to reality in this account of the exploits of a king of long ago; and if Kalidasa had lived in the reign of Skandagupta when the fortune of the royal house was evidently tottering to a fall, it would be difficult to understand the calm contentment with the established order which marks all his works."

The other view held by many Indian scholars puts Kalidasa in the first century before our era, and makes him a contemporary and a protege of King Vikramaditya, the founder of the Samvat Era–57 B. C. That there is nothing implausible in the assumption is clear when on the strong testimony of Patanjali's Mahabhashya it has been possible to put back the beginning of court poetry in general by a few centuries of the Christian Era. And "Epigraphy not merely confirms the evidence of the Mahabhashya that artificial poetry originated before the commencement of our era, but shows that that poetry continued to be cultivated throughout the succeeding centuries." Already in the days of Kanishka (78 A. D.) Ashvaghosha wrote his Buddhacarita in the artificial style and called it a Mahakavya.

In connexion with this writer it is interesting to observe that there is a striking resemblance between his poetry and the poetry of Kalidasa. Not only is there a close parallelism between a few isolated passages and descriptions, but between ideas and expressions fairly distributed over the poem. As Prof. R. N. Apte has observed these close resemblances warrant the conclusion that "one of the poets is using the other." It must be remembered that Ashvaghosha is a philosopher first and a poet afterwards; while Kalidasa is an original poet The probability, therefore, is that Ashvaghosha is the borrower and Kalidasa his original. Cowell's theory of Kalidasa's indebtedness to Ashvaghosha rests upon the view that Kalidasa belongs to Gupta period. The hollowness of this view, has, however, been shown by Prof. Shembavnekar in an article on 'the Date of Kalidasa' contributed to "the Journal of the University of Bombay" (Vol. I. Part VI. P. 232–246) who points out that the Gupta theory is based on the assumption that Candragupta II was the first monarch who bore the name Vikramaditya, whereas on the testimony of the Rajput Chronicles and the Kathasaritsagara the first king to bear that appellation was King Vikramaditya of the Paramara dynasty, the hero of countless legends, the ruler of Ujjayini in Kalidasa's day. It is held by many that the title 'Vikramorvashiya' is chosen by the poet in order to glorify and immortalize his patron's name. According to Kathasaritsagara the father of Vikramaditya was Mahendraditya. It is curious to note that the word Mahendra as an epithet of Indra is repeated by the poet no less than fourteen times in the play and in one place it is particularly significant to find the names of the father and son linked up: (दिष्टया महेंद्रोपकारपर्याप्तेन विक्रममहिम्ना वर्धसे भवान्।) It is possible as Prof. Shembavnekar suggests, that the play was written at the time of the intended retirement of Mahendra from active life, and the coronation of Vikrama as king (Kathasaritsagara XVIII. 59–60). The last act of the play, therefore, where prince Ayus is installed as the young king is but a poetic reflex of the actual course of events of the times

There is nothing in the arguments adduced by European scholars which is repugnant to this theory that

Kalidasa lived in the 1st century before our era at the court of King Vikrama of Ujjayini who founded the Samvat era. Prof. Keith's view that 'the conclusive evidence displayed in the work preserved to us of elaborate training in all the learning available to a Brahmin student of the Gupta era from the science of politics to astrology and the Kamasutra....everything points to his flourishing in the time of Gupta glory" is only a dogmatic assertion. With regard to the astronomical terms, such as the names of the signs of the Solar Zodiac which are supposed to be of Greek origin and on which European critics lay so much emphasis, it has already been proved by scholars like S. P. Pandit, R. N. Apte, that there is nothing to show that they were unknown to the people of India a few centuries before the Christian Era. While the occurrence of un-Paninian expressions and grammatical forms such as पातयां प्रथममास; प्रभ्रंशयां यो नहुषं चकार, दाश्वान्. कामयान, in Kalidasa can be satisfactorily explained only on the assumption that he belonged to a time when the Paninian grammar had not obtained a complete vogue.

The foregoing discussion is enough to justify the truth and the the vitality of the age-long tradition that the poet belongs to the days of the glorious King Vikramaditya of Ujjayini–the founder of the Samvat era (57 B. C.)

With regard to the external details of the poet's life, we know next to nothing; the numerous legends told about him are but empty figments, and only bear testimony to the greatness and extreme popularity of the poet in the land of his birth. "The truly great stand upon no middle ledge; they are either famous or unknown."

But Kalidasa is both famous and unknown. We look in vain in his works for knowledge about the facts of his life. The impression that we gather about him from them is that of a man, deeply learned in literature and philosophy and other traditional lore of the times, and more deeply learned in the book of nature. Ujjayini was the city of his heart and he is delighted to sing of her glories and of the romantic loves of her maidens. He sings of this Gem of Avanti, rich with the storied legends of Udayana and the consecrated past, this radiant bit of heaven, with her flower-sweet balconies, and black-eyed maidens; of the dread shrine of Shiva, Mahakala, of her rich gardens and lotus-lakes that send their fugitive sweetness through the dark; and his fondness for the city is so evident in his loving and lingering description of her varied charms that one might legitimately conclude that the poet must have spent at least a part of his life in this city. Further he was a widely-travelled man and was a keen observer of nature—not only of her sublime and wild aspects, but also of her mild and minute manifestations. "Rarely has a man walked our earth who observed the phenomena of living nature as accurately as he, though his accuracy was of course that of a poet, not that of the scientist."

He was essentially an eclectic in his religion and philosophy: for if the Kumarasambhava is distinctly Shivaistic, the Raghuvamsa is no less distinctly Vishnuite in tendency; while Vedantic monism or Samkhya dualism, or the active devotion of Yoga equally engaged his regard; so that, as Ryder says, "Kalidasa moved among the jarring sects with sympathy for all, fanaticism for none." A pleasing trait of his personality is his modesty which Coleridge recognises as a sure sign of great genius. Above all, his writings are coloured with the suffusion of a charmed equanimity and give the impression of a man who walked the earth with a serene and god-like tread, with mind and senses keenly responsive to every form of beauty, and accepting life and the good things it offers in a spirit of sublime acquiescence.

Of his seven works which have come down to us, three are dramas, two epics, one a lyrical piece and one a descriptive poem. It is possible to fix the chronology of his dramas, the Malavikagnimitra being the composition of his salad days, the Vikramorvashiya coming next, and the Shakuntala composed when he was in the prime of his manhood. There can be no reasonable doubt that the Rtusamhara was a juvenile piece; while with regard to the two epics Raghuvamsha and Kumarasambhava, opinions differ, for whereas the introductory stanzas of the Raghu suggest that it was written before Kumara, the abrupt and undignified ending of it suggests that the hand that wrote it was cold before it was finished; but then we have to remember the tradition that in its original form it consisted of twenty-five cantos, of which only nineteen have come down to us. In general it would be only reasonable to assume that the great works on which his fame chiefly rests–the Shakuntala, the Raghuvamsha, the Kumarasambhava and the Meghaduta—belong to a period of his life when his genius had attained to the fullest maturity of its powers.

Vikramorvashiya: its Sources.

The romance of Pururavas and Urvashi, which Kalidasa has dramatized in the Vikramorvashiya, is one of the most ancient and popular stories that we have in the literature of India. For we find it recorded in the form of a dialogue in the Rigveda, which is regarded as the oldest literary monument of Indo-European civilization. And although, in the course of its transmigration of thousands of years in Indian literature, it has undergone several changes in single points of detail, it has remained almost the same in all its essential features—so profound has been its hold upon the Indian mind.

Let us here consider the oldest and the most poetic form of this beautiful romance—the one that has been preserved to us in the Rigveda (X. 95).

King Pururavas, a mortal, and the Apsaras Urvashi find themselves irresistibly in mutual love. Urvashi consents to live with Pururarvas on earth as his wife, but only on the definite agreement, that she should never behold him divested of his apparel. This agreement (समय) is the central point of the whole story and at the same time the rock on which the matrimony must sometime be wrecked. After the loving couple have lived together for a period of four years, giving themselves up entirely to the enjoyment of conjugal happiness, the Gandharvas, who have a more ancient claim upon Urvashi and who do not wish her to stay away from themselves any more, come one night to the residence of Pururavas and produce a sound as of the bleating of lambs. Urvashi fancies that her pet lambs are being stolen away by some one and calls upon Pururavas to rescue them. As soon as Pururavas jumps out of his bed in order to pursue the supposed thief, the Gandharvas send forth a flash of lightning, and in its light Urvashi sees Pururavas stark naked. The compact is broken and Urvashi ruthlessly abandons Pururavas, whom she has loved loyally and sincerely so long, and vanishes forthwith.

Full of despair and frantic with grief, Pururavas wanders about here and there in search of her, until at last he meets her accidently. He implores her to come back to him, dwelling, in plaintive numbers, upon the memories of past happiness in her company and pleading with her by her duty as a wife and even by a threat of suicide. She, however, cold and relentless, rejects his entreaties, saying that she is hard to catch like the wind (दुरापना वात इवाहमस्मि । St. 2). With scant ceremony she asks him to go back to his house as it is impossible that he should have her again (परेहि अस्तंनहि मूरमाप: । St. 13), and advises him against laying violent hands upon his life for the sake of a woman. "For" says she, "with woman there can be no lasting friendship: hearts of wolves are the hearts of women!" Though at last she yields to compassion and comforts him with the hopes of a distant future happiness, the story remains, as indeed it is bound to, a tragedy--the tragedy of love between human and divine.

We find this very romance of Pururavas and Urvashi narrated with more or less variation in details, in the following and several other texts:

(i) शतपथब्राह्मण, 11, 5.

(ii) वेदार्थदीपिका, (a commentary on the सर्वानुक्रमणी of the Rigveda by षड्गुरुशिष्य), introductory remarks on Rigiveda X. 95.

(iii) हरिवंश, X. 26 ff.

(iv) विष्णुपुराण, IV. 6.

(v) भागवत, IX 14.

(vi) मत्स्यपुराण, XXIV.

Some of these texts (*e. g.* वेदार्थदीपिका, विष्णुपुराण, भागवत) give us, as it were the previous history of the romance. Mitra and Varuna had received consecration for a certain sacrifice and were consequently bound to observe *Brahmacarya.* But then the Apsaras Urvashi appeared there on the scene, and was rather guilty of a human weakness towards the two Gods. Enraged there at, they cursed and banished her from heaven to live in the world of mortals to expiate her sin. And then she fell in love with Pururavas.

In many of these texts again (*e.* g. शतपथब्राह्मण, हरिवंश, विष्णुपुराण, भागवत), the original story suffers a very important change in that its tragic character is entirely given up, and we are told that Urvashi, taking pity upon Pururavas, allowed him to visit her once a year, or that Pururavas performed a certain sacrifice, and as a consequence of that the Gods allowed Urvashi to live with him to the end of his life, or that, finally, as a result of the same sacred rite Pururavas was exalted to the position of the Gandharvas and remained there never again to be separated from Urvashi.

Such is then the beautiful romance that Kalidasa has dramatized in the Vikramorvashiya. Considerations of art have of course led him to make several deviations from, and modifications in, the original story. In the first place one will not fail to notice, that in consonance with a tendency which had already set in as early as the time of the शतपथब्राह्मण, and in obedience to a very important rule of Indian dramatic technique, according to which a tragedy is strictly forbidden on the stage, Kalidasa had to change the original tragic story into one of blissful union between the hero and the heroine. Other important changes introduced by him in the original story are: (i) The abduction of Urvashi by the demon Keshin and her deliverance by Pururavas; (ii) The episode of the love-letter, the enragement of the Queen and her final reconciliation; (iii) The episode of the heavenly drama, the curse pronounced upon Urvashi by the sage Bharata and its modification by Indra; (iv) Urvashi's flight from Pururavas in a spasm of jealousy, her metamorphosis into a creeper and her subsequent recovery through the power of the gem of reunion; (v) The incident of the loss of the gem and the restoration to Pururavas of his son Ayus, occasioned by its discovery; and (vi) The final removal of Urvashi's curse even in its modified form. The bungling clown (विदूषक), the artful Nipunika, the whole paraphernalia of the royal court, the celestial friends of Urvashi, the venerable Cyavana, the old Tapasi, the sage Narada all these owe their existence entirely to the inventive genius of Kalidasa. In short he has done all that was necessary in the interests of dramatic art to turn the ancient tragic story into a noble drama of intensely human interest.*

The Vikramorvashiya: its Recensions.

The immense popularity which this drama has enjoyed in India has given rise to numerous divergences in the transmission of its text. These divergences are of such a fundamental character, that we can easily distinguish between two recensions: The northern Recension repesented by Bengali and Nagari Mss., and the Southern Recension represented by most of the South Indian Mss. The former is commented upon by Ranganatha, who wrote his विक्रमोर्वशीप्रकाशिका in 1712 (Ca. 1656 or 1790 A. D., according as we take it to be the Samvat or the Shaka era), while the latter by Katayavema, the Minister of the Reddi Prince Kumaragiri of Kondavidu (Ca. 1400 A. D.). Katayavema calls his commentary कुमारगिरिराजीय after the name of his King and patron. In the Northern Recension the play is called विक्रमोर्वशी and is spoken of as a त्रोटक. In the Southern Recension, however, it is called विक्रमोर्वशीय and is designated as a नाटक. (On the meaning of the word त्रोटक *vide* "Technical Names.")

On comparing the two recensions we find, that generally speaking the Northern Recension shows a marked

---

* The version of the story of Pururavas and Urvashi as found in the Matsya Purana shows a good many affinities to the drama of Kalidasa. As however, the age of the Puranas in general is unsettled and as their texts have been tampered with by later writers, one cannot say for certain that Kalidasa used the Matsya Purana in writing the present play. On the contrary it is quite possible, that the version of the story as contained in the Matsya Purana is a Pauranic adaptation of the drama of Kalidasa.

tendency towards amplifying the matter contained in the southern Recension. This is the case especially with several prose passages which appear in a terse form in the Southern Recension, while in the Northern we find them swollen and amplified by means of the addition of words which scarcely improve the sense. In regard to metrical portions the Northern Recension shows considerable deviations from the Southern Recension. Thus in the Northern Recension we find the following four stanzas in excess of those appearing in the Southern Recension :

(1) After श्रूयते in I. 2.6

मत्तानां कुसुमरसेन षट्पदानां शब्दोऽयं परभृतनाद एष धीरः ।
आकाशे सुरगणसेविते समंतात् किं नार्यः कलमधराक्षरं प्रगीताः ॥

(2) After तथाहि in I. 5.4

मन्दारकुसुमदाम्ना गुरुरस्याः सूच्यते हृदयकम्पः ।
मुहुरुच्छ्वसता मध्ये परिणाहवतोः पयोधरयोः ॥

(3) After मार्गस्य in IV. 29.5

अभिनवकुसुमस्तबकिततरुवरस्य परिसरे
मदकलकोकिलकूजितमधुपझंकारमनोहरे ।
नन्दनविपिने निजकरिणोविरहानलेन संतप्तो
विचरति गजाधिपतिरैरावतनामा ॥

(4) After. V. 24.

सर्वस्तरतु दुर्गाणि सर्वो भद्राणि पश्यतु ।
सर्वः कामानवाप्नोतु सर्वः सर्वत्र नन्दतु ॥

In addition to these stray stanzas we find in the Northern Recension in act IV, thirty-one stanzas in Maharashtri and Apabhramsha (six in Maharashtri, and twenty-five in Apabhramsha) in various metres. as also directions in prose as to the way in which they are to be sung to the accompaniment of music and danoe. In the Southern Recension, however, we have nothing corresponding to these.

The existence of these Maharashtri and Apabhramsha stanzas in the Northern Recension alone raises a very important problem in the textual criticism of the Vikramorvashiya. It is a problem that has not yet been solved finally. Most of the scholars (S. P. Pandit, Th. Bloch, H. Jacobi etc.) think that the stanzas in question are spurious. Mr. Pandit (Ed. Vikramorvashiya, Introd. p. 8 f.), for instance, gives the following reasons :

(1) Throughout his commentary on the fourth Act, Katayavema observes complete silence about these stanzas, showing thus that he was not aware of their existence.

(2) Many of these stanzas are obviously to be recited by the King. But then it is unwarrantable to put Prakrit stanzas in the mouth of the King, who, being an उत्तमपात्र must not speak in Prakrit.

(3) In several cases these stanzas are superfluous, since they only repeat the sense of Sanskrit verses preceding or following them.

(4) Many of them, though obviously forming part of the King's soliloquy, are full of indirect description, vague allusions and references in the third person to some one in the situation of the king rather than to himself.

(5) But the strongest reason for holding these stanzas as spurious is that not only are they superfluous to the action of the play, but several of them also seriously

interfere with the free and natural flow of the sentiments expressed in the Sanskrit stanzas.

Sten Konow (Das Indische Drama, p. 64.) urges against the genuineness of these stanzas the further consideration that in none of the many later imitations of this very Act (*e. g.* Malatimadhava, Act IX; Balaramayana, Act V; Prasannaraghava, Act VI; Mahanataka, Act IV, etc.) do we come across any Apabhramsha stanzas.

It must however be confessed, that all these considerations have no probative value at all, and, for aught we know, these stanzas may have come from the pen of Kalidasa. If it is true, then we must say that from the very first they were never intended to be recited by the King at all, but that they were to be sung, from time to time by some one behind the scenes to the accompaniment of music and dance, in order just to create the proper atmosphere that was so very necessary for heightening the effect of the mournful lamentations of the King plunged in grief for the loss of his beloved.

Development of the Plot.

We shall now consider how very skilfully the poet has developed the story. In the first act which is a sort of induction setting forth the circumstances in which the germ of the love finds soil, the two lovers are fond of each other and we at once see the end in the beginning—for we know that such a reciprocity of passion must lead to union. Yet there are several obstacles to be got over—several problems to be solved; and these problems are not thrust on the reader but they come as natural issues of the story, though often the reader is taken by surprise by these issues. Thus at the end of the first act we are sure that the lovers will meet and have their desire. But as soon as we proceed to the second act and listen to the dialogue between Nipunika and Manavaka our interest deepens; for now we begin to realize the problems raised by the love of the King for the nymph of heaven—one of them being how the chief Queen, the sole wardress of the King's heart, will receive this reckless errantry of her husband. Here again there is considerable ironic humour in the King's dearest friend being tricked by the artful maid into betraying the secret of the King's passion and with breathless interest we await the issue.

There are also other complications in the story. Urvashi to assure her doubting lover of her feelings towards him, writes her love message on a *bhurja* leaf and throws it towards the King before revealing herself. Secondly when the two meet and are feasting on the presence of each other, there is announced the mandate of heaven's lord that Urvashi was to be back to *swarga* to dance to the tune of her master's humour. In the meanwhile the addle-pated companion of the King has carelessly dropped the missive of love and it falls into the hands of the Queen. Armed with this documentary evidence of her husband's breach of his avowals of fidelity, the already incensed Queen confronts that delinquent; and he has no recourse save to yield, to confess, and sue for pardon. The Queen leaves him all in a tantrum only to be afterwards reconciled to the superior rival in her husband's love, which she does apparently with a good grace in the third act.

Thus in the second act we see that there are two difficulties to be solved: How was the celestial damsel, if their union was to be permanent, to be free to act her own will and follow the lead of her heart, and secondly how was the King to pacify the irate Queen, the rival of his love.

The third act resolves these complications. The Queen, who conforms to the Hindu ideal of a wife, is weighed down by the enormity of her crime in insulting her husband and gives him freedom to indulge his vagaries; while the curse which is pronounced by Urvashi's preceptor in heaven for her unconsious substitution of her lover's name in the rehearsal of her part in the drama, Lakshmi-swayamvara, which was represented by herself and her aery companions before heaven's lord, is a blessing in disguise; for thereby she could find joy in her lover's embraces till she was with child by him.

The end of the third act has a finality about it, and the reader is likely to suppose that the drama comes to a close with the union of Pururavas and Urvashi. He thinks that no thread now remains to connect the sequel with the story so far as he has followed it. But this will be only a hasty conclusion. We know that the union of the lovers is but the memory of a sweet dream, for it is conditioned by what lovers at that stage of their love would regard as an accident of their union—the birth of a child; and the poet has to see that the beloved is not torn from the embraces of her lover by anything save their own desires. Secondly the connection appears still more organic if we look to the character of Pururavas of which more anon.

The fourth act, which is unique in several respects finds that Urvashi has left her mortal lover in a spasm of jealousy and while wandering in the dull stupor of her own distress has entered on proscribed grounds and immediately been transformed into a jasmine creeper. The King, all woe-begone, with his frail reason snapped by the shock of his sudden misery, wanders in search of her and at last finds the jewel by whose touch she is brought back to herself, and together they enter the city of Pratishthana to enjoy each other's company.

In the fifth act we learn that Urvashi has a son, and that her term of life with him comes to a close; the revelation of this fact is skilfully managed by the short episode of the vulture pouncing upon the Sangamaniya jewel and carrying it away. The vulture was killed by an arrow on which was incised the name of आयुस्, the son of Pururavas. Then while the lovers are lamenting the perversity of fate and while the king is resolving to take to sack-cloth and ashes, there enters Narada on the stage and announces the pleasure of Indra that Urvashi was his to the end of his life and the action of the drama comes to a close.

Thus from act to act our expectation is ever upward—our interest never flags. In every act we feel that we are on the verge of a catastrophe and find it skilfully averted; and what at first sight looks a simple story opens up so many complications which are still natural.

The Vikramorvashiya: Time Analysis.

The only indication of time that we get in the first Act is that its action commences in the early morning, as is evident from the following words of Pururavas: सूर्योपस्थानात्प्रतिनिवृत्तं पुरूरवसं मामुपेत्य कथ्यतां कुतो भवत्यः परित्रातव्या इति।

(I. 3. 8). He is returning just after paying his morning visit to the sphere of the Sun.

We have absolutely no means of determining the interval of time that passes between Act I and II. The incidents of the second act commence on a morning in early spring and close slightly after midday. That the spring has only recently set in can be gathered from the following passages among others: II. 6. 6. (विदूषकः । प्रेक्षतां भवान् वसन्तावतारसूचकं अस्याभिरामतरं प्रमदवनस्य ।); II. 7. अग्रे स्त्रीनखपाटलं e e.); II, 6 (इदमसुलभवस्तु etc.) and II. 19. 24 (भगवन् वसन्तप्रिय मलयानिल ।) alluding to the Malaya breeze.

That the action of the second Act commences in the morning and ends slightly after midday is shown by the following passages:

II. 1. 5 (विदूषकः । एष कार्यासनादुत्थित इत एवागच्छति वयस्यः ।). The King is just returning from the council hall. It must, therefore, be at least 10 A. M. int he morning, as Mr. Pandit suggests (Notes p. 38).

II. 2. 15. (विदूषकः । तत्र पंचविधस्याभ्यवहारस्य उपनतसंभारस्य योजनां etc.) This shows that preparations for the midday meal are going on apace in the kitchen.

II. 17. 7. (राजा । कथमर्धं गतं दिवसस्य ।) II. stanza 22 which describes the moon.

The dialogue between the pupils of Bharata, which takes place in the first scene of the third Act shows, by a remark occurring towards its end, that the evening is approching. Witness III. 1. 45 (पल्लवः । कथाप्रसंगेन अपराद्धा अभिषेकवेला । The अभिषेक is here of course the evening. *Vide* III. 1. 5. रमणीयःखलु दिवसावसानवृत्तान्तो राजवेश्मनि ।) and III. stanza 2 (उत्कीर्णा इव etc). It is the first or second day in the dark fortnight since the moon has not yet risen See III. 5.9. (विदूषकः । भोः प्रत्यासन्नेन चन्द्रोदयेन भवितव्यम् ।) And when the moon rises, her orb is not full and complete but with a slight portion of it broken off. See III. 6. 1 (विदूषकः । ही ही । भो एष खण्डमोदकसश्रीक उदितो राजा द्विजातीनाम् ।) We learn from a remark of चित्रलेखा towards the end of the third Act (III. 17. 6.) that the spring is drawing to a close and that the summer is close at hand (वसन्तानन्तरे उष्णसमये भगवान् सूर्यो मयोपचरितव्यः ।) It would appear from this, that the action of the second and the third Act takes place within the space of two months covered by the spring season.

From a remark of चित्रलेखा in the first scene of the fourth Act (IV. o. 45), we learn that the rainy season has just set in (अनेन पुनर्निर्वृतानामपि उत्कण्ठाकारिणा मेघोदयेन अनर्थाधीनो भविष्यति ।). The second Scene of the fourth Act further contains numerous references to the rainy season. From this it becomes clear, that only two months covered by the summer season separate the third from the fourth Act.

Several years elapse between Act IV and V. Ayus, the son of Pururavas and Urvashi, who is introduced to us in the fifth Act, is already a grown up–lad, capable of bearing on his body the heavy coat of mail (कवचधरः संवृत्तः । V. 12. 16) and thoroughly educated in the different arts and sciences (गृहीतविद्यः । *ibid*). This becomes still more clear from the King's remark at V. 12. 16. (अयि वत्स उषितं त्वया पूर्वस्मिन्नाश्रमे । द्वितीयमध्यासितुं तव समयः ।). Ayus has already passed through the first Ashrama (*viz.* ब्रह्मचर्य) and is now of an age to enter upon the second (*viz.* गृहस्थाश्रम).

To sum up the whole thing we can say, that the interval between the first and the second Act is not definitcly indicated. The incidents described in the second, third and fourth Acts transpire within the space of four months covered by spring and summer. The interval between the fourth and the fifth Act is several years.

Characters.

Pururavas, the hero of the present play, is the type technically known as धीरोदात्त दक्षिण *i. e.* Valiant, dignified, and considerate in his loves. According to writers on dramaturgy, a hero of this type possesses several qualities such as nobility of heart, patience, modesty, aversion to self-flattery, self-possession and extreme courteousness towards the fair sex. To any careful reader of our play it cannot but strike that Pururavas possesses all these qualities and many more besides, and thus answers in every respect to the conception of the धीरोदात्त hero.

PURURAVAS.

Let us now, see how some of the more important of these qualities are evidenced in the play in connection with the character of Pururavas, by making reference to a couple of striking incidents.

His high sense of chivalry and courtesy towards the fair sex is shown by his impatience to learn the details of the misfortune that has befallen the Apsarases, the readiness with which he volunteers his services in order to deliver Urvashi and Citralekha from the power of the demon and the anxious concern that he feels for Urvashi's recovery from her swoon. He is extremely gentle and polite in his address to the Apsarases as also to his Queen. He is ever solicitous not to hurt the feelings of the Queen and seizes the first opportunity that he gets to make truce with her.

Next to his chivalry and courtesy his humility and aversion to self-flattery claim our attention. Although he himself has overpowered and crushed the demon Keshin by the might of his arm, he gives the credit for it entirely to the all-saving prowess of Indra (त्रिलोकरक्षी महिमा हि वज्रिणः ।) I. 5; see also I. 15.

His self-possession is in evidence when in the second Act Urvashi is called away to heaven immediately after he meets her. With wonderful self-restraint he gives her permission to depart, though not without much reluctance (cf. II. 18.10 नास्मि भवत्योरीश्वरनियोगप्रत्यर्थी । स्मर्तव्यस्त्वयं जनः।).

We can continue the examination of the play in the same way and find ample evidence in it for many more admirable qualities in the character of Pururavas. But all the same we cannot fail to notice an important weakness in him *viz.* his sensuousness. From the very first Pururavas strikes us as extremely sensuous and the nymph so airy "so pure a thing, so free from mortal touch." In the whole of the play we miss very much indeed the virility or the sani y or the judgment of a Dushyanta in our hero. He scarcely does anything save bewail his state and grow sentimental. He longs for the sight of her face, the touch of her hand, the pressure of her limbs; in all this he is so morbid, and this is a trait in his character which ultimately develops into madness in Act IV. Thus with true psychological insight the poet has from the very beginning prepared us for the abnormal state of mind in which the hero comes on the stage in Act IV.

URVASHI.

We see, then, that although Pururavas answers remakably well to the description of the conventional hero in Indian drama, his character reveals on further scrutiny certain repelling features such as his sensuousness, his morbid sentimentality and the earthly character of his passion for Urvashi. Not so, however, the case with Urvashi, the heroine of our play. She is perfectly free from the earthly part—the grossness of that passion. She finds that she could scarcely live in the stifling atmosphere of Indra's court. Her attendance on him was the forced homage of an unwilling vassal. It was only when she saw Pururavas that she awakened to life. Love is the element of her being. And she is only too jealous of her love; for she considers no sacrifice too great when it is made for the sake of love. She will not look upon her son's face, for ever so many years, for fear that their union will cease to be. Some will say hard things about her on that account; but they scarcely understand the intensity of that all-consuming passion. And besides she has chosen between two evils; if she were to disclose that a son was born to them she had instantly to forego both son and lover; if on the other hand she kept that fact concealed, she could enjoy her lover's company, while her son was brought up and educated in the severe discipline of the *Ashrama*. Kalidasa has thus given us in Urvashi altogether a rare and lovable type of womanhood, for woman is at her best when she loves and deems no sacrifice too great but she may go in for it.

VIDUSHAKA.

The only other character in the play that invites our attention is the Vidushaka, the boon companion of the King. He does not of course help the King in attaining to the fulfilment of his passion for Urvashi. If at all, he only serves to make matters worse for the King by falling an easy prey to the trickery of Nipunika and divulging the secret of the King's love for Urvashi; by dropping down Urvashi's love-letter, and thus supplying the already suspecting Queen with a written proof of the King's infidelity; and by uttering all sorts of foolish things calculated to expose the King in her eyes. He creates a good deal of humour by making constant references, in time and out of time, to the dainties of the table of which, it would seem, he is a *connoisseur*. He is so occupied all along with thoughts about food and drink, that almost each and everything he sees about himself has no meaning and reality to him except in terms of these. The rising orb of the waning Moon appeals to him simply because he can liken it in his mind to a round mass of sweetmeat with its apex broken off. (Vide III 6. 2. ही ही । भो एष खण्डमोदकसश्रीक उदितो राजा द्विजातीनाम् ।). Paradise with all its pleasures and attraction fails to charm him since, as he says, the pleasures of the table are denied to the denizens thereof (See. III. 17. 11. किं वा स्वर्गे स्मर्तव्यम् । न वा अश्यते न वा पीयते ।)

We thus see that the Vidushaka does not stand in any vital relationship with the action of the play. He could well have been dispensed with by the poet, had it not been for the fact that his appearance on the stage and the humorous remarks that he makes from time to time serve to offer to the reader or the spectator a much-needed relaxation in the midst of the sentimental effusions of the love-lorn King.

Some Technical Names.

SUTRADHARA:—

He is the principal stage-manager who arranges the cast of characters, instructs them and takes a prominent part in the Prastavana. मातृगुप्ताचार्य describes him in these terms :—

चतुरातोद्यनिष्णातोऽनेकभाषासमावृतः ।
नानाभाषणतत्त्वज्ञो नीतिशास्त्रार्थतत्त्ववित् ॥
नानागतिप्रचारज्ञो रसभावविशारदः ।
नाट्यप्रयोगनिपुणो नानाशिल्पकलान्वितः ॥
छन्दोविधानतत्त्वज्ञः सर्वशास्त्रविचक्षणः ।
तत्तद्गीतानुगलयकलातालावधारणः ॥
अवधानप्रयोक्ता च योक्तृणामुपदेशकः ।
एवंगुणगणोपेतः सूत्रधारोऽभिधीयते ॥

PRASTAVANA OR STHAPAKA :—

We are told in Natyashastra that before the commencement of a drama, an elaborate series of preliminary rites (पूर्वरङ्ग) had to be gone through, of which नान्दी formed the concluding rite. These were performed by the सूत्रधार who then left the stage and his place was taken by another similar person called स्थापक who then introduced the play to the audience.

पूर्वरङ्गं विधायादौ सूत्रधारे विनिर्गते ।
प्रविश्य तद्वदपरः काव्यमास्थापयेन्नटः ॥

Later on, with the reformation of the stage, these preliminaries were considerably shortened, and the Sutradhara alone performed both the functions of the पूर्वरङ्ग and of the prologue.

This prologue or प्रस्तावना (आमुखं) or स्थापना, as it is called in some plays of the Bhasa group, is an introductory dialogue between the सूत्रधार and the नटी or one of the actors. After giving an account of the author and his qualifications it introduces the incidents of the drama : cf.

सूत्रधारो नटीं ब्रूते मार्षं वाथ विदूषकम् ।
स्वकार्यं प्रस्तुताक्षेपि चित्रोक्त्या यत्तदामुखम् ॥

Of the many varieties of this prologue we are concerned with the प्रयोगातिशय "particular presentation" in which a character is introduced by a remark of the stage-manager:—

यदि प्रयोग एकस्मिन् प्रयोगोऽन्यः प्रयुज्यते ।
तेन पात्रप्रवेशश्चेत् प्रयोगातिशयो मतः ॥

VISHAMBHAKA It is an explanatory scene, so called from its concisely compressing (वि+स्कम्भ्) into a short space those subordinate parts of the story, not enacted before the audience, but a knowledge of which is quite essential to the comprehending of the action of the play. cf.

वृत्तवर्तिष्यमाणानां कथाशानां निदर्शकः ।
संक्षिप्तार्थस्तु विष्कम्भो मध्यपात्रप्रयोजितः ॥

It is a monologue, or a dialogue, and in the latter case it is performed by two persons or more, of the same or different classes, according as it is शुद्ध or संकीर्ण (मिश्र).

एकानेककृतः शुद्धः संकीर्णो नीचमध्यमैः ॥

It may occur at the beginning of any of the acts, even the first, just after the प्रस्तावना.

PRAVESHAKA

This also is an explanatory scene serving the same purpose as the विष्कम्भक, only with this difference that the characters taking part in this scene are exclusively of the inferior class who speak the Prakrit dialect. It must come between two acts; thus unlike the विष्कम्भक, its existence in Act I is not possible. cf.

तद्वदेवानुदात्तोक्त्या नीचपात्रप्रयोजितः ।
प्रवेशोऽङ्कद्वयस्यान्तः शेषार्थस्योपसूचकः ॥

TROTAKA

The Trotaka, which is one of the eighteen Uparupakas, is a drama having five, seven, eight or nine acts. It deals with the doings of Gods and men and the Vidushaka makes his appearance in every Act. cf.

सप्ताष्टनवपंचाङ्कं दिव्यमानुषसंश्रयम् ।
त्रोटकं नाम तत्प्राहुः प्रत्यङ्कं सविदूषकम् ॥

The rule that the Vidushaka should be presented in every act of a Trotaka is not, however, strictly observed. For example, in the Vikramorvashiya which is regarded as a Trotaka, the Vidushaka appears only in Acts II, III and V. Besides the Vikramorvashiya, there is also mentioned as a Trotaka a seven act play called स्तम्भितरम्भम्, which, unfortunately, has not come down to us.

PREFACE TO THE SECOND EDITION

The notes are thoroughly revised and amplified where necessary, and a part of the Introduction is recast; otherwise, except for the arrangement of printing the translation side by side with the text, the present edition retains most of the features of the 1st edition. Our sincere thanks are due to Prof. K. V. Abhyankar, for going through most of the proof-shects, and to Mr. R. P. Kothari who so readily agreed to bring out this revised edition.

FERGUSSON COLLEGE,
POONA.

C. R. DEVADHAR,
M. V. PATWARDHAN.

विक्रमोर्वशीयम्

VIKRAMORVAŚĪYA

॥ श्रीः ॥

विक्रमोर्वशीयम् ।

प्रथमोऽङ्कः ।

वेदान्तेषु यमाहुरेकपुरुषं व्याप्य स्थितं रोदसी
यस्मिन्नीश्वर इत्यनन्यविषयः शब्दो यथार्थाक्षरः ।
अन्तर्यश्च मुमुक्षुभिर्नियमितप्राणादिभिर्मृग्यते
स स्थाणुः स्थिरभक्तियोगसुलभो निःश्रेयसायास्तु वः ॥ १ ॥

[नान्द्यन्ते]

सूत्रधारः— [नेपथ्याभिमुखमवलोक्य] मारिष इतस्तावत् ।

[प्रविश्य पारिपार्श्वकः]

पारिपार्श्वकः—भाव अयमस्मि ।

सूत्रधारः—मारिष बहुशस्तु परिषदा पूर्वेषां कवीनां दृष्टः प्रयोगबन्धः । सोहमद्य विक्रमोर्वशीयं नामापूर्वं नाटकं प्रयोक्ष्ये । तदुच्यतां पात्रवर्गः स्वेषु स्वेषु पाठेष्वसंमूढैर्भवितव्यमिति ।

पारिपार्श्वकः—यदाज्ञापयति भावः ।

[इति निष्क्रान्तः]

सूत्रधारः—यावदिदानीमार्यमिश्रान् विज्ञापयामि ।

[प्रणिपत्य ।]

प्रणयिषु वा दाक्षिण्यादथवा सद्वस्तुपुरुषबहुमानात् ।
शृणुत मनोभिरवहितैः क्रियामिमां कालिदासस्य ॥२॥

VIKRAMORVASĪYA

PROLOGUE

ACT I.

May the Eternal One who is attainable by firm faith and meditation; who is hailed as the Supreme Spirit in the Vedanta, who pervades and is present in the whole of heaven and earth; to whom alone the name of Lord, not signifying any other being, is properly applied; and who is sought within themselves by those desirous of salvation by restraining the vital breaths Prana and others, bestow upon you the highest bliss. [1]

(*At the end of the benediction*)

THE MANAGER—Ho! Marisha, come hither.

(*Entering*)

ACTOR—Here I am, sir.

THE MANAGER—Marisha, many a time has this assembly witnessed the compositions of former bards. I, therefore, propose to stage one not hitherto exhibited, the play of Vikrama and Urvashi. Speak to the actors, therefore, to attend carefully to their respective parts.

ACTOR—As you desire, sir. (*Exit*)

THE MANAGER—I have now to make (this) request to the noble audience. (*Bowing*).

Listen to this work of Kalidasa with attentive minds, in consideration of either your regard towards (us), your humble servants, or your respect for the excellent hero of this play. [2]

नेपथ्ये। **परित्ताअदु परित्ताअदु जो सुर-पक्ख-वादी जस्स वा अम्बर-अले गदी अत्थि।** परित्रायतां परित्रायतां यः सुरपक्षपाती यस्य वा अम्बरतले गतिरस्ति।

सूत्रधारः--[कर्णं दत्त्वा] **अये किं नु खलु मद्विज्ञापनानन्तरं कुररीणामिव आकाशे शब्दः श्रूयते।** [विचिन्त्य] **भवतु। ज्ञातम्।**

ऊरूद्भवा नरसखस्य मुनेः सुरस्त्री
कैलासनाथमुपसृत्य निवर्तमाना।
बन्दीकृता विबुधशत्रुभिरर्धमार्गे
क्रन्दत्यतः शरणमप्सरसां गणोऽयम् ॥ ३ ॥

[इति निष्क्रान्तः]

प्रस्तावना।

[ततः प्रविशन्ति अप्सरसः।]

सर्वाः—**परित्ताअदु परित्ताअदु जो सुर-पक्ख-वादी जस्स वा अम्बर-अले गदी अत्थि।** परित्रायतां परित्रायतां यः सुरपक्षपाती यस्य वा अम्बरतले गतिरस्ति।

[ततः प्रविशति राजा रथेन सूतश्च।]

राजा—**अलमलमाक्रन्दितेन। सूर्योपस्थानात् प्रतिनिवृत्तं पुरूरवसं मामुपेत्य कथ्यतां कुतो भवत्यः परित्रातव्या इति।**

रम्भा—**असुरावलेवादो।** असुरावलेपात्।

राजा—**किं पुनरसुरावलेपेन भवतीनामपराद्धम्।**

मेनका—**सुणादु महाराओ। जा तवो-विसेस-परिसङ्किदस्स सुउमारं पहरणं महिन्दस्स। पच्चादेसो रूव-गव्विदाए सिरीए। अलंकारो सग्गस्स। सा णो पिअसही**

(*Behind the Scenes*)

Help ! Help ! Whoso is a friend to the gods, or has power to move in the space of heaven.

The Manager–(*Listening*). What sounds are these in the air, as of the female ospreys, that break in upon my words ! (*Reflecting*) Ah ! I know.

The celestial nymph, sprung from the thigh of the sage, the friend of Nara, is, while returning after her attendance upon the Lord of Kailasa, taken prisoner on the way by the enemies of the gods ; that is why this group of Apsarasas is crying for protection. [3]

(*Exit*)

END OF THE PROLOGUE.

(*Enter the nymphs of heaven*).

ALL—Help ! Help ! Whoso is a friend to the gods or has power to move in the space of heaven.

(*Enter King in his Chariot and the Charioteer*)

KING—Cease your cries. Come to me, Pururavas, returned from my attendance upon the Sun, and tell me against what do the ladies seek help.

RAMBHA—Against a demon's violence.

KING—What wrong have the ladies suffered through the demon's violence ?

उव्वसी कुबेर-भवणादो पडिणिवट्टमाणा समावत्तिदिट्ठेण हिरण्णउरवासिणा केसिणा दाणवेण चित्तलेहादुदीआ
१८ अद्धपहं जेव्व बन्दिग्गाहं गहिदा। श्रृणोतु महाराजः। या तपोविशेषपरिशङ्कितस्य सुकुमारं प्रहरणं महेन्द्रस्य। प्रत्यादेशो रूपगर्वितायाः श्रियः। अलकारः स्वर्गस्य। सा नः प्रियसखी उर्वशी
२१ कुबेरभवनात् प्रतिनिवर्तमाना समापत्तिदृष्टेन हिरण्यपुरवासिना केशिना दानवेन चित्रलेखाद्वितीया अर्धपथ एव बन्दिग्राहं गृहीता।

राजा—अपि ज्ञायते कतमेन दिग्भागेन गतः स जाल्म इति।

२४ सहजन्या—पुव्वुत्तरेण। पूर्वोत्तरेण।

राजा—तेन हि विमुच्यतां विषादः। यतिष्ये वः सखी-प्रत्यानयनाय।

२७ रम्भा—सरिसं खु सोमादो एक्कन्दरस्स। सदृशं खलु सोमादेकान्तरस्य।

राजा—क्व पुनर्मां भवत्यः प्रतिपालयिष्यन्ति।

३० सर्वाः—इमस्सिं हेमकूड-सिहरे। एतस्मिन् हेमकूटशिखरे।

राजा—सूत ऐशानीं दिशं प्रति चोदयाश्वानाशुगमनाय।

सूतः--यदाज्ञापयत्यायुष्मान् [इति यथोक्तं करोति।]

३३ राजा--[रथवेगं निरूपयन्] साधु साधु। अनेन रथवेगेन पूर्वप्रस्थितं वैनतेयमप्यासादयेयं किं पुनस्तमपकारिणं मघोनः। तथा हि

अग्रे यान्ति रथस्य रेणुवदमी चूर्णीभवन्तो घना
श्चक्रभ्रान्तिररान्तरेषु जनयत्यन्यामिवारावलीम्।
चित्रन्यस्तमिवाचलं हयशिरस्यायामवच्चामरं
यष्ट्यग्रे च समं स्थितो ध्वजपटः प्रान्ते च वेगानिलात् ॥४॥

[निष्क्रान्तो रथेन राजा सूतश्च]

MENAKA—Listen, your majesty: our dear friend Urvashi, the delicate weapon of the great Indra when he is frightened by the excellence of Tapas, who shames proud Shri's loveliness, who is heaven's ornament, was, while on her way from Kubera's mansion, taken captive, along with Chitralekha, by the demon Keshin of Hiranyapura, who came upon us all of a sudden.

KING—Know ye what direction the wretch took?

SAHAJANYA—The North-East.

KING—Well then, banish your fears. I shall endeavour to restore you your friends.

RAMBHA—That is worthy of the descendant of the Moon only one degree removed.

KING—Where will you await my return?

ALL—Here, on the peak of yonder Hemakuta.

KING—Charioteer, urge the horses on to the North-East that we may speedily go.

CHARIOTEER—As my lord commands. (*Does as bidden*).

KING—(*Looking at the speed of his Chariot*). Well, with this speed, I may overtake Vainateya even if he has the start of me; what then of this offender of Lord Indra. For,

These heavy clouds, being pulverized, are rising before the chariot like dust; the revolution of the wheels is creating as it were another set of spokes within the spokes; the long streamer is standing on the heads of the horses as motionless as in a picture; and by the wind (produced by) the great speed, the banner-cloth spreads out evenly between the top-point of the flag-staff and its own end. [4]

रम्भा—हला जह-णिद्दिट्ठं पदेसं संकमामो। हला यथा-निर्दिष्टं प्रदेशं संक्रामामः ।

शेषाः—तह। तथा। [इति सर्वाः शैलावतरणं नाटयित्वा स्थिताः]

रम्भा—अवि णाम सो राएसी समुद्धरे णो हिअअ-सल्लं। अपि नाम स राजर्षिः समुद्धरेद् नो हृदयशल्यम् ।

मेनका—मा दे संसओ होदु। उवट्ठिदसंपराओ महिन्दो मज्झिम-लोआदो सबहुमाणं आणाविअ तं एव्व विअ-अ-सेणा-मुहे णिओजेदि । मा ते संशयो भवतु। उपस्थित-संपरायो महेन्द्रो मध्यमलोकात् सबहुमानमानाय्य तमेव विजयसेना-मुखे नियोजयति ।

रम्भा—सव्वहा इह विअई भोदु। सर्वथा इह विजयी भवतु।

सहजन्या—[क्षणमात्रं स्थित्वा] **हला समस्ससध। समस्ससध। एसो उच्चलिद-हरिण-केदणो तस्स राएसिणो सोमदत्तो रहो दीसदि। ण खु सो अकिदत्थो णिवत्तिस्सदि** । हला समाश्वसित समाश्वसित । एष उच्चलितहरिणकेतनस्तस्य राजर्षेः सोमदत्तो रथो दृश्यते । न खलु सोऽकृतार्थो निवर्तिष्यते । [सर्वा उच्चक्षुषो विलोकयन्ति ।]

[ततः प्रविशति राजा सूतश्च । चित्रलेखावलम्बितहस्ता भयनिमीलिताक्षी चोर्वशी ।]

चित्रलेखा—समस्ससदु समस्ससदु पिअ-सही। समाश्वसितु समाश्वसितु प्रियसखी ।

राजा—सुन्दरि समाश्वसिहि समाश्वसिहि।

(*Exit King with Chariot and the Charioteer.*)

RAMBHA—Now, friends, let us proceed to the place pointed out.

OTHERS—As you say. (*All gesticulate descending to the mountain-peak and making a halt.*)

RAMBHA—Will the royal sage be able to extract this dart from our hearts?

MENAKA—You make no doubt of that. For even the great Indra, when hostilities are imminent, honours him and bringing him from the world of mortals, appoints him to the command of his conquering hosts.

RAMBHA—May he succeed in every way in the present case.

SAHAJANYA—Friends, take heart, take heart. Here is to be seen his chariot, Somadatta, with its deer-emblazoned banner dancing in the wind. Surely he will not return before accomplishing his object.

(*All look with eyes upturned.*)

(*Enter King, Charioteer, and Urvashi with eyes shut in fear and supported on Chitralekha's arm.*)

CHITRALEKHA—Take cheer, take cheer, my dear friend!

गतं भयं भीरु सुरारिसंभवं
त्रिलोकरक्षी महिमा हि वज्रिणः ।
तदेतदुन्मीलय चक्षुरायतं
महोत्पलं प्रत्युषसीव पद्मिनी ॥ ५ ॥

चित्रलेखा—अम्हहे कहं ऊससिद-मेत्त-जीविदा अज्जवि
सण्णं ण पडिवज्जदि । अहो कथमुच्छ्वसितमात्रजीविता अद्यापि
३ संज्ञा न प्रतिपद्यते ।

राजा—बलवदत्रभवती परित्रस्ता । तथा हि

मुञ्चति न तावदस्याः कम्पं कुसुमसमबन्धनं हृदयम् ।
पश्य हरिचन्दनेन स्तनमध्योच्छ्वासिना कथितम् ॥६॥

चित्रलेखा—हला पज्जवत्थावेहि अत्ताणं । अणच्छरा
विअ मे पडिहासि । सखि पर्यवस्थापय आत्मानम् । अनप्सरा
३ इव मे प्रतिभासि ।

राजा—अयि प्रकृतिमापद्यते ते सखी । पश्य

आविर्भूते शशिनि तमसा मुच्यमानेव रात्रि-
र्नैशस्यार्चिर्हुतभुजइव च्छिन्नभूयिष्ठधूमा ।
मोहेनान्तर्वरतनुरियं लक्ष्यते मुक्तकल्पा
गङ्गा रोधःपतनकलुषा गृह्णतीव प्रसादम् ॥ ७ ॥

चित्रलेखा—सहि वीसद्धा होहि । पराभूदा खु तिदस-
परिपन्थिणो हदासा । सखि विश्रब्धा भव । पराभूताः खलु
३ त्रिदशपरिपन्थिनो हताशाः ।

उर्वशी—[चक्षुषी उन्मील्य] किं पहाव-दंसिणा महिन्देण ।
किं प्रभावदर्शिना महेन्द्रेण ।

६ **चित्रलेखा**—ण महिन्देण । महिन्द-सरिसाणुभावेण

KING—Fair nymph, cheer up, cheer up.

Gone, timid one, is the fear caused by the demons; for, indeed, the three worlds rest secure in Indra's greatness. Open those big eyes, even as the lotus-plant at dawn its big lotuses. [5]

CHITRALEKHA—Alas! How does she not recover consciousness yet, in whom her breath alone is what is left of life?

KING—Greatly is her ladyship troubled. For,

Behold, her heart (fluttering) like a flower on its stem does not yet forego its tremor, which is indicated by the sandal-smearings rising up between her two breasts. [6]

CHITRALEKHA—Friend, do compose yourself. Meseems you scarcely look a nymph of heaven.

(*Urvashi recovers herself*).

KING—Lady, your dear friend is coming to herself.

Look, The fair one seems well-nigh relieved of her mental stupor like the night freed from darkness when the Moon appears, or like the flame of evening fire from which the smoke has been mostly removed, or like the Ganges regaining her clearness after her waters have been soiled, by the crumbling in of her banks. [7]

CHITRALEKHA—Friend, have no fear. Vanquished are those wretches, the foes of heaven.

URVASHI—(*Opening her eyes*) By the great Indra who sees through his divine power?

इमिणा राएसिणा । न महेन्द्रेण । महेन्द्रसदृशानुभावेन अनेन राजर्षिणा ।

९ उर्वशी--[राजानं विलोक्य । आत्मगतम्] उवकिदं खु दाणवेहिं । उपकृतं खलु दानवैः ।

राजा--[प्रकृतिस्थामुर्वशीं निर्वर्ण्य । स्वगतम्] स्थाने खलु
१२ नारायणमृषिं विलोभयन्त्यस्तदूरुसंभवामिमां दृष्ट्वा व्रीडिताः सर्वा अप्सरस इति । अथ वा नेयं तपस्विनः सृष्टिर्भवितुमर्हति । तथा हि

अस्याः सर्गविधौ प्रजापतिरभूच्चन्द्रो नु कान्तप्रभः
शृङ्गारैकरसः स्वयं नु मदनो मासो नु पुष्पाकरः ।
वेदाभ्यासजडः कथं नु विषयव्यावृत्तकौतूहलो
निर्मातुं प्रभवेन्मनोहरमिदं रूपं पुराणो मुनिः ॥८॥

उर्वशी--हला सो सही-जणो कहिं खु भवे । हला स सखीजनः क्व खलु भवेत् ।

३ चित्रलेखा--महाराओ अभअ-दाई जाणादि । महाराजः अभयदायी जानाति ।

राजा--[उर्वशीमवलोकयन्] महति विषादे वर्तते । पश्यतु भवती

यदृच्छया त्वं सकृदप्यवन्ध्ययोः
पथि स्थिता सुन्दरि यस्य नेत्रयोः ।
त्वया विना सोऽपि समुत्सुको भवेत्
सखीजनस्ते किमुतार्द्रसौहृदः ॥ ९ ॥

उर्वशी--[अपवार्य] अहिजादं खु से वअणं । अहवा चन्दादो अमिअं ति किं एत्थ अच्छरिअं [प्रकाशम्]
२ अदो एव्व णं पेक्खिदुं तुवरदि मे हिअअं । अभिजातं

CHITRALEKHA—Not by Mahendra ; but by this royal sage who in his prowess is the equal of Mahendra.

URVASHI—(*Looking at the King, to herself*) Then have the demons obliged me !

KING—(*Looking at Urvashi who has regained consciousness, to himself*) How very proper that the nymphs of heaven while endeavouring to entice the sage Narayana were put to shame as they saw her spring from his thigh. Or rather, she cannot be the creation of a poor ascetic ! For,

Was the moon of lovely brightness her creator ? Or Madana himself who joys in love and love alone ? Or the vernal month ? For how could an aged anchorite who has grown dull through the study of the Vedas, and who has withdrawn himself from all worldly pleasures, fashion such a lovely form ? [8]

URVASHI—Where are our friends, my dear ?

CHITRALEKHA—The King,our protector, knows.

KING—They are greatly distressed. Look dear lady,

Even he, O fair one, within the path of whose fruitful eyes you but once moved, will feel a yearning in your absence : what then of your friends, ever full of love (for you) ? [9]

खल्वस्य वचनम् । अथवा चन्द्रादमृतमिति किमत्राश्चर्यम् । अत एवैनं प्रेक्षितुं त्वरते मे हृदयम् ।

राजा—[हस्तेन दर्शयन्]

एताः सुतनु मुखं ते सख्यः पश्यन्ति हेमकूटगताः ।
प्रत्यागतप्रसादं चन्द्रमिवोपप्लवान्मुक्तम् ॥ १० ॥

चित्रलेखा—**हला पेक्ख** । हला पश्य ।

उर्वशी—[राजानं सस्पृहं पश्यन्ती] **सम-दुक्खो पिबइ व्व मं णयणेहिं** । समदुःखः पिबतीव मां नयनाभ्याम् ।

चित्रलेखा—[साकूतम्] **अयि को** । अयि कः ।

उर्वशी—**सहि-अणो** । सखीजनः ।

रम्भा—[सहर्षम्] **एसो चित्तलेहा-दुदिअं उव्वसिं गेण्हिअ विसाहा-समीव-गदो विअ चन्दो उवट्ठिदो राएसी** । एष चित्रलेखाद्वितीयामुर्वशीं गृहीत्वा विशाखासमीपगत इव चन्द्रः उपस्थितो राजर्षिः ।

मेनका—[निर्वर्ण्य] **दुवे वि णो पिआणि उवणदाणि । इअं पच्चाणीदा सही अअं च अपरिक्खदो महाराओ त्ति ।** द्वे अप्यस्माकं प्रिये उपनते । इयं प्रत्यानीता सखी अयं चापरिक्षतो महाराज इति ।

सहजन्या—**सुट्ठु भणासि । दुज्जआ खु दाणवा ।** सुष्ठु भणसि । दुर्जयाः खलु दानवाः ।

राजा—**सूत इदं तच्छैलशिखरम् । अवतार्यतां रथः ।**

सूतः—**यदाज्ञापयत्यायुष्मान्** [इति यथोक्तं करोति]

राजा—[चक्रोद्घातं रूपयित्वा । आत्मगतम्] **हन्त दत्तफलो मे विषमावतारः ।**

URVASHI—(*Aside*) How noble his words ! Or what wonder that nectar (should flow) from the moon ! (*aloud*) That is why my heart is eager to meet them.

KING—(*Pointing by his hand*).

These your friends are watching your face—O fair one—from Hemakuta, like the Moon emerging from an eclipse and regaining its brightness. [10]

CHITRALEKHA—Dear friend, look.

URVASHI—(*Longingly looking at the King*) Equal in suffering, seems to drink me up with (thirsty) eyes

CHITRALEKHA—(*Significantly*) Who, my dear ?

URVASHI—This group of my friends.

RAMBHA—Here comes the royal sage taking Urvashi and Chitralekha with him, as if he were the Moon attended by the Vishakha (stars).

MENAKA—(*Looking closely*) We joy in both the things—here is our friend restored to us, while his majesty is unhurt.

SAHAJANYA—You speak the truth ; for the demons are hard to quell.

KING—Charioteer, here is the peak of the mountain. Bring the chariot down.

CHARIOTEER—As my lord commands. (*Does as bidden.*)

KIKG—(*Gesticulating jolting of the wheel, to himself*). Ah, not vain my descent on this uneven ground :

यदयं रथसंक्षोभादंसेनांसो रथोपमश्रोण्याः ।
स्पृष्टः सरोमविक्रियमङ्कुरितं मनसिजेनेव ॥ ११ ॥

उर्वशी—[सव्रीडम्] हला किं वि परदो ओसर । सखि किमपि परतोपसर ।

चित्रलेखा—[सस्मितम्] णाहं सक्का । नाहं शक्ता ।

रम्भा—एध संभावेम्ह राएसिं । [सर्वा उपसर्पन्ति] एत संभावयामो राजर्षिम् ।

राजा—सूत स्थापय तावद् रथम् ।

यावत् पुनरियं सुभ्रूरुत्सुकाभिः समुत्सुका ।
सखीभिर्याति संपर्कं लताभिः श्रीरिवार्तवी ॥ १२ ॥

[सूतस्तथा करोति ।]

सर्वाः—दिट्ठिआ महाराओ विअएण वड्ढदि । दिष्ट्या महाराजो विजयेन वर्धते ।

राजा—भवत्यश्च सखीसमागमेन ।

उर्वशी—[चित्रलेखादत्तहस्ता रथादवतीर्य] हला एध पीडिदं मं परिस्सजध । ण खु मे आसा आसि भूओवि सहीअणं पेक्खिस्सं ति । हला एत पीडितं मां परिष्वजध्वम् । न खलु मम आशासीद् भूयोऽपि सखीजनं द्रक्ष्यामीति ।

सत्वरं परिष्वजन्ते ।

रम्भा—सव्वहा महाराओ कप्प-सदाइं पुहविं पालअन्तो होदु । सर्वथा महाराजः कल्पशतानि पृथ्वीं पालयिता भवतु ।

सूतः—आयुष्मन् पूर्वस्यां दिशि महता रथवेगेनोपदर्शितः शब्दः ।

अयं च गगनात् कोपि तप्तचामीकराङ्गदः ।
अवरोहति शैलाग्रं तडित्वानिव तोयदः ॥ १३ ॥

That my shoulder should have rubbed the shoulder of that lovely damsel in the joltings of the chariot, so as to thrill me (with joy) looks as if love hath sprouted (within). [11]

URVASHI—(*Bashfully*). Well friend, will you move a bit.

CHITRALEKHA—I cannot.

RAMBHA—Come along—let us honour the royal sage.

(*All approach*).

KING—Charioteer, stop the chariot,

So that like the beauty of spring coming to the plants, she—this fair one—may hasten to meet her eager companions. [12]

(*The charioteer does as bidden*)

ALL—We congratulate your majesty upon your victory.

KING—And your ladyships too (are to be congratulated) upon the recovery of your friend.

URVASHI—(*Helped by Chitralekha with her arm, alighting from the chariot*). Friends come press me closely. Little did I hope to meet my friends again.

(*They quickly embrace*).

RAMBHA—May the King protect the earth a hundred *Kalpas* !

CHARIOTEER—My lord, from the East is indicated the sound of a rushing chariot.

And here is some one descending to the peak of the mountain from the sky—his armlet gleaming like heated gold, like a cloud (adorned by) lightning. [13]

(*The Nymphs look*).

[पश्यन्त्यप्सरसः ।]

सर्वाः—अम्मो चित्तरहो । अहो चित्ररथः ।

[ततः प्रविशति चित्ररथः ।]

चित्ररथः—[राजानं दृष्ट्वा सबहुमानम्] दिष्ट्या महेन्द्रोपकारपर्याप्तेन विक्रममहिम्ना वर्धते भवान् ।

राजा—अये गन्धर्वराजः [रथादवतीर्य] स्वागतं प्रियसुहृदे [परस्परं हस्तौ स्पृशतः]

चित्ररथः—वयस्य केशिना हृतामुर्वशीं नारदादुपश्रुत्य प्रत्याहरणार्थमस्याः शतक्रतुना गन्धर्वसेना समादिष्टा । ततो वयमन्तरा चारणेभ्यस्त्वदीयं जयोदाहरणं श्रुत्वा त्वामिहस्थमुपागताः । स भवानिमां पुरस्कृत्य सहास्माभिर्मघवन्तं द्रष्टुमर्हति । महत् खलु तत्रभवतो मघोनः प्रियमनुष्ठितं भवता । पश्य

पुरा नारायणेनेयमतिसृष्टा मरुत्वते ।
दैत्यहस्तादपाच्छिद्य सुहृदा संप्रति त्वया ॥ १४ ॥

राजा—मा मैवम् ।

ननु वज्रिण एव वीर्यमेतद्
विजयन्ते द्विषतो यदस्य पक्ष्याः ।
वसुधाधरकन्दराभिसर्पी
प्रतिशब्दोपि हरेर्भिनत्ति नागान् ॥ १५ ॥

चित्ररथः—युक्तमेतत् । अनुत्सेकः खलु विक्रमालंकारः ।

राजा—सखे नायमवसरो मम शतक्रतुं द्रष्टुम् । त्वमेवात्रभवतीं प्रभोरन्तिकं प्रापय ।

चित्ररथः—यथा भवान् मन्यते । इत इतो भवत्यः ।

[अप्सरसः प्रस्थिताः ।]

ALL—Behold ! it is Chitraratha.

(*Then enter Chitraratha*).

CHITRARATHA—(*Looking at the King respectfully*). I congratulate you on the greatness of your prowess which sufficeth to confer obligations on the great Indra.

KING—Ah, the King of the Gandharvas. (*Alighting from his chariot*). Welcome, my dear friend.

(*They touch each other's hands*).

CHITRARATHA—Friend, having heard from Narada that Urvashi was abducted by Keshin, Indra ordered the army of the Gandharvas to her rescue. So on our way we heard your panegyrics sung by the bards and now come to wait upon you here. It behoves you therefore, to meet Indra with us, taking her with you. Great is the service you have rendered to Indra. See,

Formerly she was presented to Indra by Narayana—and now is she being presented by you, his friend, by rescuing her from the demon's violence. [14]

KING—Do not think thus.

It is, indeed, Indra's might that enables his friends to conquer his foes: the very echo of the lion's roar, as through the rocky caves it spreads (and deepens) appals the mighty elephants. [15]

CHITRARATHA—That is proper. Humility is ever found the ornament of valour.

KING—Friend, I do not think this a proper occasion for me to see Lord Indra. Do you, therefore, take this nymph to my Lord.

CHITRARATHA—As my friend thinks. This way, ladies, this way.

उर्वशी—[जनान्तिकम्] **हला चित्तलेहे उवआरिणं पि राएसिं ण सक्कुणोमि आमन्तेदुं। ता तुमं मे मुहं होहि।** हला चित्रलेखे उपकारिणमपि राजर्षिं न शक्नोमि आमन्त्रयितुम्। तत् त्वं मम मुखं भव।

चित्रलेखा—[राजानमुपेत्य] **वअस्स उव्वसी विण्णवेदि महाराएण अब्भणुण्णादा इच्छामि पिअ-सहिं विअ महाराअस्स कित्तिं महिन्द-लोअं णेदुं ति।** वयस्य उर्वशी विज्ञापयति महाराजेन अभ्यनुज्ञाता इच्छामि प्रियसखीमिव महाराजस्य कीर्तिं महेन्द्रलोकं नेतुमिति।

राजा—गम्यतां पुनर्दर्शनाय।

[सर्वाः सगन्धर्वा आकाशोत्पतनं रूपयन्ति।]

उर्वशी—[उत्पतनभङ्गं रूपयित्वा] **अम्हहे लदा-विडवे मे एआवली लग्गा।** [परिवृत्य] **चित्तलेहे मोआवेहि दाव णं।** अहो लताविटपे ममैकावली लग्ना। चित्रलेखे मोचय तावदेनाम्।

चित्रलेखा—[सस्मितम्] **दिढं खु लग्गा। दुम्मोआ विअ मे पडिहादि। होदु जदिस्सं दाव।** दृढं खलु लग्ना। दुर्मोचनीयेव प्रतिभाति। भवतु यतिष्ये तावत्।

उर्वशी—सुमरेहि दाव एदं अत्तणो वअणं। स्मर तावदेतदात्मनो वचनम्।

[चित्रलेखा मोचनं नाटयति।]

राजा—[स्वगतम्]

प्रियमाचरितं लते त्वया मे
गमनेऽस्याः क्षणविघ्नमाचरन्त्या।
यदियं पुनरप्यपाङ्गनेत्रा
परिवृत्तार्धमुखी मयाद्य दृष्टा॥ १६॥

(*The nymphs set out*).

URVASHI—(*Aside*). Friend Chitralekha, I cannot bid adieu to this royal sage even though he is my benefactor. Do you, therefore, speak for me.

CHITRALEKHA—(*Approaching the King*). Friend, Urvashi requests leave of my Lord to take with her to heaven, as a dearly cherished friend, your fame.

KING—Adieu, till we meet again!

(*All gesticulate flying up into the heavens*).

URVASHI—(*Showing as if she is impeded in her flight*). Oh, this my necklace has got entangled in the thicket of creepers. (*Turning round*). Chitralekha, do extricate it.

CHITRALEKHA—(*Smiling*). Seems too deeply entangled to be set free. Well, I will try.

URVASHI—Be mindful of your words.

(*Chitralekha acts as if she is extricating it*).

KING—(*To himself*). A kind turn you have done me, O plant, by causing a moment's obstacle in her way. For thus I could behold her once again, with her sidelong glances and her half-averted face. [16]

सूतः—आयुष्मन् ।

अदः सुरेन्द्रस्य कृतापराधान्
प्रक्षिप्य दैत्यान् लवणाम्बुराशौ ।
वायव्यमस्त्रं शरधिं पुनस्ते
महोरगः श्वभ्रमिव प्रविष्टम् ॥ १७ ॥

राजा—तेन ह्युपश्लेषय रथं यावदारोहामि ।

[रथमुपश्लेषयति । राजा नाट्येन रथमारूढः ।
उर्वशी राजानं विलोक्य सनिःश्वासं सह सख्या निष्क्रान्ता चित्ररथश्च ।]

राजा—[उर्वशीमार्गोन्मुखः] अहो नु खलु दुर्लभाभिनिवेशी मदनः ।

एषा मनो मे प्रसभं शरीरात्
पितुः पदं मध्यममुत्पतन्ती ।
सुराङ्गना कर्षति खण्डिताग्रात्
सूत्रं मृणालादिव राजहंसी ॥ १८ ॥

[इति निष्क्रान्ताः सर्वे]

विक्रमोर्वशीये नाटके प्रथमोऽङ्कः समाप्तः ॥

CHARIOTEER—Royal sir,

Having hurled deep in the salt ocean the demon foes that offended against the King of the Gods, this Vayavya shaft now comes to rest in your quiver as comes the snake to its (wonted) covert. [17]

KING—Well then bring close to us the chariot, so that we might ascend.

(*The charioteer drives the chariot close to the King. The King acts ascending it. Urvashi sighingly looks at the King and departs with her friends and Chitraratha*).

KING—(*Looking after her*) What unattainable object doth Love attach one to!

This nymph of heaven bears off my heart forcibly out of my body, as through the mid-region of her sire she flies; so flies the swan with a fibre from the lotus-stalk, the end of which is broken. [18]

[*Exeunt Omnes*].

HERE ENDS ACT ONE.

द्वितीयोऽङ्कः ।

[ततः प्रविशति विदूषकः ।]

विदूषकः—ही ही भो णिमन्तणोवाअणेण बम्हणो विअ राअरहस्सेण फुट्टमाणो ण सक्कुणोमि आइण्णे अत्तणो जीहं रक्खिदुं । ता जाव तत्तभवं वअस्सो कज्जासणादो उट्ठेदि दाव इमस्सिं विरल-जण-संवादे विमाणुच्छङ्ग-परिसरे चिट्ठिस्सं । [परिक्रम्य स्थितः]

ही ही भो निमन्त्रणोपायनेन ब्राह्मण इव राजरहस्येन स्फोटमानो न शक्नोमि आकीर्णे आत्मनो जिह्वां रक्षितुम् । तद्यावत् तत्रभवान् वयस्यः कार्यासनादुत्तिष्ठति तावदेतस्मिन् विरल-जनसंपाते विमानोत्सङ्गपरिसरे स्थास्यामि ।

[प्रविश्य ।] **चेटी—आणत्तम्हि देवीए कासि-राअ-पुत्तीए हञ्जे णिउणए जदो-पहुदि भअवदो अक्कस्स उवत्थाणं करिअ पडिणिवुत्तो अज्जउत्तो तदो आरहिअ सुण्ण-हिअओ विअ लक्खीअदि । ता तस्स पिअ-वअस्सादो अज्ज-माणवआदो जाणाहि दाव से उक्कण्ठा-कालणं ति । कहं खु मए बम्ह-बन्धू अदिसंधेओ । अहवा विरल-तण-लग्गं विअ अवस्साअसलिलं चिरं तस्सिं रहस्सं ण चिट्ठदि । जाव णं अण्णेसामि** [परिक्रम्य अवलोक्य च] **एसो आलिहिदो वाणरो विअ किं पि तुण्हि-भूदो अज्जमाणवओ चिट्ठदि, जाव णं उवसप्पामि** [उपसृत्य] **अज्ज वन्दामि ।** आज्ञप्तास्मि देव्या काशीराजपुत्र्या हञ्जे निपुणिके यतःप्रभृति भगवतः अर्कस्योपस्थानं कृत्वा प्रतिनिवृत्त आर्यपुत्रस्तत आरभ्य शून्यहृदय

ACT. II.

(*Enter Vidushaka*).

VIDUSHAKA—Bursting as I am with the King's secret like a Brahmin with the presents he has had at some invitation, I shall not be able to set guard upon my tongue when in company. So I will bide here in the precincts of this Vimanaotsanga palace, but sparsely attended by people, until my friend comes forth from the council chamber.

(*Walks about and stands apart*).
(*Enter Nipunika, an attendant*).

NIPUNIKA—My Queen, the daughter of the King of Kashi, has bidden me: Girl Nipunika, since my Lord returned after his attendance upon the Sun, he looks absent-minded.

इव लक्ष्यते । तत् तस्य प्रियवयस्यादार्यमाणवकाज्जानीहि तावदस्योत्कण्ठाकारणमिति । कथं खलु मया ब्रह्मबन्धुरतिसंधेयः । अथवा विरलतृणलग्नमिव अवश्यायसलिलं चिरं तस्मिन् रहस्यं न तिष्ठति । यावदेनमन्विष्यामि । एष आलिखितो वानर इव किमपि तूष्णींभूतः आर्यमाणवकस्तिष्ठति । यावदेनमुपसर्पामि । आर्य वन्दे ।

विदूषकः—सत्थि भोदीए। [आत्मगतम्] **इमं दुट्ठ-चेडिअं पेक्खिअ तं राअरहस्सं हिअअं भिन्दिअ णिक्कमदि ।** [प्रकाशम्] **णिउणिए संगीद-वावारं उज्झिअ कहिं पत्थिदा सि** । स्वस्ति भवत्यै । इमां दुष्टचेटिकां दृष्ट्वा तद् राजरहस्यं हृदयं भित्वा निष्क्रामति । निपुणिके संगीतव्यापारमुज्झित्वा क्व प्रस्थितासि ।

निपुणिका—देवीए वअणेण अज्जं एव्व पेक्खिदुं । देव्या वचनेन आर्यमेव द्रष्टुम् ।

विदूषकः—किं तत्तहोदी आणवेदि। किं तत्रभवत्याज्ञापयति।

निपुणिका—देवी भणादि सदा वि अज्जो मइ पक्खवादी ण मं अणुइद-वेअणा-दुक्खिदं उवेक्खदित्ति । देवी भणति सदाप्यार्यो मयि पक्षपाती न मामनुचितवेदनादुःखितामुपेक्षत इति।

विदूषकः—[सवितर्कम्] **किं वा वअस्सेण तत्तभोदीए पडिऊलं आचरिदं** । किं वा वयस्येन तत्रभवत्याः प्रतिकूलमाचरितम् ।

निपुणिका—अज्ज जं-णिमित्तं भट्टा उक्कण्ठिदो ताए इत्थिआए णामधेएण भट्टिणा देवी आलविदा । आर्य यन्निमित्तं भर्ता उत्कण्ठितस्तस्याः स्त्रिया नामधेयेन भर्ता देवी आलपिता।

विदूषकः—[स्वगतम्] कहं सअं एव्व तत्तभवदा रहस्स—**भेदो किदो । किं दाणिं अहं जीहा-जन्तणेण दुक्खं**

Do you, therefore, know the cause of his anxiety from his dear friend, the noble Manavaka. But how may I trick that fool of a Brahmin? Or rather a secret can rest no longer in his breast, than morning dew upon the point of a thin grass-blade. I will, therefore, find him out. (*Walking about and looking*). There is he sitting silent owing to some cause or other, the very picture of a monkey. So I will go to him. (*Approaching*). Arya Manavaka, I salute you.

VIDUSHAKA—Prosperity attend you! (*Apart*). How the King's secret is bursting out of my heart at the sight of this wicked girl! (*Aloud*) Well, Nipunika, where are you going leaving your practice of music?

NIPUNIKA—Just to see you, at the Queen's bidding.

VIDUSHAKA—What are the commands of Her Majesty?

NIPUNIKA—The Queen says that you have been ever a friend of hers, and therefore will not be indifferent to her in her present anxiety which is due to some unusual distress.

VIDUSHAKA—(*Guessing*). May it be that my friend has done anything to offend her?

NIPUNIKA—Noble Sir, the King addressed the Queen by the name of the very woman who has been the source of his anxiety.

अणुहवामि । [प्रकाशम्] किं आमन्तिदा तत्तहोदी उव्वसी त्ति। ताए दंसणेण उम्मादिदो तत्तभवं ण केवलं तत्तभोर्दि मं पि विणोद-विमुहो दढं पोडेदि। कथ स्वयमेव तत्रभवता रहस्यभेदः कृतः । किमिदानीमहं जिह्वायन्त्रणेन दुःखमनुभवामि। किमामन्त्रिता तत्रभवती उर्वशीति। तस्या दर्शनेन उन्मादितस्तत्रभवान् न केवलं तत्रभवतीं मामपि विनोदविमुखो दृढं पीडयति ।

णिपुणिका—[आत्मगतम्] **किदं मए भेदणं भट्टिणो रहस्स-दुग्गस्स** [प्रकाशम्] **अज्ज किं दाव देवीए णिवेदेमि।** कृतं मया भेदनं भर्तू रहस्यदुर्गस्य। आर्य किं तावद् देव्यै निवेदयामि।

विदूषकः—णिउणिए विण्णवेहिं तत्तभोर्दि । जदामि दाव मिअतिण्हिआदो णिवत्तेदुं वअस्सं तदो देवीए मुहं पेक्खिस्सं ति । निपुणिके विज्ञापय तत्रभवतीम् । यते तावद् मृगतृष्णिकाया निवर्तयितुं वयस्यं ततो देव्या मुखं द्रक्ष्यामीति ।

निपुणिका—जं अज्जो आणवेदि । यदार्य आज्ञापयति ।

[इति निष्क्रान्ता ।]

[नेपथ्ये वैतालिकः ।] **जयतु देवः ।**

आ लोकान्तात् प्रतिहततमोवृत्तिरासां प्रजानां
तुल्योद्योगस्तव दिनकृतश्चाधिकारो मतो नः ।
तिष्ठत्येष क्षणमधिपतिर्ज्योतिषां व्योममध्ये
षष्ठे भागे त्वमपि दिवसस्यात्मनश्छन्दवर्ती ॥ १ ॥

विदूषकः—[कर्णं दत्वा] **एसो कज्जासणादो उट्ठिदो इदो एव्व आअच्छदि वअस्सो जाव से पासवत्ती होमि ।**

[इति निष्क्रान्तः ।]

एष कार्यासनादुत्थित इत एव आगच्छति वयस्यः। यावदस्य पार्श्ववर्ती भवामि ।

VIDUSHAKA—(*To himself*). How has His Majesty let out the secret himself! What need that I should suffer by putting restraint upon my tongue? (*Aloud*). What. did he call the Queen-Urvashi? Ever since he saw her he has been out of his senses, and has annoyed not only Her Majesty but me also by setting his face against all recreations.

NIPUNIKA—(*To herself*). Here have I made a breach in the fortress of the royal secret. (*Aloud*). Noble sir, what may I say to the Queen?

VIDUSHAKA—Say to Her Grace: 'I shall endeavour to wean His Majesty from this (chase of the) mirage. and then will I see the Queen's face

NIPUNIKA—As the noble sir says. [*Exit*].

(*Behind the scenes a bard*).

Glory to the King!

Your power and that of the Sun appear to us to do similar work—for you suppress the evil tendencies of your subjects all over the world as the Sun drives away darkness beyond its confines (for the benefit of the people); the Lord of luminaries rests for a moment in the middle of the sky, and you too follow your own inclination in the sixth part of the day. [1]

VIDUSHAKA—(*Listening*). My friend has left the council-chamber and is coming in this very direction so I will join him. [*Exit*]

END OF THE INTRODUCTORY SCENE.

प्रवेशकः ।

[ततः प्रविशति उत्कण्ठितो राजा विदूषकश्च ।]

राजा—

आ दर्शनात् प्रविष्टा सा मे सुरलोकसुन्दरी हृदयम् ।
बाणेन मकरकेतोः कृतमार्गमवन्ध्यपातेन ॥ १ ॥

विदूषकः—[आत्मगतम्] संपीडिदा खु दाव तवस्सिणी कासिराअउत्ती । संपीडिता खलु तावत् तपस्विनी काशीराजपुत्री ।

राजा—अपि रक्ष्यते रहस्यनिक्षेपः ।

विदूषकः—[सविषादमात्मगतम्] हद्धी हद्धी अहिसंधिदो म्हि दासीए । अण्णधा ण वअस्सो एव्वं पुच्छदि । हा धिक् हा धिक् अभिसंहितोऽस्मि दास्या । अन्यथा न वयस्य एवं पृच्छति ।

राजा—[साशङ्कम्] किं भवांस्तूष्णीमास्ते ।

विदूषकः—एव्वं मए णिअन्तिदा जीहा जं भवदो वि सहसा पडिवअणं ण देमि । एवं मया नियन्त्रिता जिह्वा यद् भवतोपि सहसा प्रतिवचनं न ददामि ।

राजा—युक्तम् । अथ क्वेदानीमात्मानं विनोदयेयम् ।

विदूषकः—महाणसं गच्छम्ह । महानसं गच्छावः ।

राजा—किं तत्र ।

विदूषकः—तहिं पञ्च-विहस्स अब्भवहारस्स उवणद-संभारस्स जोअणं पेक्खमाणेहिं सक्कं उक्कण्ठा विणोदेदुं । तत्र पञ्चविधस्य अभ्यवहारस्य उपनतसंभारस्य योजनां प्रेक्षमाणाभ्यां शक्यमुत्कण्ठा विनोदयितुम् ।

राजा—[सस्मितम्] तत्रेप्सितसंनिधानाद् भवान् रंस्यते । मया खलु दुर्लभप्रार्थनः कथमात्मा विनोदयितव्यः ।

(Enter King in a love-lorn condition and the Vidushaka)

KING—Ever since I saw her, that celestial one has enthroned herseslf in my heart to which access was given to her by the unerring shafts of Love. [2]

VIDUSHAKA—(*To himself*). Surely the poor (Queen) daughter of the King of Kashi must have been deeply annoyed.

KING—I hope you keep the secret entrusted to you.

VIDUSHAKA—(*Ruefully-to himself*). Alas! Alas! I am excellently tripped up by that wench. How else would my friend ask such a question?

KING—(*Alarmed*). How! you are silent?

VIDUSHAKA—I have so (effectively) restrained my tongue, that I cannot answer off-hand even your inquiries.

KING—Well done. Where shall I divert myself?

VIDUSHAKA—We shall proceed to the kitchen.

KING—What for?

VIDUSHAKA—There the very sight of the preparation of the five kinds of dishes with all their materials put together will be sufficient to dissipate all distressing thoughts.

KING—(*Smilingly*). There you will surely find much diversion, because what you covet will be at hand. But with my heart longing for an unattainable object, how may I find diversion?

विदूषकः—णं भवं तत्तहोदीए उव्वसीए दंसण-पहं गदो। ननु भवांस्तत्रभवत्या उर्वश्या दर्शनपथं गतः।

राजा—ततः किम्।

विदूषकः—ण खु सा दुल्लह त्ति समत्थेमि। न खलु सा दुर्लभेति समर्थये।

राजा—पक्षपातोयमवधार्यताम्।

विदूषकः—एत्तिअं मन्तअन्तेण भवदा वड्ढिदं मे कोदूहलं। किं तत्तभोदी उव्वसी अदुदिआ रूवेण अहं विअ विरूवदाए। एतावद् मन्त्रयमाणेन भवता वर्धितं मे कौतूहलम्। किं तत्रभवत्युर्वशी अद्वितीया रूपेण अहमिव विरूपतया।

राजा—माणवक प्रत्यवयवमशक्यवर्णनां तामवेहि। समासतः श्रूयताम्।

विदूषकः—अवहिदो म्हि। अवहितोस्मि।

राजा—

आभरणस्याभरणं प्रसाधनविधेः प्रसाधनविशेषः।
उपमानस्यापि सखे प्रत्युपमानं वपुस्तस्याः ॥ ३ ॥

विदूषकः—अदो खु भवदा दिव्व-रसाहिलासिणा चादअव्वदं गहिदं। अतः खलु भवता दिव्यरसाभिलाषिणा चातकव्रतं गृहीतम्।

राजा—विविक्तादृते नान्यदुत्सुकस्य शरणमस्ति। तद् भवान् प्रमदवनमार्गमादेशयतु।

विदूषकः—[आत्मगतम्] **का गदी** [प्रकाशम्] **इदो इदो भवं** [परिक्रम्य] **एदेण पमद-वण-चोदिदेण विअ पच्चुग्गदो भवं आअन्तुओ दक्खिण-मारुदेण।** का गतिः। इत इतो भवान्। एतेन प्रमदवनचोदितेनेव प्रत्युद्गतो भवानागन्तुको दक्षिणमारुतेन।

VIDUSHAKA—Has the lady Urvashi seen my friend?

KING—What then?

VIDUSHAKA—Why, then, I should think her not quite unattainable.

KING—Remember, this is your partiality for me.

VIDUSHAKA—What Your Highness says only adds to my curiosity. What! Is she without a peer in beauty as I in deformity?

KING—Manavaka, I assure you, words cannot paint the loveliness of each part of her body; so hear her (described) in brief.

VIDUSHAKA—I am all attention.

KING—Her form is the ornament of ornaments,
an excellent decoration of decorations, and, my friend,
a standard of comparison to the (accepted) standards. [3]

VIDUSHAKA—That is why you have taken the vow of the *Chataka*, yearning as you do for heavenly drink.

KING—To one smarting under love's pain, there is no other solace than solitude. Do you, therefore, lead the way to the Pramadavana.

VIDUSHAKA—(*To himself*). What help! (*Aloud*). This way, this way, my Lord. (*Walking about*). This southern breeze, as if deputed by the Pramadavana advances to greet you, its guest.

राजा—[विलोक्य] उपपन्नं विशेषणमस्य वायोः। अयं हि

निषिञ्चन् माधवीमेतां लतां कौन्दीं च नर्तयन् ।
स्नेहदाक्षिण्ययोर्योगात् कामीव प्रतिभाति मे ॥ ४ ॥

विदूषकः—ईरिसो एव्व दे अहिणिवेसो होदु [परिक्रामितकेन] एदं पमदवण-दुवारं । पविसदु भवं । ईदृश
३ एव तवाभिनिवेशो भवतु । एतत् प्रमदवनद्वारम् । प्रविशतु भवान् ।

राजा—प्रविशाग्रतः ।

उभौ प्रविशतः ।

६ **राजा**—[अग्रतो विलोक्य] वयस्य मया न साधु समर्थितमापत्प्रतीकारः किल प्रमदवनोद्यानप्रवेश इति ।

विविक्षुर्यदहं तूर्णमुद्यानं तापशान्तये ।
स्रोतोजवोह्यमानस्य प्रतीपतरणं हि तत् ॥ ५ ॥

विदूषकः—कहं विअ । कथमिव ।

राजा—

इदमसुलभवस्तुप्रार्थनादुर्निवारं
प्रथममपि मनो मे पञ्चबाणः क्षिणोति ।
किमुत मलयवातोन्मूलितापाण्डुपत्रै-
रुपवनसहकारैर्दर्शितेष्वङ्कुरेषु ॥ ६ ॥

विदूषकः—अलं परिदेविदेण । अइरेण दे इच्छिअसंपादइत्तओ अणङ्गो एव्व सुहदो भविस्सदि । अलं
३ परिदेवितेन । अचिरेण तव इष्टसंपादयिता अनङ्ग एव सुखदो भविष्यति ।

राजा—प्रतिगृहीतं ब्राह्मणवचनम् ।

परिक्रामतः ।

६ **विदूषकः**—पेक्खदु भवं वसन्तोदारसूअअं अहिरामत्तणं पमदवणस्स । पश्यतु भवान् वसन्तावतारसूचकमभिरामत्वं प्रमदवनस्य ।

KING—(*Looking*). This is but a proper epithet for this breeze. For,

Impregnating this Madhavi creeper and making the Kaundi dance, he appears to me like a lover, as he combines in himself love (to one) and kindness (to the other). [4]

VIDUSHAKA—Let your love also be such and no other. (*Walking*). Here is the entrance to the Pramadavana; please you to enter.

KING—Go ahead.

(*Both enter*).

KING—(*Looking ahead*). Well, my friend, I was not right when I imagined that to enter this Pramadavana garden would yield relief to my affliction.

For the thought of entering this garden so quickly to dispel my anguish is (as vain as) the swimming against the current by one who is borne backwards by the stream. [5]

VIDUSHAKA—How so?

KING—Already the five-arrowed god has pierced my heart which is difficult to be withdrawn from its desire for the unattainable: what then when the mango-trees of the garden, whose pallid leaves have been blown away by the Malaya breeze, are showing fresh sprouts? [6]

VIDUSHAKA—Away with your lamentations! Before long this very Love will be agreeable to you by yielding you the object of your desire.

KING—I accept these words of a Brahmin.

(*They pace about*).

VIDUSHAKA—Let my friend notice the beauty of this garden (Pramadavana) heralding the advent of spring.

राजा—ननु प्रतिपादपमेवावलोकयामि । अत्र हि

अग्रे स्त्रीनखपाटलं कुरबकं श्यामं द्वयोर्भागयो-
र्बालाशोकमुपोढरागसुभगं भेदोन्मुखं तिष्ठति ।
ईषद्बद्धरजःकणाग्रकपिशा चूते नवा मञ्जरी
मुग्धत्वस्य च यौवनस्य च सखे मध्ये मधुश्रीः स्थिता ॥७॥

विदूषकः—एसो मणि सिला-पट्टअ-सणाहो अदिमुत्त-लदामण्डवो भमर-संघट्ट-पडिदेहिं कुसुमेहिं सअं विअ किदोवआरो भवन्तं पडिच्छदि । अणुगेण्हीअदु दाव एसो । एष मणिशिलापट्टकसनाथः अतिमुक्तलतामण्डपो भ्रमरसंघट्टपतितैः कुसुमैः स्वयमिव कृतोपचारो भवन्तं प्रतीच्छति । तदनुगृह्यतां तावदेषः ।

राजा—यथा भवते रोचते । [परिक्रम्योपविष्टौ]

विदूषकः—इह सुहासीणो भवं ललिद-लदा-विलोहीअमाणणअणो उव्वसी-गदं उक्कण्ठं विणोदेदु । इह सुखासीनो भवान् ललितलताविलोभ्यमाननयनः उर्वशीगतामुत्कण्ठां विनोदयतु ।

राजा—[निःश्वस्य]

न मम कुसुमितास्वपि सखे नोपवनलतासु नम्रविटपासु ।
चक्षुर्बध्नाति धृतिं तद्रूपालोकदुर्ललितम् ॥ ८ ॥

तदुपायश्चिन्त्यतां यथा सफलप्रार्थनो भवेयम् ।

विदूषकः—[विहस्य] भो अहल्ला-कामुअस्स महिन्दस्स वेज्जो उव्वसीपज्जुस्सुअस्स भवदो अहं वि दुवे एत्थ उम्मत्तआ । भोः अहल्याकामुकस्य महेन्द्रस्य वैद्य उर्वशीपर्युत्सुकस्य भवतोहमपि द्वावत्रोन्मत्तौ ।

राजा—मा मैवम् । अतिस्नेहः खलु कार्यदर्शी ।

विदूषकः—एसो चिन्तेमि । मा उण परिदेविदेण मम

KING—Well! I mark it on every tree. For,

Here is the *Kurabaka* flower red at the tip like a woman's nails, and black at the sides; the young *Ashoka* bud charming owing to increased redness, is ready to burst (into flower); the new blossom of the mango is yellow at the ends as the pollen is yet imperfectly formed; (thus) the Beauty of spring stands, my friend, between childhood and youth. [7]

VIDUSHAKA—The Jasmine-bower yonder, with its slab of marble, seems itself to present you with flowers which have been dropped down by the bees coming into contact with them, and offers you welcome. Please you to favour it.

KING—As you please.

(*They walk about and seat themselves*).

VIDUSHAKA—Now, seated comfortably in this place, you may dissipate your longing for Urvashi with your eyes captivated by these lovely creepers.

KING—(*Sighing*). My eye, grown fastidious by looking on her charms, does not find any pleasure in these garden-plants with their branches bent, although they have now flowered. [8]

So, think of an expedient to secure me the object of my wishes.

VIDUSHAKA—(*Laughing*). Well, the physician to the great Indra who was enamoured of Ahalya, and I to you pining for Urvashi, both are madmen in this affair.

KING—Nay, do not say so. Genuine affection ever counsels wisely.

VIDUSHAKA—Well, I will turn the matter over in my mind; but then you must not disturb my meditation by your sighs.

समाधिं भञ्जिस्ससि [चिन्तां रूपयति] एष चिन्तयामि । मा पुनः परिदेवितेन मम समाधिं भङ्क्ष्यसि ।

९ **राजा**—[निमित्तं सूचयित्वा आत्मगतम् ।]

न सुलभा सकलेन्दुमुखी च सा
किमपि चेदमनङ्गविचेष्टितम् ।
अभिमुखीष्विव काङ्क्षितसिद्धिषु
व्रजति निर्वृतिमेकपदे मनः ॥ ९ ॥

[जाताशास्तिष्ठति । ततः प्रविशत्याकाशयानेन उर्वशी चित्रलेखा च ।]

चित्रलेखा—हला कहिं अणिद्दिट्ठकालणं गच्छीअदि ।
३ हला क्व अनिर्दिष्टकारणं गम्यते ।

उर्वशी—सहि तदा हेमऊड-सिहरे लदा-विडवेण खण-विग्घिदाआसगमणं मं ओहसिअ किं दाणिं पुच्छसि ।
६ सखि तदा हेमकूटशिखरे लताविटपेन क्षणविघ्निताकाशगमनां मामुपहस्य किमिदानीं पृच्छसि ।

चित्रलेखा—किं तस्स राएसिणो पुरूरवस्स सआसं
९ **पत्थिदा सि ।** किं तस्य राजर्षेः पुरूरवसः सकाशं प्रस्थितासि ।

उर्वशी—अअं मे अवहत्थिद-लज्जो ववसाओ। अयं मम अपहस्तितलज्जो व्यवसायः ।

१२ **चित्रलेखा—को उण सहीए पुढमं पेसिदो ।** कः पुनः सख्या प्रथमं प्रेषितः ।

उर्वशी—हिअअं । हृदयम् ।

१५ **चित्रलेखा—सअं एव्व साहु संपधारीअदु दाव् ।** स्वयमेव साधु संप्रधार्यतां तावत् ।

उर्वशी—मअणो खु मं णिओएदि । किं एत्थ संपधा-

(*Vidushaka acts as if he is meditating*).

KING—(*Showing that he has perceived an omen, to himself*).

The damsel with her face lovely as the full-orbed
moon, is far beyond my reach ; and yet here is this act
of Love for some reason or another ; for, all of a sudden,
my mind feels relief as it would when the fulfilment of
its desire was nigh [9].

(*Feels hope revived within him. Enter Urvashi and Chitralekha in the air*).

CHITRALEKHA—Tell me, dear girl, whither we are going for some unknown purpose.

URVASHI—How can you ask me such a question, friend, having chaffed me at that time on the peak of the *Hemakuta*, where owing to the branch of some plant I felt a moment's obstacle in my flight in the sky ?

CHITRALEKHA—Are you going to meet the royal sage, Pururavas ?

URVASHI—Yes, such my venture, and I have thrown to the winds all shame about it.

CHITRALEKHA—And, pray, whom hath my friend sent ahead ?

URVASHI—Well, my heart.

CHITRALEKHA—Think well, beforehand, yourself.

URVASHI—Love leads me on : what is there to be considered ?

रीअदि । मदनः खलु मां नियोजयति । किमत्र संप्रधार्यते ।

चित्रलेखा--अदो वरं णत्थि मे उत्तरं । अतः परं नास्ति ममोत्तरम् ।

उर्वशी--तेण हि आदिसीअदु मग्गो जह गच्छन्तीणं अन्तराओ ण भवे । तेन हि आदिश्यतां मार्गो यथा गच्छन्त्योरन्तरायो न भवेत् ।

चित्रलेखा--सहि वीसद्धा होहि । णं भअवदा देवगुरुणा अवराइदं णाम सिहा-बन्धण-विज्जं उवदिसन्तेण तिदस-पडिवक्खस्स अलङ्घणिज्जा कदम्ह। सखि विश्रब्धा भव । ननु भगवता देवगुरुणा अपराजितां नाम शिखाबन्धनविद्यामुपदिशता त्रिदशप्रतिपक्षस्य अलङ्घनीये कृते स्वः ।

उर्वशी--अहो विसुमरिदं मे हिअअं । अहो विस्मृतं मम हृदयम् ।

[सिद्धमार्गमासाद्य ।]

चित्रलेखा--एदं भअवदीए भाईरहीए जउँणा-संगम-विसेस-पावणेसु सलिलेसु ओलोअन्तस्स विअ अत्ताणअं पइट्ठाणस्स सिहाभरण-भूदं राएसिणो भवणं उवट्ठिदम्ह । एतद् भगवत्या भागीरथ्या यमुनासंगमविशेषपावनेषु सलिलेष्ववलोकयत इव आत्मानं प्रतिष्ठानस्य शिखाभरणभूतं राजर्षेर्भवनमुपस्थिते स्वः ।

उर्वशी--[विलोक्य] **णं वत्तव्वं ठाणन्तर-गदो सग्गो त्ति ।** [विचार्य] **हला कहिं णु खु सो आवण्णाणुकम्पी भवे ।** ननु वक्तव्यं स्थानान्तरगतः स्वर्ग इति । हला क्व नु खलु स आपन्नानुकम्पी भवेत् ।

चित्रलेखा--एदस्सिं णन्दण-वणेक्कदेसे विअ पमद-वणे ओदरिअ जाणिस्सामो । एतस्मिन् नन्दनवनैकदेश इव प्रमदवने अवतीर्य ज्ञास्यावः ।

CHITRALEKHA—Well then, I make no further question.

URVASHI—Advise me, then, which way we should proceed, so that we may not meet with any impediment on our way.

CHITRALEKHA—Have no fear, dear girl. Have not we two been made inviolable of the enemy of the gods by the revered preceptor of the immortals by imparting to us the mystic art of tying up the hair called the *Aparajita ?*

URVASHI—How could I be so forgetful!

(*Coming to the path of the Siddhas*).

CHITRALEKHA—Here have we come to the palace of the royal sage, the crest-borne gem of Pratisthana, which appears as it were to look at its own reflection in the waters of the divine Ganges, rendered particularly holy by her confluence with the Yamuna.

URVASHI—(*Looking*). Rather it should be said that the heavens have been transferred to another place! (*Reflecting*). But friend, where shall we find him—that pitying friend of the helpless?

CHITRALEKHA—Let us first alight in this Pramadavana which looks like a part of the garden of heaven, and we shall find out.

[उभे अवतरतः ।]

चित्रलेखा—[दृष्ट्वा सहर्षम्] **हला एसो खु पढमोदिदो विअ चन्दो कोमुदिं विअ तुमं पडिच्छदि ।** सखि एष खलु प्रथमोदित इव चन्द्रः कौमुदीमिव त्वां प्रतीक्षते ।

उर्वशी—[विलोक्य] **हला दाणिं पुढम-दंसणादो सविसेसं पिअदंसणो महाराओ पडिहादि ।** सखि इदानीं प्रथमदर्शनात् सविशेषं प्रियदर्शनो महाराजः प्रतिभाति ।

चित्रलेखा—जुज्जदि । ता एहि उवसप्पम्ह । युज्यते । तदेहि उपसर्पावः ।

उर्वशी—तिरक्खरिणी-पडिच्छण्णा पासगदा से भविअ सुणिस्सं दाव । पास-पडिवत्तिणा वअस्सेण सह विअणे किं पि मन्तअन्तो चिट्ठदि । तिरस्करिणीप्रतिच्छन्ना पार्श्वगता अस्य भूत्वा श्रोष्यामि तावत् । पार्श्वपरिवर्तिना वयस्येन सह विजने किमपि मन्त्रयमाणस्तिष्ठति ।

चित्रलेखा—जह दे रोअदि । [यथोक्तमनुतिष्ठतः ।] यथा ते रोचते ।

विदूषकः—भो चिन्तिदो मए दुल्लह-प्पणइणी-समाअमोवाओ । भोः चिन्तितो मया दुर्लभप्रणयिनीसमागमोपायः ।

[राजा तूष्णीभास्ते ।]

उर्वशी—का णु खु एसा इत्थिआ इमिणा पत्थीअमाणा अत्ताणअं विकत्थेदि । का नु खल्वेषा स्त्री अनेन प्रार्थ्यमाना आत्मानं विकत्थते ।

चित्रलेखा—किं उण माणुस्सअं विडम्बीअदि । किं पुनर्मानुष्यं विडम्ब्यते ।

(*Both alight*).

CHITRALEKHA—(*Looking with joy*). Friend, here is he expecting you, like the newly-risen moon expecting moonlight.

URVASHI—(*Observing*) My dear, does not he look more graceful now than when first he met my gaze ?

CHITRALEKHA—Quite so; well then, come along, let us approach.

URVASHI—Let me for a while remain hidden by the power of the *tiraskarini* charm, and approaching him, listen. He seems to be talking something to his friend who is near, in this solitary place.

CHITRALEKHA—As you like it.

(*They do, as said*).

VIDUSHAKA—Well, friend, I have thought out a plan for securing you an interview with the person you love, although she is inaccessible.

(*The King remains silent*).

URVASHI—What woman thinks much of herself (that she should hold out) even when made love to, by him ?

CHITRALEKHA—But why do you act the part of a mortal ?

उर्वशी—भयामि सहसा पभावादो विण्णादुं । बिभेमि सहसा प्रभावाद् विज्ञातुम् ।

विदूषकः—णं भणामि चिन्तिदो उवाओ त्ति । ननु भणामि चिन्तित उपाय इति ।

राजा—तेन हि कथ्यताम् ।

विदूषकः—सिविण-समाअम-आरिणिं णिद्दं सेवदु भवं। अहवा तत्थभोदीए उव्वसीए पडिकिदिं आलिहिअ ओलोअन्तो चिट्ठ । स्वप्नसमागमकारिणीं निद्रां सेवतां भवान् । अथवा तत्रभवत्या उर्वश्याः प्रतिकृतिमालिख्य अवलोकयंस्तिष्ठ ।

उर्वशी—[सहर्षम्] **होण-सत्त हिअअ समस्सस समस्सस ।** हीनसत्त्व हृदय समाश्वसिहि समाश्वसिहि ।

राजा—उभयमप्यनुपपन्नम् ।

हृदयमिषुभिः कामस्यान्तः सशल्यमिदं सदा
कथमुपलभे निद्रां स्वप्ने समागमकारिणीम् ।
न च सुवदनामालेख्येपि प्रियामसमाप्य तां
मम नयनयोरुद्बाष्पत्वं सखे न भविष्यति ॥ १० ॥

चित्रलेखा—सुदं तुए । श्रुतं त्वया ।

उर्वशी—सुदं । ण उण पज्जत्तं हिअअस्स । श्रुतम् । न पुनः पर्याप्तं हृदयस्य ।

विदूषकः—एत्तिओ मे मदि-विहवो । एतावान् मम मतिविभवः ।

राजा—[सनिःश्वासम्]

नितान्तकठिनां रुजं मम न वेद सा मानसीं
प्रभावविदितानुरागमवमन्यते वापि माम् ।
अलब्धफलनीरसान् मम विधाय तस्मिञ्जने
समागममनोरथान् भवतु पञ्चबाणः कृती ॥ ११ ॥

URVASHI—But I fear too soon to know through my power.

VIDUSHAKA—Well, I say, I have hit upon a plan.

KING—Well then, tell me.

VIDUSHAKA—Let Your Majesty enjoy a nap, which will effect your union in dreams ; or delineate a likeness of the lady Urvashi and remain gazing upon the picture.

URVASHI—(*With joy*). Be of good cheer, my timid heart.

KING—Both are impracticable, (I fear).

For the shafts of love are ever rankling inside my breast · how then can I enjoy sleep which in dreams might effect our union ? And even before I have completed the picture of the beloved one with the lovely face, tears would surely not fail to start in my eyes. [11]

CHITRALEKHA—Have you heard ?

URVASHI—Yes I have ; but that scarcely sufficeth to comfort my heart.

VIDUSHAKA—Well, my ingenuity extends only so far.

KING—(*Sighing*).

Perhaps she does not know the very keen anguish of my heart ; or knowing my love through her supernatural power, she but despises me. Let the God of the five shafts feel happy by making my desires of union with that person void of any pleasure on account of their fruitlessness. [11]

चित्रलेखा--सुदं तुए । श्रुतं त्वया ।

उर्वशी--हद्धी हद्धी । मं एव्वं अवगच्छदि । असमत्थ-म्हि अग्गदो भविअ से पडिवअणस्स । पहाव-णिम्मि-देण भुज्ज-वत्तेण संपादिदुत्तरा होदुं इच्छामि । हा धिक् हा धिक् । मामेवमवगच्छति । असमर्थास्मि अग्रतो भूत्वा अस्य प्रतिवचनस्य । प्रभावनिर्मितेन भूर्जपत्रेण संपादितोत्तरा भवितुमिच्छामि ।

चित्रलेखा--अणुमदं मे । अनुमतं मम ।

[उर्वशी ससंभ्रमं गृहीत्वा यथोक्तं करोति ।]

विदूषकः--[दृष्ट्वा] **अविहा अविहा । भो किं णु खु एदं भुअङ्ग-णिम्मोअं विअ संमुहे णो णिवडिदं ।** अविहा अविहा । भोः किं नु खल्वेतद् भुजङ्गनिर्मोक इव संमुखे आवयोः निपतितम् ।

राजा--[विभाव्य] **भूर्जपत्रगतोयमक्षरविन्यासः ।**

विदूषकः--ण खु अदिट्ठाए तत्तहोदीए उव्वसीए भवदो परिदेविदं सुणिअ समाणाणुराअ-सूअआइं अक्खराइं विसज्जिआइं होन्ति । न खल्वदृष्टया तत्रभवत्या उर्वश्या भवतः परिदेवितं श्रुत्वा समानानुरागसूचकान्यक्षराणि विसृष्टानि भवन्ति ।

राजा--नास्त्यगतिर्मनोरथानाम् [गृहीत्वा अनुवाच्य । सहर्षम् ।] **सखे प्रसन्नस्ते तर्कः ।**

विदूषकः--भवं दाणिं पसीददु । एत्थ लिहिदं सुणिदुं इच्छामि । भवान् इदानीं प्रसीदतु । अत्र लिखितं श्रोतुमिच्छामि ।

उर्वशी--साहु अज्ज णाअरिओ सि । साधु आर्य नागरिकोसि ।

राजा--श्रूयताम् । [वाचयति]

सामिअ संभाविआ जह अहं तुए अमुणिआ ।
तह अणुरत्तस्स जइ णाम तुह उवरि ॥ १२ ॥

CHITRALEKHA—Have you heard?

URVASHI—Alas! Alas! He takes me to be thus! I cannot confront him and give him answer; so I desire to make answer to him by means of a Bhurja leaf which I will produce through my power.

CHITRALEKHA—I agree.

(Urvashi takes it in haste and does as said).

VIDUSHAKA—(*Seeing*). Holla! What is here, in front of us, that looks like the slough of a snake?

KING—(*Looking closely*). This is some letter written upon a Bhurja-leaf.

VIDUSHAKA—May it be that the lady Urvashi, unperceived, has overheard, your lamentation and has sent this letter indicating therein her equal love for you?

KING—There is nothing to which desires do not soar. *(Takes and reads it; with joy).* Very happy was your guess, my friend.

VIDUSHAKA—Please to favour me; for I desire to hear what may be written on it.

URVASHI—Well said, sir; you have proved yourself a town-gallant.

KING—Listen. (*Reads*).

"Lord, if I am indeed, what in your ignorance, you make me out to be, towards you who love me, how

णं मे लुलिअ-पारिजाअ-सअणिज्जयम्मि होन्ति ।
णन्दण-वण-वाआ वि अच्चुण्हआ सरीरए ॥ १३ ॥

स्वामिन् संभाविता यथाहं त्वया अज्ञाता ।
तथानुरक्तस्य यदि नाम तवोपरि ॥ १२ ॥
ननु मम लुलितपारिजातशयनीये भवन्ति ।
नन्दनवनवाता अप्यत्युष्णकाः शरीरके ॥ १४ ॥

उर्वशी—किं णु खु संपदं भणिस्सदि । किं नु खलु सांप्रतं भणिष्यति ।

३ चित्रलेखा—णं भणिदं एव्व कमल-णालाअमाणेहिं अङ्गेहिं । ननु भणितमेव कमलनालायमानैरङ्गैः ।

विदूषकः—दिट्ठिआ मए विअ बुभुक्खिदेण सोत्थि-
६ वाअणं उवलद्धं भवदा समासासणं । दिष्ट्या मयेव बुभुक्षितेन स्वस्तिवाचनमुपलब्धं भवता समाश्वासनम् ।

राजा—समाश्वासनमिति किमुच्यते ।

तुल्यानुरागपिशुनं ललितार्थबन्धं
पत्रे निवेशितमुदाहरणं प्रियायाः ।
उत्पक्ष्मणो मम सखे मदिरेक्षणाया-
स्तस्याः समागतमिवाननमाननेन ॥ १४ ॥

उर्वशी—एत्थ णो सम-विभाआ पीदी । अत्र आवयोः समविभागा प्रीतिः ।

३ राजा—वयस्य अङ्गुलीस्वेदेन दूष्येरन्नक्षराणि । धार्यतामयं प्रियायाः स्वहस्तः ।

विदूषकः—[गृहीत्वा] किं दाणिं तत्तभोदी उव्वसी भवदो
६ मणोरहाणं कुसुमं दंसिअ फले विसंवददि । किमिदानीं तत्रभवत्युर्वशी भवतो मनोरथानां कुसुमं दर्शयित्वा फले विसंवदति ।

is it that even the heavenly breezes are felt to be so hot to my body even while reclining on a bed of crushed *Parijata* flowers ? [12—13]

URVASHI—What, indeed, would he say now ?

CHITRALEKHA—Has not he already said, with his limbs acting the part of the lotus-stalk ?

VIDUSHAKA—Fortunately now my friend has as much cause for comfort as I should have if I receive a present (*just*) when I feel hungry.

KING—How say you ! cause for comfort ?

This song of the beloved one, indicative of equal love, and charming in its import, which is put on this leaf, is, as it were, the face of her, with its upturned eyelashes and its bewitching eyes, coming close to my face. [14]

URVASHI—Ours, then, is a case of reciprocal love.

KING—Friend, the sweat of my fingers might soil the characters ; do you, therefore, hold this my beloved's autograph.

VIDUSHAKA—(*Holding*). Will the lady Urvashi, now when she has shown you the blossom of your desires, fail to show you the fruit thereof ?

उर्वशी—हला जाव उवगमण-कादरं हिअअं पज्जवत्थावेमि दाव तुमं से अत्ताणं दंसिअ जं मे खमं तं भणाहि। हला यावदुपगमनकातरं हृदयं पर्यवस्थापयामि तावत् त्वमस्मै आत्मानं दर्शयित्वा यन्मम क्षमं तद् भण ।

चित्रलेखा—[तिरस्करिणीमपनीय राजानमुपेत्य] जेदु जेदु महाराओ । जयतु जयतु महाराजः ।

राजा—[सहर्षम्] स्वागतं भवत्यै । भद्रे

न तथा नन्दयसि मां सख्या विरहिता तया ।
संगमे पूर्वदृष्टेव यमुना गङ्गया विना ॥ १५ ॥

चित्रलेखा—णं पढमं मेह-राई दीसदि पच्छा विज्जुल्लदा। ननु प्रथमं मेघराजिर्दृश्यते पश्चाद् विद्युल्लता ।

विदूषकः—[अपवार्य] कहं ण एसा उव्वसी । ताए तत्तहोदीए अहिमदा सहअरी । कथं नैषा उर्वशी । तस्यास्तत्रभवत्या अभिमता सहचरी ।

चित्रलेखा—उव्वसी महाराअं सिरसा पणमिअ विण्णवेदि । उर्वशी महाराजं शिरसा प्रणम्य विज्ञापयति ।

राजा—किमाज्ञापयति ।

चित्रलेखा—मह सुरारि-संभवे दुज्जादे महाराओ एव्व सरणं आसि । सा अहं तुह दंसण-समुत्थेण मअणेण बलिअं बाहीअमाणा भूओ वि महाराएण अणुकम्पणीअ त्ति । मम सुरारिसंभवे दुर्जाते महाराज एव शरणमासीत् । साहं तव दर्शनसमुत्थेन मदनेन बलवद् बाध्यमाना भूयोऽपि महाराजेन अनुकम्पनीयेति ।

राजा—भद्रमुखि

पर्युत्सुकां कथयसि प्रियदर्शनां ता-
मार्तं न पश्यसि पुरूरवसं तदर्थे ।

URVASHI—Well, friend, while I compose my heart which has grown faint at the prospect of meeting him, do you disclose yourself and say what is proper about me.

CHITRALEKHA—(*Removing the Tiraskarini and approaching the King*). Glory, Glory, to our Lord!

KING—(*With joy*). Welcome, dear Lady. Fair lady,

In the absence of that dear friend of yours, you give me no more joy than does the Yamuna, first seen at the confluence, in the absence of the Ganges. [15]

CHITRALEKHA—Well, the clouds come first, and then the lightening.

VIDUSHAKA—(*Aside*). How! This is not the lady Urvashi; but the dear friend of Her Ladyship!

CHITRALEKHA—Urvashi bows down her head before the King, and makes the request—

KING—What are her commands?

CHITRALEKHA—That in her (former) peril caused by the enemy of the gods, Your Majesty gave her protection; she, therefore, prays that on this occasion, too, when fiercely assailed by love that has arisen at your sight, Your Majesty should take compassion on her.

KING—Dear Lady,

You tell me that the fair one is pining in love, but you do not see how Pururavas is afflicted on her account. Alike is our request to the God of love; hot iron deserves to be welded with hot iron. [16]

साधारणोयमुभयोः प्रणयः स्मरस्य
तप्तेन तप्तमयसा घटनाय योग्यम् ॥ १६ ॥

चित्रलेखा—[उर्वशीमुपेत्य] हला एहि । तुवत्तो विणिद्दअदरं मअणं देक्खिअ पिअदमस्स दे दूदि म्हि संवुत्ता । सखि एहि । त्वत्तोपि निर्दयतरं मदनं दृष्ट्वा प्रियतमस्य ते दूत्यस्मि संवृत्ता ।

उर्वशी—[तिरस्करिणीमपनीय] अम्महे लहुअं तुए उज्झिदम्हि । अहो लघु त्वया उज्झितास्मि ।

चित्रलेखा—इदो मुहुत्तादो जाणिस्सं का कं उज्झिस्सदित्ति । आआरं दाव पडिवज्ज । इतो मुहूर्तात् ज्ञास्यामि का कामुज्झिष्यतीति । आचारं तावत् प्रतिपद्यस्व ।

उर्वशी—[सव्रीडम्] जेदु जेदु महाराओ । जयतु जयतु महाराजः ।

राजा—सुन्दरि

मया नाम जितं यस्य त्वयायं समुदीर्यते ।
जयशब्दः सहस्राक्षादगतः पुरुषान्तरम् ॥ १७ ॥

[हस्ते गृहीत्वा एनामुपवेशयति ।]

विदूषकः—भोदि रण्णो पिअ-वअस्सो बम्हणो किं ण वन्दीअदि । भवति राज्ञः प्रियवयस्यो ब्राह्मणः किं न वन्द्यते ।

[उर्वशी सस्मितं प्रणमति ।]

विदूषकः—सत्थि भोदीए । स्वस्ति भवत्यै ।

देवदूतः—[नेपथ्ये] चित्रलेखे त्वरयोर्वशीम् ।

मुनिना भरतेन यः प्रयोगो
भवतोष्वष्टरसाश्रयो नियुक्तः ।
ललिताभिनयं तमद्य भर्ता
मरुतां द्रष्टुमनाः सलोकपालः ॥ १८ ॥

CHITRALEKHA—(*Approaching Urvashi*). Come, friend; seeing that Love afflicts him more relentlessly than he does you, I have become the messenger of your beloved.

URVASHI—(*Removing the Tiraskarini*). Ah, how suddenly have you deserted me!

CHITRALEKHA—I will soon see who deserts whom. But now offer your salutation.

URVASHI—(*Bashfully*). Victory to the King!

KING—Fair Lady,

Surely have I triumphed, since the word 'victory' which from your lips has never hailed any other person save the thousand-eyed Indra, has now been used by you for (greeting) me. [17]

(*Takes her by the hand and leads her to a seat*).

VIDUSHAKA—Fair lady, here is the dear friend of the King, a Brahmin, who remains unsaluted.

(*Urvashi bows to him smiling*).

VIDUSHAKA—Prosperity attend you!

(*Behind the scenes a messenger of the Gods*)—

Chitralekha, hasten Urvashi.

The Lord of the Gods, together with the guardians of the quarters, desires to witness to-day the play, (so) gracefully acted, which the sage Bharata has taught you, and which contains (all) the eight poetic flavours. [18].

[सर्वे कर्णं ददति । उर्वशी विषादं नाटयति]

चित्रलेखा—सुदं पिअ-सहीए देव-दूदस्स वअणं । अणुमाणीअदु महाराओ । श्रुतं प्रियसख्या देवदूतस्य वचनम् । अनुमान्यतां महाराजः ।

उर्वशी—णत्थि मे वाआ । नास्ति मे वाक् ।

चित्रलेखा—महाराअ पर-वसो अअं जणो । ता महाराएण अब्भणुण्णादा इच्छदि देवेसु अणवरद्धं अत्ताणअं कादुं । महाराज परवशोयं जनः । तद् महाराजेनाभ्यनुज्ञाता इच्छति देवेष्वनपराद्धमात्मानं कर्तुम्

राजा—[कथंचिद् वाचं व्यवस्थाप्य] **नास्मि भवत्योरीश्वरनियोगप्रत्यर्थी । स्मर्तव्यस्त्वयं जनः ।**

[उर्वशी वियोगदुःखं रूपयन्ती सह सख्या निष्क्रान्ता ।]

राजा—[सनिःश्वासम्] **सखे वैयर्थ्यमिव चक्षुषः संप्रति ।**

विदूषकः—[पत्रं दर्शयितुकामः] **णं एदं** [इत्यर्धोक्ते आत्मगतम् ।] **हद्धी हद्धी उव्वसो-दंसण-विम्हिदेण मए तं भुज्ज-वत्तअं पब्भट्ठं पि हत्थादो पमादेण ण विण्णादं ।** नन्वेतत्–हा धिक् हा धिक् । उर्वशीदर्शनविस्मितेन मया तद् भूर्जपत्रं प्रभ्रष्टमपि हस्तात् प्रमादेन न विज्ञातम् ।

राजा—भद्र किमसि वक्तुकाम इव ।

विदूषकः—मा भवं अङ्गाइं मुञ्चदु । दढं खु तुइ बद्ध-भावा उव्वसी । ण सा इदो-गदं अणुराअं सिढिलेदि । मा भवानङ्गानि मुञ्चतु । दृढं खलु त्वयि बद्धभावा उर्वशी । न सा इतोगतमनुरागं शिथिलयति ।

(*All Listen; Urvashi gesticulates disappointment*).

CHITRALEKHA—Has my dear friend heard the message of the Gods' messenger? So take your leave of my Lord.

URVASHI—I cannot speak.

CHITRALEKHA—My Lord, this person is subservient to another's will; hence by My Lord's leave she desires not to offend the Gods.

KING—(*Composing his speech with great difficulty*). I do not wish to interrupt the task which your Lords assign you. Only do not forget me.

(*Urvashi gesticulates sorrow at the parting, and departs with her companion*).

KING—(*Sighingly*). In vain, indeed, are we now gifted with sight.

VIDUSHAKA—(*Desiring to show the letter*) Why, this—(*When half through the words—to himself*). Why, bless me, I was so fascinated by the presence of Urvashi, that I did not mark that the Bhurja-leaf slipped unconsciously out of my hands.

KING—Friend, you were about to say something.

VIDUSHAKA—Let not my friend yield to despair. Urvashi is firmly attached to you; she will not relax her attachment towards you.

राजा—ममाप्येतदाशंसि मनः । तया खलु प्रस्थाने

अनीशया शरीरस्य हृदयं स्ववशं मयि ।
स्तनकम्पक्रियालक्ष्यैर्न्यस्तं निःश्वसितैरिव ॥ १९ ॥

विदूषकः—[आत्मगतम्] **वेवदि मे हिअअं इमं वेलं तत्तभवदा तस्स भुज्ज-वत्तस्स णाम गेण्हिदव्वं भविस्सदि त्ति ।** वेपते मे हृदयमिमां वेलां तत्रभवता तस्य भूर्जपत्रस्य नाम ग्रहीतव्यं भविष्यतीति ।

राजा—केनेदानीं दृष्टिं विलोभयामि । [स्मृत्वा] **आ उपनयतु भवान् भूर्जपत्रम् ।**

विदूषकः—[विषादं नाटयति ।] **हन्त ण दीसदि । गदं उव्वसीए मग्गेण ।** हन्त न दृश्यते । गतमुर्वश्या मार्गेण ।

राजा—सर्वत्र प्रमादी वैधेयः । ननु विचिनोतु भवान् ।

विदूषकः—[उत्थाय] **णं इदो भवे इदो भवे** [इति विचेतव्यं नाटयति] नन्वितो भवेदितो भवेत् ।

[ततः प्रविशति काशीराजपुत्री सपरिवारा देवी ।]

देवी—हञ्जे णिउणिए सच्चं तुए भणिदं इमं लदा-गेहं पविसन्तो अज्ज-माणवअ-सहाओ अज्जउत्तो दिट्ठो त्ति । हञ्जे निपुणिके सत्यं त्वया भणितमिदं लतागेहं प्रविशन्नार्यमाणवकसहाय आर्यपुत्रो दृष्ट इति ।

निपुणिका—किं अण्णहा भट्टिणी मए विण्णविद-पुव्वा । किमन्यथा भट्टिनी मया विज्ञापितपूर्वा ।

देवी—तेण हि लदन्तरिदा सुणिस्सं दाव से वीसद्धामन्तिदाणि । जं तुए कहिदं तं सच्चं ण व त्ति । तेन हि लतान्तरिता श्रोष्यामि तावदस्य विश्रब्धामन्त्रितानि । यत् त्वया कथितं तत् सत्यं न वेति ।

KING—My mind, too, is filled with the same hope. For at the time of departing, she,

Not mistress of her own person, seemed to lodge her heart in mine, free as she was to dispose of it, through her sighs indicated by the panting of her bosom. [19]

VIDUSHAKA—(*To himself*). How my heart trembles lest my friend should now mention that Bhurja-leaf !

KING—What shall now console my eyes ? (*Remembering*). Well, friend, give me the Bhurja-leaf.

VIDUSHAKA—(*Gesticulates despair*). Dear me, it is not to be seen--has gone after Urvashi.

KING—A blundering fool, everywhere ! Will you not search for it ?

VIDUSHAKA—(*Rising*). May be, it is here, may be, it is there.

(*Gesticulates searching it*).

(*Enter Queen, the daughter of the King of Kasi, together with her retinue*).

QUEEN—Girl Nipunika, did you tell me the truth when you said you saw my noble Lord entering this arbour with the noble Manavaka ?

NIPUNIKA—Have I ever told a falsehood to my mistress ?

QUEEN—Well, then, screening myself behind the creepers, I will just hear his confidential talk--whether what you told me is right or not.

निपुणिका--जं भट्टिणी आणवेदि । यद् भट्टिनी आज्ञापयति।

देवी--[परिक्रम्य] **हञ्जे णिउणिए किं एदं जिण्ण-चीरं विअ इदोमुहं दक्खिण-मारुदेण आणीअदि** । हञ्जे निपुणिके किमेतज्जीर्णचीरमिव इतोमुखं दक्षिणमारुतेन आनीयते ।

निपुणिका--[विभाव्य] **भट्टिणि पडिवत्तण-विभाविदक्खरं भुज्ज-वत्तं खु एदं । हन्त भट्टिणीए एव्व णेउर-कोडीए लग्गं** । [गृहीत्वा] **कहं । वाईअदु** । भट्टिनि परिवर्तनविभाविताक्षरं भूर्जपत्रं खल्वेतत् । हन्त भर्त्र्या एव नूपुरकोट्या लग्नम् । कथम् । वाच्यताम् ।

देवी--अणुवाएहि दाव णं । जदि अविरुद्धं तदो सुणिस्सं । अनुवाचय तावदेतत् । यदि अविरुद्धं ततः श्रोष्यामि ।

निपुणिका--[तथा कृत्वा] **भट्टिणि तं एव्व कोलीणं विअ पडिहादि । भट्टारअं उद्दिसिअ उव्वसीए कव्व-बन्धो त्ति तक्केमि । अज्जमाणवअ-पमादेण अम्हाणं हत्थं गदो त्ति** । भट्टिनि तदेव कौलीनमिव प्रतिभाति । भर्तारमुद्दिश्य उर्वश्या काव्यबन्ध इति तर्कयामि । आर्यमाणवकप्रमादेन आवयोर्हस्तं गत इति ।

देवी--तेण हि से गहिदत्था होमि । तेन ह्यस्य गृहीतार्था भवामि ।

[निपुणिका राज्ञा पूर्ववाचितं वाचयति ।]

देवी--एत्थ इमिणा एव्व उवाअणेण अच्छरा-कामुअं पेक्खामि । [इति परिजनसहिता लतागृहं परिक्रामति।] अत्र अनेनैव उपायनेन अप्सरःकामुकं पश्यामि ।

विदूषकः--भो वअस्स किं एदं पमद-वण-समीव-गद-कीलापव्वद-पज्जन्ते दीसदि । भो वयस्य किमेतत् प्रमदवनसमीपगतक्रीडापर्वतपर्यन्ते दृश्यते ।

NIPUNIKA—As the mistress commands.

QUEEN—(*Moving about*). Girl Nipunika what could this be that is driven along towards us by the southern breeze—looking like a tattered shred of a garment?

NIPUNIKA—(*Looking closely*). Mistress, this is surely a Bhurja-leaf on which are to be seen some characters when it is turned round (by the wind). Why, it has clung to the end of my mistress' anklet. How! Shall I read (it)?

QUEEN—Read it to yourself. If there is nothing objectionable, I will hear it.

NIPUNIKA—(*Doing as bidden*). Mistress, it is that same (story)-what looks like a scandal. It seems to me to be some song of Urvashi addressed to my Lord. It has fallen into our hands by the heedlessness of the noble Manavaka.

QUEEN–Well then, I should like to know its contents. (*Nipunika reads what was formerly read out by the King*).

QUEEN—Well, I will see this nymph-enamoured person here, with this very present.

(*She goes round the arbour along with her retinue*).

VIDUSHAKA—Well, friend, what do you see yonder at the edge of the pleasure-mound near the Pramadavana?

राजा—[उत्थाय] भगवन् वसन्तप्रिय दक्षिणवायो ।

वासार्थं हर संभृतं सुरभिणा पौष्पं रजो वीरुधां
किं मिथ्या भवतो हृतेन दयितास्नेहस्वहस्तेन मे ।
जानीते हि मनोविनोदनफलैरेवंविधैर्धारितं
कामार्तं जनमङ्गनां प्रति भवानालक्षितप्रार्थनः ॥२०॥

निपुणिका—भट्टिणि एदस्स एव्व अण्णेसणा वट्टदि । भट्टिनि एतस्यैवान्वेषणा वर्तते ।

देवी—पेक्खामि । पश्यामि ।

विदूषकः—भो मिलाअमाण-केसरच्छविणा मोर-पिच्छेण विप्पलद्धो म्हि । भो म्लायमानकेसरच्छविना मयूरपिच्छेन विप्रलब्धोस्मि ।

राजा—सर्वथा हतोस्मि ।

देवी—[उपेत्य] अज्जउत्त अलं आवेएण । एदं तं भुज्जवत्तं । आर्यपुत्र अलमावेगेन । एतत् तद् भूर्जपत्रम् ।

राजा—[ससंभ्रमम्] अये देवी । स्वागतं देव्यै ।

विदूषकः—[अपवार्य] दुरागदं दाणिं संवुत्तं । दुरागतमिदानीं संवृत्तम् ।

राजा—[जनान्तिकम्] सखे किमत्र प्रतिविधेयम् ।

विदूषकः—लोत्तेण गहिदस्स कुम्भीलअस्स अत्थि वा पडिवअणं । लोत्रेण गृहीतस्य कुम्भीरकस्य अस्ति वा प्रतिवचनम् ।

राजा—देवि नेदं मया मृग्यते । स खलु परसमन्वेषणार्थमारम्भोयम् ।

देवी—जुज्जदि अत्तणो सोहग्गं पच्छादेदुं । युज्यत आत्मनः सौभाग्यं प्रच्छादयितुम् ।

KING—(*Rising*). Noble breeze of the south, the friend of spring,

You may remove from the plants the flowery-pollen produced by spring for (scattering). perfume ; but why vainly rob me of those characters written through love by my beloved with her own hand ? For surely you, who are known to have loved Anjana, know that a love-afflicted person lives on such means intended to solace his heart. [20]

NIPUNIKA—Mistress, they are searching this very thing.

QUEEN—I see.

VIDUSHAKA—O, I was deceived by a peacock-feather of the colour of a faded Kesara flower.

KING—So I am ruined everyway !

QUEEN—(*Approaching*). Noble Lord do not grieve. Here is the Bhurja-leaf.

KING—(*Confusedly*) Oh, the Queen. Welcome, Queen.

VIDUSHAKA—(But) now it is the reverse of welcome.

KING—(*Aside*). Friend, how to meet the present (situation) ?

VIDUSHAKA—How can a thief answer for himself, when caught with a portion of the stolen article on his person ?

KING—Queen, this was not the object of my search; but I was searching some other object.

QUEEN—It is but proper to conceal one's good fortune.

विदूषकः—भोदि तुवरेहि से भोअणं जं पित्तोवसमण-समत्थं होदि। भवति त्वरयास्य भोजनं यत् पित्तोपशमनसमर्थं भवति ।

देवी—णिउणिए सोहणं खु बम्हणेण आसासिदो वअस्सो। निपुणिके शोभनं खलु ब्राह्मणेन आश्वासितो वयस्यः ।

विदूषकः—भोदि णं पेक्ख आसासिदो पिसाओ वि भोअणेण । भवति ननु पश्य आश्वासितः पिशाचोपि भोजनेन ।

राजा—मूर्ख बलादपराधिनं मामापादयसि ।

देवी—णत्थि भवदो अवराहो। अहं एव्व एत्थ अवरद्धा। जा पडिऊल-दंसणा भविअ अग्गदो दे चिट्ठामि। इदो अहं गमिस्सं । [कोपं नाटयित्वा प्रस्थिता।] नास्ति भवतोपराधः । अहमेवात्र अपराद्धा । या प्रतिकूलदर्शना भूत्वा अग्रतस्ते तिष्ठामि। इताह गमिष्यामि ।

राजा—

अपराधी नामाहं प्रसीद रम्भोरु विरम संरम्भात् ।
सेव्यो जनश्च कुपितः कथं नु दासो निरपराधः ॥२१॥

[इति पादयोः पतति ।]

देवी—[आत्मगतम्] **मा खु लहु-हिअआ अहं अणुणअं बहु मण्णे । किं दु अदक्खिण्ण-किदस्स पच्छादावस्स भाएमि ।** [राजानमपहाय सपरिवारा निष्क्रान्ता ।] **मा खलु** लघुहृदयाहमनुनयं बहु मन्ये । किं तु अदाक्षिण्यकृतात् पश्चात्तापाद् बिभेमि

विदूषकः—पाउस-णदी विअ अप्पसण्णा गदा देवी । उट्ठेहि । प्रावृण्नदीव अप्रसन्ना गता देवी । उत्तिष्ठ ।

राजा—[उत्थाय] **वयस्य नेदमनुपपन्नम् । पश्य**

प्रियवचनशतोपि योषितां
दयितजनानुनयो रसादृते ।

VIDUSHAKA—Madam, quickly get ready his dinner, which will be an effectual remedy for his bile.

QUEEN—Nipunika, how well has the Brahmin consoled his friend !

VIDUSHAKA—Madam, don't you see even a ghost is laid by dinner.

KING—Blockhead, how falsely you represent me as guilty !

QUEEN—It is not your fault. It is I that am at fault, since I stand before you even when my presence is disagreeable. I will go from hence.

(*Gesticulates anger and starts to go*).

KING—I confess my guilt; be pleased, O fair one, curb your resentment ; for when the master is angry it cannot be but that the servant is at fault. [21]

(*Prostrates himself at her feet*).

QUEEN—(*To himself*). I am not so light-hearted as to take his importunities seriously. But I am afraid of the remorse that would be caused by my incivility (*Leaves the King, and departs along with her retinue*).

VIDUSHAKA—Like a turbid river in the rains, Her Majesty has gone off in (high) dudgeon. Rise

KING—(*Rising*). Friend, this is not unreasonable.

The solicitations of a favoured person although full of hundreds of flattering compliments will not

प्रविशति हृदयं न तद्विदां
मणिरिव कृत्रिमरागयोजितः ॥ २२ ॥

विदूषकः—अणुऊलं एत्थभवदो एदं । ण हु अक्खिदुक्खिदो अहिमुहे दीव-सिहं सहेदि । अनुकूलमत्रभवत एतत् । न खल्वक्षिदुःखितः अभिमुखे दीपशिखां सहते ।

राजा—मा मैवम् । उर्वशीगतमनसोपि मे स एव देव्यां बहुमानः । किं तु प्रणिपातलङ्घनादहमस्यां धैर्यमवलम्बिष्ये ।

विदूषकः—चिट्ठदु दाव भवदो धीरदा । बुभुक्खिदस्स बम्हणस्स जीविदं अवलम्बदु भवं । समओ खु ण्हाण-भोअणं सेविदुं । तिष्ठतु तावद् भवतो धीरता । बुभुक्षितस्य ब्राह्मणस्य जीवितमवलम्बतां भवान् । समयः खलु स्नानभोजनं सेवितुम् ।

राजा—[ऊर्ध्वमवलोक्य] गतमर्धं दिवसस्य ।

उष्णालुः शिशिरे निषीदति तरोर्मूलालवाले शिखी
निर्भिद्योपरि कर्णिकारमुकुलान्यालीयते षट्पदः ।
तप्तं वारि विहाय तीरनलिनीं कारण्डवः सेवते
क्रीडावेश्मनि चैष पञ्जरशुकः क्लान्तो जलं याचते ॥२३॥

[इति निष्क्रान्ताः सर्वे ।]

इति द्वितीयोऽङ्कः ।

---

touch a woman's heart in the absence of (real) love; just as a gem artificially coloured finds little favour with those who are the connoisseurs (of that art). [22]

VIDUSHAKA—This is quite agreeable to you. For a person whose eyes are dazzled will not bear the lamp-flame in his face.

KING—Do not think thus. Although my heart is given to Urvashi, yet I retain my former regard for the Queen. Only I will face her courageously now, since she has so disdained my prostrations.

VIDUSHAKA—Talk not of your courage. But please to sustain the life of a famished Brahmin It is indeed (high) time to bathe and eat.

KING—(*Looking upwards*). Half the day is over.

Exhausted by the heat the peacock now rests in the cool basin round the root of (yonder) tree; the bees lie snugly inside the Karnikara buds, having forced them open at the top, the water-fowl leaves the heated water and lurks in the lotus-plant on the brink; while the drooping parrot in its cage in the pleasure-house calls for water [23]

(*Exeunt Omnes*)

HERE ENDS THE SECOND ACT

तृतीयोऽङ्कः ।

[ततः प्रविशतो भरतशिष्यौ ।]

प्रथमः—सखे पल्लव महेन्द्रसदनं गच्छतोपाध्यायेन त्वमासनं प्रतिग्राहितः । अग्निशरणसंरक्षणाय स्थापितोहम् । अतः खलु पृच्छामि । अपि गुरोः प्रयोगेण दिव्या परिषदाराधिता ।

द्वितीयः—गालव ण आणे आराहिदा ण वत्ति । तस्सिं उण सरस्सई-किद-कव्व-बन्धे लच्छी-सअंवरे तेसु तेसु रसन्तरेसु तम्मआ आसि । किं तु—गालव न जाने आराधिता न वेति । तस्मिन् पुनः सरस्वतीकृतकाव्यबन्धे लक्ष्मीस्वयंवरे तेषु तेषु रसान्तरेषु तन्मयी आसीत् । किं तु--

प्रथमः—सदोषावकाश इव ते वाक्यशेषः ।

द्वितीयः—आम । तहिं उव्वसीए वअणं पमाद-क्खलिदं आसि । आम् । तस्मिन्नुर्वश्या वचनं प्रमादस्खलितमासीत् ।

प्रथमः—कथमिव ।

द्वितीयः—लच्छी-भूमिआए वट्टमाणा उव्वसी वारुणी-भूमिआए वट्टमाणाए मेणआए पुच्छिदा । सहि समाअदा एदे तेलोक्कसुपुरिसा सकेसवा लोअ-वाला । कदमस्सिं दे भावाहिणिवेसो त्ति । लक्ष्मीभूमिकायां वर्तमाना उर्वशी वारुणीभूमिकायां वर्तमानया मेनकया पृष्टा । सखि समागता एते त्रैलोक्यसुपुरुषाः सकेशवा लोकपालाः । कतमस्मिस्ते भावाभिनिवेश इति ।

प्रथमः—ततस्ततः ।

द्वितीयः—तदो ताए पुरिसोत्तमे त्ति भणिदव्वे पुरूरवे

ACT III

(Enter two disciples of Bharata).

FIRST—Friend Pallava, you were asked to carry the seat by our preceptor when he had gone to Indra's palace, while I was left behind to keep watch over the holy fire. That is why I ask: Was the assembly of the Immortals pleased with the performance of our master?

SECOND—I do not know whether it was pleased or not. But then it quite lost itself in the various emotions of that play of Lakshmisvayamvara composed by Sarasvati. But—

FIRST—The rest of your sentence seems to imply that there is something wrong.

SECOND—Yes, for Urvashi stumbled in her part.

FIRST—How was it?

SECOND—Urvashi who played the part of Lakshmi was questioned by Menaka who played Varuni's part: Friend here are assembled the best men in the three worlds--the guardians of the spheres together with Keshava To whom inclines your heart?

FIRST—What then?

SECOND—Her reply should have been 'to Purushotta-

२४ त्ति णिग्गदा वाणी । ततस्तया पुरुषोत्तम इति भणितव्ये पुरूरवसीति निर्गता वाणी ।

प्रथमः—भवितव्यानुविधायीनीन्द्रियाणि । न खलु तामभिक्रुद्धो गुरुः ।
२७

द्वितीयः—सा खु सत्ता उवज्झाएण । महिन्देण उण अणुगहिदा । सा खलु शप्ता उपाध्यायेन । महेन्द्रेण पुनरनुगृहीता ।

३० **प्रथमः**—कथमिव ।

द्वितीयः—जेण मम उवदेसो तुए लङ्घिदो तेण ण दे दिव्वं ठाणं हविस्सदि त्ति उवज्झाअस्स सावो । महि-
३३ न्देण उण पेक्खणावसाणे लज्जावणद-मुही भणिदा जस्सिं बद्धभावा सि तस्स मे रण-सहाअस्स राए-
सिणो पिअं एत्थ करणिज्जं । सा तुमं जहा-कामं पुरू-
३६ रवसं उवचिट्ठ जाव सो तुह दिट्ठसंताणो भोदि त्ति ।
येन ममोपदेशस्त्वया लङ्घितस्तेन न ते दिव्यं स्थानं भविष्यतीति उपाध्यायस्य शापः । महेन्द्रेण पुनः प्रेक्षणावसाने लज्जावनतमुखी
३९ भणिता यस्मिन् बद्धभावासि तस्य मे रणसहायस्य राजर्षेः प्रियमत्र करणीयम् । सा त्वं यथाकामं पुरूरवसमुपतिष्ठस्व यावत् स त्वयि दृष्टसंतानो भवेदिति ।

४२ **प्रथमः**—सदृशं पुरुषान्तरविदो महेन्द्रस्य ।

द्वितीयः—[सूर्यमवलोक्य] कधा-पसङ्गेण अम्हेहिं अवरद्धा अहिसेअ-वेला क्खु उवज्झाअस्स । ता एहि से पास-
४५ परिवत्तिणो होम । कथाप्रसङ्गेन अस्माभिरपराद्धा अभिषेकवेला खलूपाध्यायस्य । तदेह्यस्य पार्श्वपरिवर्तिनौ भवावः ।

[इति निष्क्रान्तौ ।]

मिश्रविष्कम्भकः ॥

ma,' but instead, the words 'to Pururavas' escaped her lips.

FIRST—The senses are but the slaves of destiny. Was not our preceptor highly displeased with her

SECOND—Yes, he denounced a curse upon her, but she found favour with Mahendra.

FIRST—How so?

SECOND—'Since you have forgotten my instruction, you shall lose your divine place;' that was the curse of the preceptor; Mahendra, however, at the end of the performance said to her as she stood with her face bowed in shame, "The royal sage on whom you have set your heart, my ally in battles, is entitled to my favour. Do you, then, as you desire, remain with Pururavas till he beholds the child you will bear him."

FIRST—This was like Mahendra who knows other men's hearts.

SECOND—(*Looking at the Sun*). In the course of the talk, we have indeed passed over our preceptor's time of bathing. Come, then, let us approach him. (*Exeunt*)

END OF THE INTRODUCTORY SCENE

[ततः प्रविशति कञ्चुकी ।

कञ्चुकी—

सर्वः कल्ये वयसि यतते लब्धुमर्थान् कुटुम्बी
पश्चात्पुत्रैरपहृतभरः कल्पते विश्रमाय ।
अस्माकं तु प्रतिदिनमियं सादयन्ती शरीरं
सेवाकारा परिणतिरहो स्त्रीषु कष्टोऽधिकारः ॥ १ ॥

[परिक्रम्य ।] आदिष्टोऽस्मि सनियमया काशीराजपुत्र्या व्रतसंपादनार्थं मया मानमुत्सृज्य निपुणिकामुखेन पूर्वं याचितो महाराजः । तदेव मद्वचनाद् विज्ञापयेति । यावदिदानीमवसितसंध्याजाप्यं महाराजं पश्यामि । [परिक्रम्य अवलोक्य च] रमणीयः खलु दिवसावसानवृत्तान्तो राजवेश्मनि । इह हि

उत्कीर्णा इव वासयष्टिषु निशानिद्रालसा बर्हिणो
धूपैर्जालविनिःसृतैर्वलभयः संदिग्धपारावताः ।
आचारप्रयतः सपुष्पबलिषु स्थानेषु चार्चिष्मतीः
संध्यामङ्गलदीपिका विभजते शुद्धान्तवृद्धाजनः ॥२॥

[नेपथ्याभिमुखं दृष्ट्वा] अये इत एव प्रस्थितो देवः ।

परिजनवनिताकरार्पिताभिः
परिवृत एष विभाति दीपिकाभिः ।
गिरिरिव गतिमानपक्षलोपा-
दनुतटपुष्पितकर्णिकारयष्टिः ॥ ३ ॥

यावदेनमवलोकनमार्गे स्थितः प्रतिपालयामि ।

[ततः प्रविशति यथानिर्दिष्टो राजा विदूषकश्च ।]

राजा—[आत्मगतम्]

(Then Enter a Chamberlain)

CHAMBERLAIN—As long as life is vigorous, a married man strives to acquire wealth, and afterwards relieved by his sons of the burden (of family cares) he takes rest; but to persons like us old age is a veritable servitude that saps the body every day! Alas, for the duty of watching over women! [1]

(Walking about), I have been told by the daughter of the King of Kashi who has engaged herself in a vow, that for the fulfilment of that vow she having laid aside all sense of pride, has already requested His Majesty's presence through Nipunika. I have been now asked to make the same request on her behalf. So I will see my Lord who has now finished his evening prayer.

(Walking about and observing). The scene at the palace at the close of the day is certainly so delightful For here,

The peacocks drowsing at the approach of night look like sculptured (figures) on their perches; the pigeons on the terrace-tops are scarcely disting shable from the incense that flows through the lattices: and the old matrons of the inner apartment ready to perform the customary acts (of the hour) are distributing in places adorned with flower-offerings the auspicious lights of evening that are burning brightly. [2]

(Looking towards the curtain)-Ah My Lord is coming hither.

Surrounded by the torches borne in their hands by the female attendants, he looks like a mountain moving because its wings are unclipt, that has the tall, thin, Karnikara trees in full blossom on both its sides. [3]

I shall, therefore, keeping him within sight, wait for him.

(Enter King as described and Vidushaka).

KING—*(To himself)*.

कार्यान्तरितोत्कण्ठं दिनं मया नीतमनतिकृच्छ्रेण ।
अविनोददीर्घयामा कथं नु रात्रिर्गमयितव्या ॥ ४ ॥

कञ्चुकी—[उपगम्य] जयतु जयतु देवः । देवी विज्ञापयति मणिहर्म्यपृष्ठे सुदर्शनश्चन्द्रः । तत्र संनिहितेन देवेन प्रतिपालयितुमिच्छामि यावद् रोहिणीसंयोग इति ।

राजा—आर्य लातव्य विज्ञाप्यतां देवी यस्ते छन्द इति ।

कञ्चुकी—यदाज्ञापयति देवः ।

[इति निष्क्रान्तः]

राजा—वयस्य किं परमार्थत एव देव्या व्रतनिमित्तोऽयमारम्भः स्यात् ।

विदूषकः—भो तक्केमि जाद-पच्छादावा तत्तभोदी वदावदेसेण भवदो पणिपाद-लङ्घणं पमज्जिदु-काम त्ति । भोः तर्कयामि जातपश्चात्तापा तत्रभवती व्रतापदेशेन भवतः प्रणिपातलङ्घनं प्रमार्ष्टुकामेति ।

राजा—उपपन्नं भवानाह । तथा हि

अवधूतप्रणिपाताः पश्चात्संतप्यमानमनसोऽपि ।
निभृतैर्व्यपत्रपन्ते दयितानुनयैर्मनस्विन्यः ॥ ५ ॥

तदादेशय मणिहर्म्यपृष्ठमार्गम् ।

विदूषकः—इदो इदो भवं । इमिणा गङ्गा-तरङ्ग-सस्सिरीएण फलिहमणि-सोवाणेण आरोहदु भवं पदोसावसररमणिज्जं मणिहम्मिअं । इत इतो भवान् । एतेन गङ्गातरङ्गसश्रीकेण स्फटिकमणिसोपानेन आरोहतु भवान् प्रदोषावसररमणीयं मणिहर्म्यम् ।

राजा—आरोहाग्रतः ।

[सर्वे सोपानारोहणं रूपयन्ति ।]

विदूषकः—[विलोक्य] भो पच्चासण्णेण चन्दोदएण

I could pass the day without much difficulty as the cares of state drowned all anxious thoughts of love; but how am I to pass the night which, on account of the absence of any diversion, will be (drearily) long in its watches ? [4]

CHAMBERLAIN—(*Approaching.*) Glory to our Lord ! Her Majesty requests : "The terrace of the crystal pavilion affords a glorious view of the Moon; so in the presence of My Lord I desire to wait there till the Moon enters the asterism Rohini."

KING—Noble Latavya, say to the Queen, "(Do) as it pleases you."

CHAMBERLAIN—As Your Majesty commands.

(*Exit*).

KING—Friend, do you think it is really on account of a vow that the Queen undertakes these proceedings ?

VIDUSHAKA—Well, my view is that her ladyship, stung with remorse, wishes to efface the indignity with which she treated your prostration, under the pretext of her (present) vow.

KING—You speak the truth; for,

Proud women having slighted the prostrations of their lord, are subsequently filled with repentance; yet with all this they are secretly ashamed of doing any acts conciliating their beloved ones. [5]

VIDUSHAKA—This way, this way, sir. Here, up the flight of crystal steps gleaming (white) like the waves of the Ganges, do you, sir, ascend the crystal palace which looks so lovely at eventide.

KING—Do you ascend first.

(*All act ascending the flight of steps*).

होदव्वं । जह तिमिर-रेईअमाणं पुव्व-दिसा-मुहं आ-
लोअ-सुहअं दीसदि । भोः प्रत्यासन्नेन चन्द्रोदयेन भवितव्यम् ।
१२ यथा तिमिररिच्यमानं पूर्वदिशामुखमालोकसुभगं दृश्यते ।

राजा--सम्यगाह भवान् ।

उदयगूढशशाङ्कमरीचिभिस्तमसि दूरमितः प्रतिसारिते ।
अलकसंयमनादिव लोचने हरति मे हरिवाहनदिङ्मुखम् ॥६॥

विदूषकः--ही ही । भो एसो खण्ड-मोदअ-सस्सिरीओ
उदिदो राआ दुआदीणं । ही ही। भोः एष खण्डमोदकसश्रीक
उदितो राजा द्विजातीनाम् ।

राजा—[सस्मितम] सर्वत्रौदरिकस्य अभ्यवहार्यमेव
विषयः [प्राञ्जलिः प्रणिपत्य] भगवन्क्षपानाथ

रविमावसते सतां क्रियायै सुधया तर्पयते सुरान् पितॄंश्च ।
तमसां निशि मूर्छतां निहन्त्रे हरचूडानिहितात्मने नमस्ते ॥७॥

[उत्तिष्ठति]

विदूषकः—भो बम्हणसंकामिदक्खरेण दे पिदामहेण
३ अब्भणुण्णादो आसण-ट्ठिदो होहि जाव अहं पि सुहा-
सीणो होमि। भोः ब्राह्मणसंक्रामिताक्षरेण ते पितामहेन अभ्यनुज्ञात:
आसनस्थितो भव यावदहमपि सुखासीनो भवामि ।

६ राजा—[विदूषकवचनं परिगृह्य उपविष्टः । परिजनं विलोक्य]
अभिव्यक्तायां चन्द्रिकायां किं दीपिकापौनरुक्त्येन ।
विश्राम्यन्तु भवत्यः ।

परिजनः—जं देवो आणवेदि । यद् देव आज्ञापयति ।

[इति निष्क्रान्तः ।]

VIDUSHAKA—O, the Moon is just about to rise since the Eastern horizon, relieved of darkness is so lovely to view.

KING—You spoke the truth.

For, now that the (evening) gloom retires before the rays of the Moon that is hid behind the rising mountain, the face of the East captivates my eyes as though her (masses of) hair are pound up. [6]

VIDUSHAKA—Ha! Ha! Yonder riseth the King of the twice-born, looking like a broken ball of sweets!

KING—(*Smiling*). A gourmet thinks of nothing else but food everywhere.

(*Bowing with folded hands*) Divine Lord of the Night

Bow to you who dwell in the sun to enable the righteous to perform the religious rites; who regale the gods and the Manes with ambrosia; who destroy darkness prevailing at night, and who have placed yourself in the crest of Hara. [7]

(*Rises*)

VIDUSHAKA—Sir, through this Brahmin to whom he communicates his words, your grand-sire bids you sit, that I too, may repose myself.

KING—(*Saying 'yes sits; looking at the attendants*). When the Moon shines splendidly, why the superfluous light of lamps? Rest ye.

ATTENDANTS—As Your Majesty commands.

(*Exeunt*)

राजा—[चन्द्रमसमवलोक्य] वयस्य परं मुहूर्तादागमनं देव्याः । तद् विविक्ते कथयिष्यामि स्वामवस्थाम् ।

विदूषकः—णं दीसदि एव्व सा किं दु तारिसं अणुराअं पेक्खिअ सक्कं आसा-बन्धेण अत्ताणं धारेदुं । ननु दृश्यत एव सा किं तु तादृशमनुरागं दृष्ट्वा शक्यमाशाबन्धेन आत्मानं धारयितुम् ।

राजा—एवमेतत् । बलवान् पुनर्मम मनसोभितापः ।

नद्या इव प्रवाहो विषमशिलासंकटस्खलितवेगः ।
विघ्नितसमागमसुखो मनसिशयः शतगुणोभवति ॥८॥

विदूषकः—जहा परिहीयमाणेहिं अङ्गेहिं अहिअं सोहसि तहा अदूरे पिअ-समागमं ते पेक्खामि । यथा परिहीयमानैरङ्गैरधिकं शोभसे तथा अदूरे प्रियासमागमं ते पश्यामि ।

राजा—[निमित्तं सूचयित्वा] वयस्य

वचोभिराशाजननैर्भवानिव गुरुव्यथम् ।
अयं मां स्पन्दितैर्बाहुराश्वासयति दक्षिणः ॥ ९ ॥

विदूषकः—ण हु अण्णहा बम्हणस्स वअणं । न खलु अन्यथा ब्राह्मणस्य वचनम् ।

[राजा सप्रत्याशस्तिष्ठति]

[प्रविश्य आकाशयानेन अभिसारिकावेषा उर्वशी चित्रलेखा च ।]

उर्वशी—[आत्मानं विलोक्य] हला चित्तलेहे अवि रोअदि दे अअं मे अप्पाभरण-भूसिदो णीलंसुअ-परिग्गहो अहिसारिआ-वेसो । हला चित्रलेखे अपि रोचते तेयं मे अल्पाभरणभूषितो नीलांशुकपरिग्रहोभिसारिकावेषः ।

चित्रलेखा—णत्थि मे वाआ-विहवो पसंसिदुं । इदं तु

KING—(*Looking at the Moon*). Friend, the Queen will be coming after a while; so now, in this solitude I will describe to you my condition.

VIDUSHAKA—Why, that is so manifest. But it is possible to keep up your spirits with hope considering the intensity of Urvashi's love for you.

KING—That is true; and yet severe is the agony of my heart.

My fond desire becomes more fervid as (fresh) impediments obstruct the pleasure of union, as the current of a river, checked by uneven rocks, splits itself into hundred streams. [8]

VIDUSHAKA—Since even with limbs attenuated you look more handsome, therefore, I argue that your meeting with the beloved is not far distant.

KING—(*Showing that he perceives an omen.*) Friend my right arm by its pulsations soothes me that am heavily suffering, like you with hope-inspiring words. [9]

VIDUSHAKA—Surely the words of a Brahmin will never be falsified

(*The King is filled with hope revived*).

(*Enter in the air Urvashi dressed as an Abhisarika and Chitralekha*).

URVASHI—(*Looking at herself*). Now dear Chitralekha, what say you to these blue robes of an Abhisarika thus scantily trimmed with ornaments?

चिन्तेमि । अवि णाम अहं पुरूरवा भवेअं ति । नास्ति मे वाग्विभवः प्रशंसितुम् । इदं तु चिन्तयामि । अपि नामाहं पुरूरवा भवेयमिति ।

उर्वशी—सहि मदणो खु तुमं आणवेदि ! सिग्घं णेहि मं तस्स सुहअस्स वसदिं । सखि मदनः खलु त्वामाज्ञापयति । शीघ्रं नय मां तस्य सुभगस्य वसतिम् ।

चित्रलेखा—णं एदं परिवत्तिदं विअ केलास-सिहरं पिअदमस्स दे भवणं उवगद म्ह । नन्वेतत् परिवर्तितमिव कैलासशिखरं प्रियतमस्य ते भवनमुपगते स्वः ।

उर्वशी—तेण हि पहावदो जाणाहि दाव कहिं सो मम हिअअचोरो किं वा अणुचिट्ठदि त्ति । तेन हि प्रभावात् जानीहि तावत् क स मम हृदयचौरः किं वानुतिष्ठतीति ।

चित्रलेखा—[ध्यात्वा । आत्मगतम्] **भोदु कीलिस्सं दाव एदाए ।** [प्रकाशम्] **हला एसो मणोरह-लद्ध-पिआ-समाअम-सुहं अणुहवन्तो उवहोअ-क्खमे ओआसे चिट्ठदि ।** भवतु क्रीडिष्यामि तावदेतया । हला एष मनोरथलब्धप्रियासमागमसुखमनुभवन्नुपभोगक्षमेऽवकाशे तिष्ठति ।

[उर्वशी विषादं नाटयति ।]

चित्रलेखा—मुद्धे का उण अण्णा चिन्ता पिआ-समाअमस्स । मुग्धे का पुनरन्या चिन्ता प्रियासमागमस्य ।

उर्वशी—[सोच्छ्वासम्] **अदक्खिणं संदेहदि मे हिअअं ।** अदक्षिणं संदिग्धे मे हृदयम् ।

चित्रलेखा—[विलोक्य] **एसो मणि-हम्मिअ-गदो वअस्स मेत्त-सहाओ राएसी । ता एहि उवसप्पाम णं ।** एष मणिहर्म्यगतो वयस्यमात्रसहायो राजर्षिः । तदेहि । उपसर्पाव एनम् ।

उभे अवतरतः ।

राजा—वयस्य रजन्या सह विजृम्भते मदनबाधा ।

CHITRALEKHA—Words fail me to describe it. But this is what is in my mind Would that I were Pururavas!

URVASHI—Dear, Love himself bids you-take me quick to that loved one's dwelling.

CHITRALEKHA—Here we come to your lover s palace which looks like the summit of Kailasa changed into another form

URVAS —Know, then, through your power where he is, that thief who has stolen my heart, and what employs him.

CHITRALEKHA—(*Contemplating to herself*). Well, I shall chaff her a bit. (*Aloud*) Friend, here he is in a place fit for enjoyment, happy in the company of his beloved whom he has obtained according to his wishes.

(*Urvashi expresses despair*).

CHITRALEKHA—Child, but why any other thought about the company of the beloved?

URVASHI—(*Sighing*). My unkind heart becomes suspicious.

CHITRALEKHA—Here is the royal sage with his friend as his only attendant in the crystal palace. So come let us advance towards him.

(*They descend*).

KING—Friend, how do the torments of Love increase with the night!

उर्वशी--अणिब्भिण्णत्थेण इमिणा वअणेण आकम्पिदं मे हिअअं । अन्तरिदा एव्व सुणाम से सेरालावं जाव णो संसअ-च्छेदो होदि । अनिर्भिन्नार्थेन अनेन वचनेन आकम्पितं मम हृदयम् । अन्तरिते एव शृणुवः अस्य स्वैरालापं यावदावयोः संशयच्छेदो भवति ।

चित्रलेखा--जं दे रोअदि । यत् ते रोचते ।

विदूषकः--णं इमे अमिअ-गब्भा सेवीअन्तु चन्द-वादा । नन्वेते अमृतगर्भाः सेव्यन्तां चन्द्रपादाः ।

राजा--वयस्य एवमादिभिरनुपक्रम्योयमातङ्कः । पश्य ।

कुसुमशयनं न प्रत्यग्रं न चन्द्रमरीचयो
न च मलयजं सर्वाङ्गीणं न वा मणियष्टयः ।
मनसिजरुजं सा वा दिव्या समालगपोहितुम्-

उर्वशी--का वा अवरा । का वापरा ।

राजा--

रहसि लघयेदारब्धा वा तदाश्रयिणी कथा ॥ १० ॥

उर्वशी--हिअअ दाणिं मं उज्झिअ इदो संकन्तेण तुए फलं उवलद्धं । हृदय इदानीं मामुज्झित्वा इतः संक्रान्तेन त्वया फलमुपलब्धम् ।

विदूषकः--आम । हंपि जदा मिट्ठ-हरिणी-मंस-भोअणं ण लहे तदा णं पत्थअन्तो संकित्तअन्तो आसासेमि । आम् । अहमपि यदा मिष्टहरिणीमांसभोजनं न लभे तदा एतत प्रार्थयमानः संकीर्तयन्नाश्वसिमि ।

राजा--संपद्यत इदं भवतः ।

विदूषकः--भवं पि तं अचिरेण पाविस्सदि । भवानपि तामचिरेण प्राप्स्यति ।

URVASHI—My heart is all in a flutter at these dubious words; let us, therefore, remain invisible and overhear his unreserved utterances till doubt be all dispersed.

CHITRALEKHA—Just as you please.

VIDUSHAKA—You should enjoy the rays of the Moon that are charged with ambrosia.

KING—Friend, small is the power of such remedies to mitigate this malady. Mark,

Neither fresh flower-beds, nor the rays of the Moon, nor sandal-smearing all over the body nor jewel-necklaces will allay the pangs of Love; she alone - that woman divine can do it——

URVASHI—And who else?

KING—Or secret converse regarding her can mitigate (the suffering). [10]

URVASHI—My heart, now have you reaped the fruit of having gone over to him after deserting me.

VIDUSHAKA—Quite so. I too, when I do not get a dinner of dainty venison, but feel a desire for it, take comfort in speaking about it.

KING—But you get that.

VIDUSHAKA—And you too will get her in a short time.

राजा—सखे एवं मन्ये—

चित्रलेखा—सुणु असंतुट्ठे सुणु । शृणु असंतुष्टे शृणु ।

विदूषकः—कहं विअ । कथमिव ।

राजा—

अयं तस्या रथक्षोभादंसनांसो निपीडितः ।
एकः कृती शरीरेऽस्मिन् शेषमङ्गं भुवो भरः ॥ ११ ॥

चित्रलेखा—किं दाणिं विलम्बीअदि । किमिदानीं विलम्ब्यते ।

उर्वशी—[सहसोपसृत्य] हला अग्गदो वि मम गदाए उदासीणो विअ महाराओ । हला अग्रतोपि मम गताया उदासीन इव महाराजः ।

चित्रलेखा—[सस्मितम्] अदितुवरिदे अणुक्खित्त-तिरक्खरिणीआ सि । अतित्वरिते अनुत्क्षिप्ततिरस्करिणीकासि ।

[नेपथ्ये ।] इदो इदो भट्टिणो । इत इतो भर्त्री ।

[सर्वे कर्णं ददति ।]

[उर्वशी सह सख्या विषण्णा ।]

विदूषकः—अविहा अविहा उवट्ठिदा देवी । ता वाअंजमो होहि । अविहा अविहा उपस्थिता देवी । तद् वाचंयमो भव ।

राजा—भवानपि संवृताकारमास्ताम् ।

उर्वशी—हला किं एत्थ करणिज्जं । हला किमत्र करणीयम् ।

चित्रलेखा—अलं आवेएण । अन्तरिदा वयं । उववासणिअमवेसा राएसि-महिसी दीसदि । ता ण एसा चिरं चिट्ठिस्सदि । अलमावेगेन । अन्तर्हिते आवाम् । उपवासनियमवेषा राजर्षिमहिषी दृश्यते । तन्नैषा इह चिरं स्थास्यति ।

[ततः प्रविशति औपहारिकहस्तपरिजना देवी ।]

देवी—[परिक्रम्य अवलोक्य च] हञ्जे णिउणिए एसो रोहिणी-संजोएण अहिअं सोहदि भअवं मिअ-लञ्छणो ।

KING—Friend, I think that——

CHITRALEKHA—Hear, unsatisfied that you are, hear.

VIDUSHAKA—What ?

KING—This shoulder that was pressed by hers owing to the jolting of the chariot is the only limb that exists with reason; the rest is a mere burden to the earth. [11]

CHITRALEKHA—Why do you delay now ?

URVASHI—(*Suddenly advancing*) Friend, although I stand in his presence, he deigns not to regard me !

CHITRALEKHA—(*Smiling*). O impatient one, you have not put off the Tiraskarini.

(*Behind the Scenes*).

This way, mistress, this way,

(*All Listen*).

(*Urvashi and her friend feel despair*).

VIDUSHAKA—Holla, the Queen is here: you had better be mute.

KING—You, too, should conceal the expression of your face

URVASHI—What may we do now, dear ?

CHITRALEKHA—Don't you worry. We are invisible. The Queen of the royal sage wears a dress befitting the observance of a fast: she will, therefore, not tarry here long.

(*Enter Queen with attendants carrying materials of worship*).

QUEEN—(*Walking about and seeing*). Girl Nipunika

हञ्जे निपुणिके एष रोहिणीसंयोगेन अधिकं शोभते भगवान् मृगलाञ्छनः ।

चेटी—णं देवी-सहिदो भट्टा विसेस-रमणिज्जो [परिक्रामति] ननु देवीसहितो भर्ता विशेषरमणीयः ।

विदूषकः—[दृष्ट्वा] **भो ण जाणामि सोत्थि-वाअणं देइ त्ति आदु भवदो वद-व्ववदेसेण मुक्क-रोसा पणि-पाद-लङ्घणं पमज्जिदुकाम त्ति अज्ज मे अक्खीणं सुह-दंसणा देवी ।** भो न जानामि स्वस्तिवायनं ददातीति अथवा भवतो व्रतव्यपदेशेन मुक्तरोषा प्रणिपातलङ्घनं प्रमार्ष्टुकामेति अद्य ममाक्ष्णोः शुभदर्शना देवी ।

राजा—[सस्मितम्] **उभयमपि घटते । तथापि भवता यत् पश्चादभिहितं तन्मां प्रति भाति । यदत्रभवती**

सितांशुका मङ्गलमात्रभूषणा
पवित्रदूर्वाङ्कुरलाञ्छितालका ।
व्रतापदेशोज्झितगर्ववृत्तिना
मयि प्रसन्ना वपुषेव लक्ष्यते ॥ १२ ॥

देवी—[उपगम्य] **जदु जेदु अज्जउत्तो ।** जयतु जयतु आर्यपुत्रः ।

परिजनः—जेदु जेदु भट्टा । जयतु जयतु भर्ता ।

विदूषकः—सत्थि भोदीए । स्वस्ति भवत्यै ।

राजा—स्वागतं देव्यै [तां हस्तेन गृहीत्वा उपवेशयति]

उर्वशी—हला इअं ठाणे देवी-सद्देण उवअरीअदि । ण किं पि परिहीअदि सचीए ओजस्सिदाए । हला इयं स्थाने देवीशब्देनोपचर्यते । न किमपि परिहीयते शच्या ओजस्वितया ।

this union with the constellation of Rohini yields new brilliance to the divine Moon.

ATTENDANT—Does not His Majesty in the company of the Queen look so beautiful?

VIDUSHAKA—I do not know whether because she is to offer a present, or because using the occasion of the vow to lay aside her anger she (in fact) wishes to obliterate the recollection of her contemptuous treatment of your prostration–but Her Majesty to my eyes looks very charming to-day.

KING—(*Looking*). Both are likely; but what you said last appears to my mind to be the truth; her ladyship,

> Clad in white garments, wearing only (a few) auspicious ornaments, and with the tresses of her hair marked by the sprouts of holy Durva grass, appears to be reconciled to me by her very bodily appearance which has dismissed its haughty bearing under the pretext of a vow. [12]

QUEEN—(*Approaching*) Glory to my noble Lord!

ATTENDANTS—Glory to our Lord!

VIDUSHAKA—Prosperity attend your Ladyship!

KING—Queen, welcome. (*Takes her by the hand and leads her to a seat*).

URVASHI—Friend, how properly is she called "Devi"; for she does not fall short of Shachi in dignity.

चित्रलेखा—साहु असूआ-परम्मुहं मन्तिदं । साधु असूयापराङ्मुखं मन्त्रितम् ।

देवी—अज्जउत्तं पुरो करिअ को वि वद-विसेसो मए संपादणीओ । ता मुहुत्त उवरोहो सहीअदु । आर्यपुत्रं पुरस्कृत्य कोपि व्रतविशेषो मया संपादनीयः । तद् मुहूर्तमुपरोधः सह्यताम् ।

राजा—मा मैवम् । अनुग्रहः खलु नोपरोधः ।

विदूषकः—ईरिसो सोत्थि-वाअणवन्तो उवरोहो बहुसो होदु । ईदृशः स्वस्तिवायनवानुपरोधो बहुशो भवतु ।

राजा—किंनामधेयमेतद् देव्या व्रतम् ।

[देवी निपुणिकामवेक्षते।]

निपुणिका—भट्टा पिआणुप्पसादणं णाम । भर्तः प्रियानुप्रसादनं नाम ।

राजा—[देवीं विलोक्य] **यद्येवम्**

अनेन कल्याणि मृणालकोमलं
व्रतेन गात्रं ग्लपयस्यकारणम् ।
प्रसादमाकाङ्क्षति यस्तवोत्सुकः
स किं त्वया दासजनः प्रसाद्यते ॥ १३ ॥

उर्वशी—महन्तो खु से इमस्सिं बहु-माणो । महान् खल्वस्य एतस्यां बहुमानः ।

चित्रलेखा—अइ मुद्धे अण्ण-संकन्त-प्पेम्माणो णाअरिआ अधिअं दक्खिणा होन्ति । अयि मुग्धे अन्यसंक्रान्तप्रेमाणो नागरिका अधिकं दक्षिणा भवन्ति ।

देवी—[सस्मितम्] **णं इमस्स वद-परिग्गहस्स अअं पहावो जं एत्तिअं मन्ताविदो अज्जउत्तो ।** नन्वेतस्य व्रतपरिग्रहस्य अयं प्रभावः यदेतावद् मन्त्रित आर्यपुत्रः ।

CHITRALEKHA—Good, you speak without envy.

QUEEN—I have to fulfil a certain vow with my noble Lord's help: bear with the moment's inconvenience it may cause.

KING—Do not speak thus. It is, indeed, a favour and no inconvenience.

VIDUSHAKA—Would that such inconvenience often befall, that I might each time receive presents!

KING—What is the name of the Queen's vow?

(*Queen looks at Nipunika*).

NIPUNIKA—My Lord, the conciliation of the beloved.

KING—(*Looking to the Queen*). If that is so,

Then it is needless, O fair one, to wear this form, delicate as the lotus-stem, with this vow. How, do you propitiate this slave of yours who eagerly seeks your favour! (13)

URVASHI—Great indeed is his regard for her.

CHITRALEKHA—You simple one, these citizens when they transfer their affections to other women, become, indeed, very courteous (to their wives).

QUEEN—(*Smiling*). Such the effect of the vow that My Lord is made to speak thus.

विदूषकः—विरमदु भवं । ण जुत्तं सुहासिदं पच्चाचरिदुं । विरमतु भवान् । न युक्तं सुभाषितं प्रत्याचरितुम् ।

देवी—दारिआओ उवणेध ओवहारिअं जाव मणि-हम्मिअ-गदे चन्द-पादे अच्चेमि । दारिका उपनयत औपहारिकं यावद् मणिहर्म्यगतांश्चन्द्रपादानर्चामि ।

परिजनः—एसो गन्ध-कुसुमादिउवहारो । एष गन्धकुसुमाद्युपहारः ।

देवी—[नाटयेन गन्धपुष्पादिभिश्चन्द्रपादानभ्यर्च्य] **हञ्जे एदे ओवहारिअ-मोदए अज्ज-माणवअं लम्भावेहि ।** हञ्जे एतानौपहारिकमोदकानार्यमाणवकं लम्भय ।

परिजनः—जं देवी आणवेदि । अज्ज-माणवअ एदं दाव दे । यद् देवी आज्ञापयति । आर्यमाणवक एतत् तावत् ते ।

विदूषकः—[मोदकशरावं गृहीत्वा] **सोत्थि भोदीए । बहु-फलो दे उववासो होदु ।** स्वस्ति भवत्यै । बहुफलस्तवोपवासो भवतु ।

देवी—अज्जउत्त इदो दाव । आर्यपुत्र इतस्तावत् ।

राजा—अयमस्मि ।

देवी—[राज्ञः पूजामभिनीय प्राञ्जलिः प्रणिपत्य] **एसा अहं देवदामिहुणं रोहिणी-मिअ-लञ्छणं सक्खी-करिअ अज्ज-उत्तं अणुप्पसादेमि । अज्ज-प्पहुदि जं इत्थिअं अज्जउत्तो पत्थेदि जा अज्जउत्तस्स समाअमप्पणइणी ताए मए पीदि-बन्धेण वत्तिदव्वं त्ति ।** एषाहं दवतामिथुनं रोहिणीमृगलाञ्छनं साक्षीकृत्य आर्यपुत्रमनुप्रसादयामि । अद्यप्रभृति यां स्त्रियमार्यपुत्रः प्रार्थयते या आर्यपुत्रस्य समागमप्रणयिनी तया मया प्रीतिबन्धेन वर्तितव्यमिति ।

VIDUSHAKA—Forbear, my friend. You ought not to oppose auspicious words.

QUEEN—Girls, bring to me the materials of worship, that I may worship the rays of the Moon that have streamed into this crystal palace.

ATTENDANT—Here are materials of worship—sandal, flowers and others.

QUEEN—(*Acting worshipping the rays of the Moon with sandal, flowers etc.*). Girl, offer these sweets used in the worship to the noble Manavaka.

ATTENDANT—As the Queen commands. Noble Manavaka, this is for you.

VIDUSHAKA—(*Taking the platter of the Sweets*). Prosperity attend your Ladyship! May your fast bear manifold fruits!

QUEEN—My Lord, please to come here.

KING—Here I come.

QUEEN—(*Acting worshipping the King, and bowing with folded hands*). In the presence of these twin divinities—Rohini and the Moon—I now conciliate my noble Lord: henceforth whatever woman attracts my Lord's regard, or desires union with him, will be treated by me with kind complacency.

उर्वशी—अम्हहे ण आणे किं-परं से वअणं ति। मम उण वीसास-विसदं हिअअं संवुत्तं। अहो न जाने किंपरमस्या वचनमिति। मम पुनर्विश्वासविशदं हृदयं संवृत्तम्।

चित्रलेखा—सहि महाणुहावाए पदिव्वदाए अब्भणुण्णादो अणन्तराओ दे पिअ-समाअमो हविस्सदि। सखि महानुभावया पतिव्रतया अभ्यनुज्ञातः अनन्तरायस्ते प्रियसमागमो भविष्यति।

विदूषकः—[अपवार्य] **छिन्न-हत्थो मच्छे पलाइदे णिव्विण्णो धीवरो भणादि धम्मो मे हविस्सदि त्ति।** [प्रकाशम्] **भोदि किं तारिसो पिओ तत्तभवं।** छिन्नहस्तो मत्स्ये पलायिते निर्विण्णो धीवरो भणति धर्मो मे भविष्यतीति। भवति किं तादृशः प्रियस्तत्रभवान्।

देवी—मूढ अहं खु अत्तणो सुहावसाणेण अज्जउत्तं णिव्वुदसरीरं कादुं इच्छामि। एत्तिएण चिन्तेहि दाव पिओ ण व त्ति। मूढ अहं खलु आत्मनः सुखावसानेन आर्यपुत्रं निर्वृतशरीरं कर्तुमिच्छामि। एतावता चिन्तय तावत् प्रियो न वेति।

राजा—

दातुं वा प्रभवसि मामन्यस्मै कर्तुमेव वा दासम्।
नाहं पुनस्तथा त्वं यथा हि मां शङ्कसे भीरु ॥ १४ ॥

देवी—होहि वा मा वा। जधा-णिद्दिट्ठं संपादिदं पिआणुप्पसादणं वदं। दारिआओ एध गच्छम्ह। [प्रस्थिता देवी] भव वा मा वा। यथानिर्दिष्टं संपादितं प्रियानुप्रसादनं व्रतम्। दारिका एत गच्छामः।

राजा—प्रिये न खलु प्रसादितोऽस्मि यदि संप्रति विहाय गम्यते।

URVASHI—Well, I am scarce able to divine her purport, yet mightily do these words assuage the apprehensions of my heart.

CHITRALEKHA—Friend, nothing will anymore impede your union with your love, now that it is assented to by this lady of such an exalted spirit, who is such a devoted wife.

VIDUSHAKA—(*Aside*). When the fish has broken loose from his hand the fisherman in despair says 'A meritorious deed would be recorded in my favour. (*Aloud*). What! Is His Majesty dear to you in that manner?

QUEEN—Fool, desiring to promote my Lord's happiness I have resigned my own. Think from this whether he was dear to me or not.

KING—Yours the power to give me away or
make me a slave to yourself. But I am indeed not
what you—O timid one–doubt me to be. [14]

QUEEN—You may be so or may not be so. I have accomplished the vow 'conciliation of the loved one' as prescribed. Girls, now, come along. (*Queen starts to go*).

KING—My dear. I am indeed not pleased if you leave me now and go.

देवी—अज्जउत्त अलङ्घिद-पुव्वो मए णिअमो । आर्यपुत्र अलङ्घितपूर्वो मया नियमः ।

[निष्क्रान्ता सपरिवारा देवी]

उर्वशी—हला पिअ-कलत्तो राएसी । ण उण हिअअं णिवत्तेदुं सक्कुणोमि । हला प्रियकलत्रो राजर्षिः । न पुनर्हृदयं निवर्तयितुं शक्नोमि ।

चित्रलेखा—किं उण तुए णिरासाए णिवत्तीअदि । किं पुनस्त्वया निराशया निवर्त्यते ।

राजा—[आसनमुपेत्य] **वयस्य न खलु दूरं गता देवी ।**

विदूषकः—भण वीसद्धं जं सि वत्तु-कामो । असज्झो त्ति वेज्जेण आदुरो विअ सेरं मुत्तो भवं तत्तहोदीए । भण विश्रब्धं यदसि वक्तुकामः । असाध्य इति वैद्येनातुर इव स्वैरं मुक्तो भवांस्तत्रभवत्या ।

राजा—अपि नामोर्वशी—

उर्वशी—अज्ज किदत्था भवे । अद्य कृतार्था भवेत् ।

राजा—

गूढा नूपुरशब्दमात्रमपि मे कान्तं श्रुतौ पातयेत्
पश्चादेत्य शनैः कराम्बुजवृते कुर्वीत वा लोचने ।
हर्म्येऽस्मिन्नवतीर्य साध्वसवशान्मन्दायमाना बला-
दानीयेत पदात् पदं चतुरया सख्या ममोपान्तिकम् ॥१५॥

उर्वशी—हला इमं दाव से मणोरहं संपादइस्सं । [पृष्ठतो गत्वा राज्ञो नयने संवृणोति] हला इमं तावदस्य मनोरथं संपादयिष्यामि ।

[चित्रलेखा विदूषकं संज्ञापयति ।]

राजा—[स्पर्शं रूपयित्वा] **सखे नारायणोरुसंभवा सेयं वरोरूः ।**

QUEEN—My noble Lord, never before have I broken a sacred rule.

(Exit Queen with retinue).

URVASHI—Friend, the royal sage is fond of his wife and yet I am not able to reclaim my heart.

CHITRALEKHA—But why should you despair and withdraw ?

KING—*(Approching his seat).* Friend, the Queen indeed has not gone far.

VIDUSHAKA—You may say whatever you wish, safely enough. You are fairly given over by her ladyship, like a sick man in despair by his physician.

KING—Would that Urvashi—

URVASHI—Find her happiness to day !

KING—Herself concealed let fall the sweet music of her anklets in mine ear ! Or that with her lotus-hands, as lightly she stole behind me, she veiled my eyes ! Or descending to this palace and yet delaying to come through fear she were brought to me, step after step, with (welcome) violence by some clever friend ! [15]

URVASHI—Friend, let me grant him his desire.

(Going behind him, covers the King's eyes).

(Chitralekha makes a sign to the Vidushaka).

KING—*(Showing that he feels the touch).* Friend, this is that fair lady sprung from the lap of the sage Narayana

विदूषकः—कहं भवं अवगच्छदि। कथं भवानवगच्छति।

राजा—किमत्र ज्ञेयम्।

अङ्गमनङ्गक्लिष्टं सुखयेदन्या न मे करस्पर्शात्।
नोच्छ्वसिति तपनकिरणैश्चन्द्रस्येवांशुभिः कुमुदम् ॥१६॥

उर्वशी— [हस्तावपनीय उत्तिष्ठति। किंचिदुपसृत्यः] जेदु जेदु महाराओ। जयतु जयतु महाराजः।

राजा—सुन्दरि स्वागतम् [एकासने उपवेशयति]

चित्रलेखा—अवि सुहं वअस्सस्स। अपि सुखं वयस्यस्य।

राजा—नन्वेतदुपपन्नम्।

उर्वशी—हला देवीए दिण्णो महाराओ। तदो से पणअवदी विअ सरीर-संपक्कं गद म्हि। मा खु मं पुरोभाइणिं समत्थेहि। हला देव्या दत्तो महाराजः। ततोस्य प्रणयवतीव शरीरसंपर्कं गतास्मि। मा खलु मां पुरोभागिनीं समर्थयस्व।

विदूषकः—कहं इह ज्जेव तुम्हाणं अत्थमिदो सुज्जो। कथमिहैव युवयोरस्तमितः सूर्यः।

राजा—[उर्वशीमवलोक्य]

देव्या दत्त इति यदि व्यापारं व्रजसि मे शरीरेऽस्मिन्।
प्रथमं कस्यानुमते चोरितमेतत् त्वया हृदयम् ॥१७॥

चित्रलेखा—वअस्स णिरुत्तरा एसा। संपदं मह विण्णप्पं सुणीअदु। वयस्य निरुत्तरैषा। साम्प्रतं मम विज्ञाप्यं श्रूयताम्।

राजा—अवहितोस्मि।

चित्रलेखा—वसन्ताणन्तरे उण्ह-समए भअवं सुज्जो मए उवअरिदव्वो। ता जहा इअं मे पिअ-सही सग्गस्स ण उक्कण्ठेदि तहा वअस्सेण कादव्वं। वसन्तानन्तरे उष्णसमये भगवान् सूर्यो मयोपचरितव्यः। तद् यथेयं मे प्रियसखी स्वर्गाय नोत्कण्ठते तथा वयस्येन कर्तव्यम्।

VIDUSHAKA—How do you know?

KING—What is there to be known!

None else would give such delight to the body, afflicted by love, through the touch of her hand. The Kumuda wakes not at the touch of the solar ray as at the touch of moonbeams. [16]

URVASHI—(*Removing her hands and rising—slightly approaching*). Glory to the King!

KING—Welcome, fair one.

(*Makes her share his seat*).

CHITRALEKHA—I hope my friend feels happiness.

KING—Why it just comes to me.

URVASHI—Friend the Queen has given (me) His Majesty. So I approach his person-like his loving wife. You will not regard me as officious—will you?

VIDUSHAKA—How, has the Sun set to you even here?

KING—(*Looking at Urvashi*).

If you approach my person, because the Queen has presented me to you, who was it that first granted you permission to rob me of my heart? [17]

CHITRALEKHA—Friend, she can proffer no reply. Now listen to my prayer.

KING—I am all attention.

CHITRALEKHA—After spring, in summer, I have to wait upon the divine Sun. See to it, therefore, that you behave in such a manner that my dear friend does not long for heaven.

विदूषकः—किं वा सग्गे सुमरिदव्वं। ण वा अण्हीअदि ण वा पीअदि । केवलं अणिमिसेहिं णअणेहिं मोणा विडम्बीअन्ति । किं वा स्वर्गे स्मर्तव्यम् । न वा अश्यते न वा पीयते । केवलमनिमिषैर्नयनैर्मीना विडम्ब्यन्ते ।

राजा—भद्रे

अनिर्देश्यसुखः स्वर्गः कस्तं विस्मारयिष्यति ।
अनन्यनारीसामान्यो दासस्त्वस्याः पुरूरवाः ॥ १८ ॥

चित्रलेखा—अणुगहिद म्हि । हला उव्वसि अकादरा भविअ विसज्जेहि मं । अनुगृहीतास्मि । हला उर्वशि अकातरा भूत्वा विसर्जय माम् ।

उर्वशी—[चित्रलेखां परिष्वज्य] सहि मा खु मं विसुमरेहि । सखि मा खलु मां विस्मर ।

चित्रलेखा—[सस्मितम्] वअस्सेण संगदा तुमं एव्व एदं मए जाचिदव्वा। वयस्येन संगता त्वमेव एतद् मया याचितव्या ।

विदूषकः— दिट्ठिआ मणोरह- संपत्तीए वड्ढदि भवं। दिष्टया मनोरथसंपत्त्या वर्धते भवान् ।

राजा—इयं तावद् वृद्धिर्मम । पश्य ।

सामन्तमौलिमणिरञ्जितशासनाङ्क-
मेकातपत्त्रमवनेर्न तथा प्रभुत्वम् ।
अस्याः सखे चरणयोरहमद्य कान्त-
माज्ञाकरत्वमधिगम्य यथा कृतार्थः ॥ १९ ॥

उर्वशी—णत्थि मे विहवो अदो पिअदरं मन्तिदुं । नास्ति मे विभवः अतः प्रियतरं मन्त्रयितुम् ।

राजा—[उर्वशी हस्तेनावलम्ब्य] अहो विरुद्धसंवर्धन ईप्सितलाभो नाम ।

VIDUSHAKA—What is there to remember of heaven? They neither eat nor drink in that place; but they only mock the fish by not closing their eyes even for a twinkle.

KING—Fair lady,

The heaven is a place of joy ineffable; who can efface its memory? But Pururavas will be a slave unto no other woman than her. [18]

CHITRALEKHA—I am beholden to you. Friend Urvashi, summon up courage and bid me adieu.

URVASHI—(*Embracing Chitralekha*). Friend, you will not forget me?

CHITRALEKHA—(*Smiling*). That I should rather beg of you now that you are united to my friend.

(*Bowing to the King, departs*).

VIDUSHAKA—I congratulate you on the accomplishment of your desire.

KING—It is true, I reach the height of joy. See, I do not feel so blest by the sovereignty of the earth in which none holds the royal umbrella save myself and in which the royal edicts are illumined by the light of the jewels in the crests of the feudatories, as I do by obtaining the fair position of a slave to her feet! [19]

URVASHI—I have no words to give expression to sentiments dearer than these.

KING—(*Holding Urvashi by the hand*). How wonderful is the accomplishment of one's wishes, giving rise to contraries!

पादास्त एव शशिनः सुखयन्ति गात्रं
बाणास्त एव मदनस्य मनोऽनुकूलाः ।
संरम्भरूक्षमिव सुन्दरि यद्यदासीत्
त्वत्संगमेन मम तत्तदिवानुनीतम् ॥ २० ॥

उर्वशी—अवरद्धम्हि चिर-कारिआ अज्जउत्तस्स । अपराद्धास्मि चिरकारिका आर्यपुत्रस्य ।

राजा—मा मैवम् ।

यदेवोपनतं दुःखात् सुखं तद् रसवत्तरम् ।
निर्वाणाय तरुच्छाया तप्तस्य हि विशेषतः ॥ २१ ॥

विदूषकः—भो सेविदा पदोस-रमणीआ चन्द-वादा । समओ खु दे वास-घर-पवेसस्स । भोः सेविताः प्रदोषर-
३ मणीयाश्चन्द्रपादाः । समयः खलु ते वासगृहप्रवेशस्य ।

राजा—तेन हि सख्यास्ते मार्गमादेशय ।

विदूषकः—इदो इदो भवदी । [इति निष्क्रामन्ति] इत इतो
६ भवती ।

राजा—सुन्दरि इयमिदानीमभ्यर्थना ।

उर्वशी—कहं विअ । कथमिव ।

९ **राजा**—

अनधिगतमनोरथस्य पूर्वं
शतगुणितेव गता मम त्रियामा ।
यदि तु तव समागमे तथैव
प्रसरति सुभ्रु ततः कृती भवेयम् ॥ २२ ॥

[इति निष्क्रान्ताः सर्वे]

तृतीयोऽङ्कः समाप्तः ॥

Those very moon-beams soothe my body, those very shafts of love are now agreeable to my mind; whatever, O fair one, was harsh (as if) through anger seems now to be reconciled to me through your union. [20]

URVASHI—I have wronged my Lord by causing delay.

KING—No, not so.

The joy that follows grief gains richer zest; the traveller who has been scorched by the fierce day can better tell how sweet is the shelter of the tree. [21]

VIDUSHAKA—Well, sir, we have enjoyed the moon-light so lovely at night. It is high time now for you to retire to the inner apartment.

KING—Well then show your friend the way.

VIDUSHAKA—This way, this way, your ladyship. (*They leave*).

KING—Beloved. this is my request now.

URVASHI—What is it?

KING–Dearest, before the fruition of my most cherished desires a hundredfold were my nights prolonged! If that were the case now that we are together, I would be happy indeed. [22]

(*Exeunt Omnes.*)

END OF ACT III.

चतुर्थोऽङ्कः ।

[ततः प्रविशति विमनस्का चित्रलेखा सहजन्या च ।]

सहजन्या—[चित्रलेखां विलोक्य] **सहि मिलाअमाण-सद-वत्तस्स विअ दे मुहस्स छाआ हिअअस्स अस्सत्थदं सूएदि। ता कहेहि णिव्वेद-कारणं। सम-दुक्खा भविदुं इच्छामि ।** सखि म्लायमानशतपत्रस्येव ते मुखस्य च्छाया हृदयस्य अस्वस्थतां सूचयति । तत् कथय निर्वेदकारणम् । समदुःखा भवितुमिच्छामि ।

चित्रलेखा—अच्छरा-वार-पज्जाएण इह भअवदो सुज्जस्स पाद-मूलोवट्ठाणं वट्टदि त्ति बलिअं खु उव्वसीए उक्कण्ठिद म्हि । अप्सरोवारपर्यायेण इह भगवतः सूर्यस्य पादमूलोपस्थानं वर्तत इति बलवत् खलूर्वश्यामुत्कण्ठितास्मि ।

सहजन्या—जाणे वो अण्णोण्ण-सिणेहं । तदो तदो । जाने युवयोरन्योन्यस्नेहम् । ततस्ततः ।

चित्रलेखा—तदो इमाइं दिवसाइं को णु खु वुत्तन्तो त्ति पणिधाण-ट्ठिदाए मए अच्चाहिदं उवलद्धं। तत एतेषु दिवसेषु को नु खलु वृत्तान्त इति प्रणिधानस्थितया मया अत्याहितमुपलब्धम् ।

सहजन्या—[सावेगम्] **कीरिसं विअ ।** कीदृशमिव ।

चित्रलेखा—उव्वसी किल तं रदि-सहाअं राएसिं अमच्चेसु णिवेसिद-रज्ज-धुरं गेण्हिअ गन्धमादण-वणं विहरिदुं गदा । उर्वशी किल तं रतिसहायं राजर्षिममात्येषु निवेशितराज्यधुरं गृहीत्वा गन्धमादनवनं विहर्तुं गता ।

Act IV

(*Enter Chitralekha dejected in mind and Sahajanya).*

SAHAJANYA—(*Looking at Chitralekha*) Your face, looking like a faded lotus-flower, speaks the sadness of your heart. Tell me, then, the cause of your distress. I wish to share half your grief.

CHITRALEKHA—By the turn of service incumbent upon the nymphs, I was engaged in attending upon the Sun, and, therefore, I felt a deep longing for Urvashi.

SAHAJANYA–I know your mutual love. Well what then?

CHITRALEKHA—Then desiring to know how it was with her during all these days I put myself in contemplation and discerned a calamity.

SAHAJANYA—(*Feelingly*). Of what sort?

CHITRALEKHA—Urvashi took with her the King, her companion in her pleasures, who had put the yoke of the kingdom upon his ministers, and went to disport in the Gandhamadana Groves.

सहजन्या—**सो णाम संभोओ जो तारिसेसु पदेसेसु। तदो तदो।** स नाम संभोगो यस्तादृशेषु प्रदेशेषु। ततस्ततः।

चित्रलेखा—**तहिं खु मन्दाइणीअ पुलिणेसु गदा सिअदा-पव्वद-केलीहिं कीलमाणा विज्जाधर-दारिआ उदयवदी णाम तेण राएसिणा णिज्झाइद त्ति कुविदा उव्वसी।** तत्र खलु मन्दाकिन्याः पुलिनेषु गता सिकतापर्वतकेलीभिः क्रीडन्ती विद्याधरदारिका उदयवती नाम तेन राजर्षिणा निध्यातेति कुपिता उर्वशी।

सहजन्या—**होदव्वं। दूरारूढो खु पणओ असहणो। तदो तदो।** भवितव्यम्। दूरारूढः खलु प्रणयः असहनः। ततस्ततः।

चित्रलेखा—**तदो भट्टिणो अणुणअं अपडिवज्जमाणा गुरु-साव-संमूढ-हिअआ इत्थिआ-जण-परिहरणिज्जं कुमार-वणं पइट्ठा। पवेसाणन्तरं च काणणोवन्त-वत्ति-लदाभा-वेण परिणदं से रूवं।** ततो भर्तुरनुनयमप्रतिपद्यमाना गुरुशाप-संमूढहृदया स्त्रीजनपरिहरणीयं कुमारवनं प्रविष्टा। प्रवेशानन्तरं च काननोपान्तवर्तिलताभावेन परिणतमस्या रूपम्।

सहजन्या—**णत्थि विहिणो अलङ्घणिज्जं। तस्स अणुरा-अस्स अअं णाम एक्क-वदे ईरिसो अणत्थो। अह किम-वत्थो सो राएसी।** नास्ति विधेरलङ्घनीयम्। तस्यानुरागस्य अयं नाम एकपदे ईदृशोऽनर्थः। अथ किमवस्थः स राजर्षिः।

चित्रलेखा—**तस्सिं एव्व काणणे पिअदमं विचिण्णन्तो अहोरत्ते अदिवाहेदि। इमिणा उण णिव्वुदाणं पि उक्कण्ठा-कारिणा मेहोदएण अणत्थाहीणो हविस्सदि।** तस्मिन्नेव कानने प्रियतमां विचिन्वन्नहोरात्रानतिवाहयति। एतेन पुन-र्निर्वृतानामपि उत्कण्ठाकारिणा मेघोदयेन अनर्थाधीनो भविष्यति।

सहजन्या—**सहि तारिसा आकिदि-विसेसा चिरं दुक्ख-भाइणो ण होन्ति। अवस्सं किं पि अणुग्गह-णिमित्तं**

SAHAJANYA—That is indeed enjoyment as is obtained in such places. What then?

CHITRALEKHA—There, the royal sage looked intently at Udayavati, a Vidyadhara damsel playing with (making) mountains of sand on the banks of the Mandakini, and that angered Urvashi.

SAHAJANYA—That is possible; for intense love is so intolerant. What next?

CHITRALEKHA—Then not accepting the apologies of her husband and with her mind darkened by the curse the preceptor had denounced her with, she entered the grove sacred to Kumara, which is forbidden to women. And after she had entered it, she was transformed into a creeper on the skirt of the grove.

SAHAJANYA—There is nothing that fate may not assail. Alas! that such dire calamity should have all of a sudden befallen such affection! And, pray, what is the condition of the royal sage?

CHITRALEKHA—He is in that same forest passing days and nights in searching her.

SAHAJANYA—Friend, but such excellent forms do not undergo misery for long. Surely there will befall some

भूओ वि समाअम-कारणं हविस्सदि । ता एहि उद्-उम्मुहस्स भअवदो सुज्जस्स उवट्ठाणं करेम्ह । सखि
५२ तादृशा आकृतिविशेषाश्चिरं दुःखभागिनो न भवन्ति । अवश्यं किमपि अनुग्रहनिमित्तं भूयोपि समागमकारणं भविष्यति । तदेहि उदयोन्मुखस्य भगवतः सूर्यस्य उपस्थानं कुर्वः ।

५५ [इति निष्कान्ते ।]

प्रवेशकः ॥

[ततः प्रविशति उन्मत्तवेषो राजा ।]

५८ **राजा—आः दुरात्मन् रक्षस्तिष्ठ तिष्ठ । क्व मे प्रियतमामादाय गच्छसि । हन्त शैलशिखराद् गगनमुत्पत्य बाणर्मामभिवर्षति ।** [विभाव्य]

नवजलधरः संनद्धोऽयं न दृप्तनिशाचरः
सुरधनुरिदं दूराकृष्टं न नाम शरासनम् ।
अयमपि पटुर्धारासारो न बाणपरंपरा
कनकनिकषस्निग्धा विद्युत् प्रिया न ममोर्वशी ॥१॥

[विचिन्त्य] । **क्व नु खलु रम्भोरूर्गता स्यात्**

तिष्ठेत् कोपवशात् प्रभावपिहिता दीर्घं न सा कुप्यति
स्वर्गायोत्पतिता भवेन्मयि पुनर्भावार्द्रमस्या मनः ।
तां हर्तुं विबुधद्विषोऽपि न च मे शक्ताः पुरोवर्तिनीं
सा चात्यन्तमदर्शनं नयनयोर्यातेति कोऽयं विधिः ॥२॥

[दिशोऽवलोक्य । सनिःश्वासम् ।] **अये परावृत्तभागधेयानां दुःखं दुःखानुबन्धि । कुतः ।**

अयमेकपदे तया वियोगः प्रियया चोपनतः सुदुःसहो मे ।
नववारिधरोदयादहोभिर्भवितव्यं च निरातपत्वरम्यैः ॥३॥

event making for reunion caused by some favourable circumstances. So come along, let us worship the divine Sun, that is just about to rise. (*Exeunt*).

END OF THE INTRODUCTORY SCENE.

(*Enter King dressed as an insane person*).

KING—Hold, you wicked fiend, hold Where are you going, taking my beloved? Ha, from the mountain-peak up-flying he rains showers of arrows on me. (*Looking closely*).

This is a fresh cloud ready to shower, and not a haughty fiend girt in armour. This here is the heavens rainbow striding a vast length and not a (warrior's) bow stretched out; and this a pelting shower of rain that is so sharp and not a volley of arrows; while this is only a flash of lightning gleaming like a streak of gold on the touch-stone, and not my beloved Urvashi. [1]

(*Reflecting*)—Where can the fair one have gone?

Has she through her power remained invisible in anger? But she will not be angry long. Has she flown up to the heavens? But her heart yearns in ever fresh love for me. While even the foes of the immortals cannot wrest her, while in my presence. And yet she is quite invisible to mine eyes! What fate is this? [2]

(*Looking into space, sighing*). Ah! How one upon another calamities whelm those whom once misfortune has assailed! For,

While all of a sudden I have suffered severance from my beloved which is unbearably painful, here the fresh clouds appear making the days so genial by mitigating their intense heat. [3]

[विहस्य] मुधैव खलु मनसः परितापवृद्धिरुपेक्ष्यते ।
यथा मुनयोऽपि व्याहरन्ति राजा कालस्य कारणमिति ।
२ तत् किमहं जलदसमयं न प्रत्यादिशामि । अथ वा
प्रावृषेण्यैरेव लिङ्गैर्मम राजोपचारः संप्रति । कथमिव ।

विद्युल्लेखाकनकरुचिरं श्रीवितानं ममाभ्रं
व्याधूयन्ते निचुलतरुभिर्मञ्जरीचामराणि ।
घर्मच्छेदात् पटुतरगिरो बन्दिनो नीलकण्ठा
धारासारोपनयनपरा नैगमाश्चाम्बुवाहाः ॥ ४ ॥

भवतु । किमेवं परिच्छदश्लाघया । यावदस्मिन् कानने
तां प्रियामन्वेषयामि [विलोक्य] हन्त व्यवसितस्य मे
३ संदीपनमिव संवृत्तम् कुतः

आरक्तराजिभिरियं कुसुमैर्नवकन्दली सलिलगर्भैः ।
कोपादन्तर्बाष्पे स्मरयति मां लोचने तस्याः ॥ ५ ॥

इतो गतेति कथं नु तत्रभवती मया सूचयितव्या ।

पद्भ्यां स्पृशेद् वसुमतीं यदि सा सुगात्री
मेघाभिवृष्टसिकतासु वनस्थलीषु ।
पश्चान्नता गुरुनितम्बतया ततोऽस्या
दृश्येत चारुपदपङ्क्तिरलक्तकाङ्का ॥ ६ ॥

[परिक्रम्य अवलोक्य च सहर्षम् ।] उपलब्धमुपलक्षणं येन
तस्याः कोपनाया मार्गोऽनुमीयते ।

हृतोष्ठरागैर्नयनोदबिन्दुभि-
र्निमग्ननाभेर्निपतद्भिरङ्कितम् ।
च्युतं रुषा भिन्नगतेरसंशयं
शकोदरश्याममिदं स्तनांशुकम् ॥ ७ ॥

(*Laughing*). Or, in vain do I bear all these troubles of my mind. For even the wise say that the King is the lord of time. Why should I not countermand the rainy season? Or rather the signs of the rainy season are the only insignia that are doing me royal honour.

Here the clouds spread my splendid canopy, shot with the gold of lightning streaks; The Nichula trees wave their (tufted) blossoms as *chowries*; the peacocks growing clamorous, now that summer is gone, are my bards; while the clouds are the (rich) merchants that proffer me tribute of rain-showers. [4]

But let it be. Why should I laud my paraphernalia? So I will search that love of mine in this forest.

(*Looking*).—Dear me? As I set about it here is something that aggravates (my troubles). For,

This fresh Kandali plant with its flowers streaked with red veins, and with water inside them painfully reminds me of her eyes with the tears starting inside them through anger. [5]

How am I to know that her ladyship has gone hence

If she were to touch the earth with her feet here in these woodland spots whose sandy soil is showered over by the clouds, then would I trace her lovely footprints marked with the Alaktaka dye, pressed deep in the soil at the back owing to the heaviness of her hips. [6]

(*Walking about and looking with joy*).—Here have I found a sign by which I can infer the way, the irate one has gone

Here is the scarf covering her breasts, dark-green like a parrot's belly, which assuredly must have slipped down as in anger she stumbled on, and marked by the tears of that fair one with a deep navel—tears which falling first upon her lips carried with them their red paint. [7]

[विभाव्य ।] कथम् । सेन्द्रगोपं नवशाद्वलमिदम् । कुतो नु खलु निर्जने वने प्रियाप्रवृत्तिरवगमयितव्या [दृष्ट्वा]
अये आसारोच्छ्वसितशैलेयस्थलीपाषाणमारूढः
आलोकयति पयोदान् प्रबलपुरोवातनर्तितशिखण्डः ।
केकागर्भेण शिखी दूरोन्नमितेन कण्ठेन ॥ ८ ॥

[उपेत्य ।] यावदेनं पृच्छामि ।

नीलकण्ठ ममोत्कण्ठा वनेऽस्मिन् वनिता त्वया ।
दीर्घापाङ्गा सितापाङ्ग दृष्टा दृष्टिक्षमा भवेत् ॥ ९ ॥

कथमदत्त्वा प्रतिवचनं नर्तितुं प्रवृत्तः । किं नु खलु हर्षकारणमस्य । [विचिन्त्य] भवतु । विदितमेतत् ।

मृदुपवनविभिन्नो मत्प्रियाया विनाशाद्
घनरुचिरकलापो निःसपत्नोऽस्य जातः ।
रतिविगलितबन्धे केशहस्ते सुकेश्याः
सति कुसुमसनाथे किं करोत्येष बर्ही ॥ १० ॥

भवतु । परव्यसननिर्वृतं न खल्वेनं पृच्छामि [परिक्रम्य] इयमातपान्तसंधुक्षितमदा जम्बूविटपमध्यास्ते परभृता । विहंगमेषु पण्डिता जातिरेषा । यावदेनामभ्यर्थये । भवति

त्वां कामिनो मदनदूतिमुदाहरन्ति
मानावभङ्गनिपुणं त्वममोघमस्त्रम् ।
तामानय प्रियतमां मम वा समीपं
मां वा नयाशु कलभाषिणि यत्र कान्ता ॥ ११ ॥

[आकाशे ।] किमाह भवती । कथं त्वामेवमनुरक्तं विहाय गतेति । शृणोतु भवती ।

(*Looking closely*).—How, this is fresh sward with the Indragopa insects! Where indeed can I get the intelligence of my love in this lonesome wild?

(*Seeing*).—Ah, here, perched on a stone in the rocky soil, bright-looking on account of rain-showers, is a peacock,

That looks (proudly) at the clouds with neck out-stretched and clamorous with rapture, his crest waved by the breezes blowing in his face. [8]

(*Approching*).—So I will inquire of him.

O blue-necked peacock, with eyes white in the corners, have you seen my love-lorn lady of broad big eyes in this forest? For her charms deserve your gaze. [9]

How he deigns no answer but simply treads a measure. What could have exhilarated him? (*Reflecting*) Well I have it.

Owing to the disappearance of my love, his beautiful, thick plumage, divided by the gentle breeze, is now without a rival; but where would be his boast, before the excellent tresses of her hair decked with flowers, when loosened in amorous sport? [10]

Let be.—I shall not ask him, who seems to be happy in another's misfortune. (*Walking about*). Here is a Koil sitting on the Jambu tree, her passions inflamed at the end of summer. She is a wise bird among the winged flock. So I will request her.

They call you the lover's messenger of love—the unfailing missile able to break down pride; do you, O sweet-tongued, bring my dearest to me, or lead me to where she is. [11]

What do you say? 'How did she leave you when you were so devoted to her?' Hear,

कुपिता न तु कोपकारणं सकृदप्यात्मगतं स्मराम्यहम् ।
प्रभुता रमणेषु योषितां न हि भावस्खलितान्यपेक्षते ॥१२॥

कथं कथाच्छेदकारिणो स्वकार्य एव सक्ता ।

महदपि परदुःखं शीतलं सम्यगाहुः
प्रणयमगणयित्वा यन्ममापद्गतस्य ।
अधरमिव मदान्धा पातुमेषा प्रवृत्ता
फलमभिमुखपाकं राजजम्बूद्रुमस्य ॥ १३ ॥

एवंगतेऽपि प्रियेव मे मञ्जुस्वनेति न कोपोऽस्याम् ।
इतो वयम्- [परिक्रामितकेन। कर्णे दत्त्वा] अये दक्षिणेन
२ प्रियाचरणनिक्षेपशंसी नूपुररवः । यावदत्र गच्छामि ।
[परिक्रम्य] अहो धिक् धिक् ।

मेघश्यामा दिशो दृष्ट्वा मानसोत्सुकचेतसाम् ।
कूजितं राजहंसानां नेदं नूपुरशिञ्जितम् ॥ १४ ॥

भवतु । यावदेते मानसोत्सुकाः पतत्रिणः सरसो नोत्प-
तन्ति तावदेतेभ्यः प्रियाप्रवृत्तिरवगमयितव्या । [उपेत्य]
३ भो भो जलविहंगमराज

पश्चात् सरः प्रति गमिष्यसि मानसं तत्
पाथेयमुत्सृज बिसं ग्रहणाय भूयः ।
मां तावदुद्धर शुचो दयिताप्रवृत्त्या
स्वार्थात् सतां गुरुतरा प्रणयिक्रियैव ॥ १५ ॥

यथोन्मुखो विलोकयति मानसोत्सुकेन मया न लक्षिते-
त्येवं वचनमाह ।

Angry I find her, but I do not remember to have even for once given her any cause for offence. The fond tyranny that women exercise over those who love them does not require any deviation from love for them to get angry. [12]

How now! She seems to mind her own business and not heed our conversation.

It is well said that howsoever great another's woe, a stranger will not be in the least affected by it Thus she disregards my request and lo! speeds to yon excellent Jambu tree to drink the (luscious) juice of its now ripe fruit, as one intoxicated (by the draught of love) to sip the honey of (roseate) lips. [13]

Although it is thus, yet I scarcely feel angry with her as she has the sweet voice of my love. Hence we—(*Going about and listening*). Ah! from the South I hear the jingle of anklets indicating the tread of my Love's feet. So I will proceed thither (*Moving about*). Oh, fie!

This is not the chime of tinkling anklets, but the cooing of swans who, seeing the space darkened with clouds, are filled inwardly with a longing to go to the Manasa lake. [14]

Well, while these birds, filled as they are with a (passionate) yearning for the Manasa lake, are not flown from the lake, let me get from them news about my Love. (*Approaching*). You, prince of aquatic birds,

After a while, you will begin your journey to the Manasa lake; forego the provender of lotus-stem; you will have that again. Do you first redeem me from despair by imparting some tidings of my beloved; for the good regard it worthier to render kindly offices to the suppliants than be mindful of their own business. [15]

Since he looks up he seems to say that in his longing for the Manasa, he has not marked her.

यदि हंस गता न ते नतभ्रूः
 सरसो रोधसि दर्शनं प्रिया मे ।
मदखेलपदं कथं नु तस्याः
 सकलं चोर गतं त्वया गृहीतम् ॥ १६ ॥

अतश्च—

हंस प्रयच्छ मे कान्तां गतिरस्यास्त्वया हृता ।
विभावितैकदेशेन देयं यदभियुज्यते ॥ १७ ॥

[विहस्य]। एष चोरानुशासी राजेति भयादुत्पतितः। [परिक्रम्य] अयमिदानीं प्रियासहायश्चक्रवाकः। तावदेनं पृच्छामि ।

रथाङ्गनामन् वियुतो रथाङ्गश्रोणिबिम्बया ।
अयं त्वां पृच्छति रथी मनोरथशतैर्वृतः ॥ १८ ॥

कथं कः क इत्याह । मा तावत् । न खलु विदितोऽह मस्य ।

सूर्याचन्द्रमसौ यस्य मातामहपितामहौ ।
स्वयं वृतः पतिर्द्वाभ्यामुर्वश्या च भुवा च यः ॥१९॥

कथं तूष्णीं स्थितः । भवतु । उपालप्स्ये तावदेनम् ।

सरसि नलिनीपत्त्रेणापि त्वमावृतविग्रहां
 ननु सहचरीं दूरे मत्वा विरौषि समुत्सुकः ।
इति च भवतो जायास्नेहात् पृथक्स्थितिभीरुता
 मयि च विधुरे भावः कान्ताप्रवृत्तिपराङ्मुखः ॥२०॥

सर्वथा मदीयानां भाग्यविपर्ययाणामयं प्रभावः। यावदन्यमवकाशमवगाहे । [पदान्तरे स्थित्वा] भवतु न तावद् गच्छामि ।

Well, O swan, if you have not seen my love with her arched eye-brows, on the bank of the lake, how could you, O thief, have wholly taken her gait, elegant through youthful pride? [16]

Therefore,

O swan, give me my Love; you have stolen her gait. He who is proved guilty as regards a part should restore the whole of what is claimed. [17]

(*Laughing*).—He has flown up fearing that a King the chastiser of thieves. is here (*Walking about*). Here is the Chakrawaka with his mate. So I will ask him.

O Chakrawaka, this warrior, here severed from his broad-hipped Love and filled with a hundred longings, asks you. [18]

How does he say "Who?" Who? That will not do It seems he knows me not.

The Sun and the Moon are my grandsires on both sides; while I am the self-chosen Lord of Urvashi and the Earth. [19]

How, he keeps quiet! Well, I will remonstrate with him.

If by so much as a lotus-leaf thy mate is screened from sight in the lake, thou wilt pour out thy plaints, all yearning for her, thinking her to be far-removed. Thus art thou apprehensive of thy mate's separation through thy fondness for her. Why, then, friend, dost thou seem so averse to giving me news about my Love, even when I am so distressed? [20]

In every respect my fortune has been so perverse to me. So I will go to another region. (*Stopping after a step*). Well, I will not go

इदं रुणद्धि मां पद्ममन्तःकूजितषट्पदम् ।
मया दष्टाधरं तस्याः ससीत्कारमिवाननम् ॥ २१ ॥

भवतु। अस्मिन्नेव कमलाभ्यासिनि मधुकरे प्रणयित्वं करिष्ये। इतो गतस्यानुशयो मा भूदिति।

मधुकर मदिराक्ष्याः शंस तस्याः प्रवृत्तिं
[विभाव्य ।]

वरतनुरथवासौ नैव दृष्टा त्वया मे ।
यदि सुरभिमपास्यस्तन्मुखोच्छ्वासगन्धं
तव रतिरभविष्यत् पुण्डरीके किमस्मिन् ॥ २२ ॥

साधयामस्तावत् [परिक्रामितकेन] एष नीपस्कन्धनिषण्णहस्तः करिणीसहायो नागराजस्तिष्ठति। अस्मात् प्रियोदन्तमुपलप्स्ये [विलोक्य] भवतु न त्वरा कार्या।

अयमचिरोद्गतपल्लवमुपनीतं प्रियकरेणुहस्तेन ।
अभिलषतु तावदासवसुरभिरसं सल्लकीभङ्गम् ॥ २३ ॥

[क्षणमात्रं स्थित्वा।] हन्त कृताह्निकः संवृत्तः। भवतु पृच्छामि।

मदकल युवतिशशिकला गजयूथप यूथिकाशबलकेशी।
स्थिरयौवना स्थिता ते दूरालोके सुखालोका ॥ २४ ॥

[सहर्षम्।] अनेन स्निग्धमन्द्रेण गर्जितेन प्रियोपलम्भशंसिना समाश्वासितोऽस्मि। साधर्म्याच्च त्वयि मे भूयसी प्रीतिः।

मामाहुः पृथिवीभृतामधिपतिं नागाधिराजो भवान्
अव्युच्छिन्नपृथुप्रवृत्ति भवतो दानं ममाप्यर्थिषु ।
स्त्रीरत्नेषु ममोर्वशी प्रियतमा यूथे तवेयं वशा
सर्वं मामनु ते प्रियाविरहजां त्वं तु व्यथां मानुभूः ॥२५॥

This lotus, here, amidst whose petals the bees are sweetly murmuring, arrests me; it is thus like my beloved's face, murmuring protest at my somewhat rudely sipping its lower lip. [21]

Well then, I shall woo this honey-sipper sitting on the lotus lest I should regret when I go hence.

Bee, give me the intelligence of that fair one with bewitching eyes.

(*Looking closely*).

Or rather, you have not seen that fair Love of mine; for had you tasted the fragrance of her delicious breath, you would certainly have scorned the lotus. [22]

I will leave, then. (*Walking about*). Here is the Lord of elephants with his mate, resting his trunk on the stem of a Nipa tree. I will get news of the dear one from him. (*Looking*). Let him be. I should not be in a hurry.

Let him eat the bough of the Sallaki with its newly-appearing shoots and its rich fragrant juice offered to him by his dear mate. [23]

(*Waiting for a moment*). Well, now he has had his meal; so I will ask him.

Lord of elephants, charming with the pride of youth, have you beheld (even) afar off that beautiful one, blooming with eternal youth, like the crescent Moon among (the stars of) women, her hair decked with the Yuthika flowers? [24]

(*With joy*). I am (mightily) consoled by this kind and gentle roar conveying some intimation of my Love. And great is my love for you because of our likeness.

For while they call me the lord of kings, you are the lord of elephants; your bounty sheds the frontal ichor profusely without break, while my wealth is lavishly showered on the needy; Urvashi is my Love among the jewels of womankind, and this gentle one your mate in the herd; thus everything of yours accords with mine. May you, however, never know the pangs of severance from your beloved. [25]

सुखमास्तां भवान्। साधयामस्तावत्। [पार्श्वतो दृष्टिं दत्त्वा] अये सुरभिकन्दरो नाम विशेषरमणीयः सानुमानालोक्यते। प्रियश्चायमप्सरसाम्। अपि नाम सुतनुरस्योपत्यकायामुपलभ्येत। [परिक्रम्य अवलोक्य च] कथमन्धकारः। भवतु। विद्युत्प्रकाशेनावलोकयामि। हन्त मदीयैर्दुरितपरिणामैर्मेघोऽपि शतह्रदाशून्यः संवृत्तः। तथापि शिलोच्चयमेतमपृष्ट्वा न निवर्तिष्ये।

अपि वनान्तरमल्पकुचान्तरा श्रयति पर्वत पर्वसु संनता।
इदमनङ्गपरिग्रहमङ्गना पृथुनितम्ब नितम्बवती तव ॥२६॥

कथं तूष्णीमास्ते। शङ्के विप्रकृष्टो न शृणोतीति। समीपेऽस्य गत्वा पुनरेनं पृच्छामि [परिक्रम्य]

सर्वक्षितिभृतां नाथ दृष्टा सर्वाङ्गसुन्दरी।
रामा रम्ये वनान्तेऽस्मिन् मया विरहिता त्वया ॥२७॥

[आकर्ण्य। सहर्षम्।] कथं यथाक्रमं दृष्टेत्याह। भवानपि अतः प्रियतरं शृणोतु। क्व तर्हि मम प्रियतमा। [नेपथ्ये तदेवाकर्ण्य।] हा धिक्। ममैवायं कन्दरमुखविसर्पी प्रतिशब्दः। [विषादं रूपयित्वा] श्रान्तोऽस्मि। अस्यास्तावद् गिरिनद्यास्तीरे स्थितस्तरङ्गवातमासेविष्ये। इमां नवाम्बुकलुषामपि स्रोतोवहां पश्यतो मे रमते मनः।

तरङ्गभ्रूभङ्गा क्षुभितविहगश्रेणिरसना
विकर्षन्ती फेनं वसनमिव संरम्भशिथिलम्।
यथाविद्धं याति स्खलितमभिसंधाय बहुशो
नदीभावेनेयं ध्रुवमसहना सा परिणता ॥ २८ ॥

May you rest in peace. I will go. (*Looking at his side*). Here is the mountain 'Surabhikandara,' particularly lovely and a loved resort of the nymphs. May it be that the fair one is to be found on it ledges? (*Moving about and observing*). Oh, how is it dark? Well, I will see with the flash of lightning. What a (sad) result of my sins that even the clouds are bereft of lightning! Still I will not return without making inquiry of this mountain.

> Does she, of close breasts, and full in the joints, and plump in the hips, resort the interior of this forest, sacred to love, O large-sided mountain? [26]

How is he silent? I am afraid he does not hear me being at a distance. I will approach him and ask him again. (*Walking about*).

> O Lord of mountains, have you seen that lovely woman, beautiful in all limbs, in this charming forest, severed from me? [27]

(*Listening; with joy*). How, in the same order, he said 'I have seen'! May you, too, hear sweeter words than these. Where, then, is my beloved? (*Hearing the same words from behind the scenes*). Ah, bless me! This is only my voice reverberating from the mouth of the cave. (*Showing despair*). I am tired. So reposing on the bank of this mountain-stream I shall enjoy the breezes from its waves. My mind is charmed as I look upon this stream although it is turbid with fresh water.

> The rippling wave is her arching brow; the fluttering line of birds her girdle; drawing along its foam, which is as it were her garment loosened through anger, it flows meanderingly, avoiding the many obstacles in the way, like my beloved who stumbles along as she remembers my faults; so surely that irascible one has been transformed into this river. [28]

भवतु । याचिष्ये तावदेनाम् । [अञ्जलिं कृत्वा]

त्वयि निबद्धरतेः प्रियवादिनः
प्रणयभङ्गपराङ्मुखचेतसः ।
कमपराधलवं मम पश्यसि
त्यजसि मानिनि दासजनं यतः ॥ २९ ॥

अथ वा परमार्थसरिदेवैषा । न खलूर्वशी पुरूरवसम-
पहाय समुद्राभिसारिणी भविष्यति । भवतु । अनिर्वे-
३ दप्राप्याणि श्रेयांसि । यावदमुमेव प्रदेशं गच्छामि यत्र
मे नयनयोः सुनयना तिरोभूता । [परिक्रम्य अवलोक्य]
हन्त दृष्टमुपलक्षणं तस्या मार्गस्य ।

रक्तकदम्बः सोऽयं प्रियया घर्मान्तशंसि यस्यैकम् ।
कुसुममसमग्रकेसरविषममपि कृतं शिखाभरणम् ॥३०॥

[विलोक्य ।] इमं तावत् प्रियाप्रवृत्तिनिमित्तं सारङ्गमासी-
नमभ्यर्थये ।

कृष्णसारच्छविर्योऽसौ दृश्यते काननश्रिया ।
वनशोभावलोकाय कटाक्ष इव पातितः ॥ ३१ ॥

[विलोक्य ।] किं नु खलु मामवधीरयन्निव अन्यतोमुखः
संवृत्तः । [दृष्ट्वा ।]

अस्यान्तिकमायान्ती शिशुना स्तनपायिना मृगी रुद्धा ।
तामयमनन्यदृष्टिर्भुग्नग्रीवो विलोकयति ॥ ३२ ॥

हंहो यूथपते

अपि दृष्टवानसि मम प्रियां वने
कथयामि ते तदुपलक्षणं शृणु ।
पृथुलोचना सहचरी यथैव ते
सुभगं तथैव खलु सापि वीक्षते ॥ ३३ ॥

Well, I will implore her. (*Folding his hands*).

I am devoted to you, ever speak agreeably to you and have a heart that has never deviated from love: so what fault, even the slightest, have I committed that you fl[illegible] from me so wholly yours? [29]

Or, rather this is really a stream; for surely Urvashi will not quit her Pururavas for the Ocean. So let it be. Fortune crowns those who yield not to despair. So I will go to the place where the fair-eyed one was lost to me. (*Walking about and observing*). Ah, now I see this indication as to the way she took.

Here is the Raktakadamba tree, one of whose flowers, uneven on account of its filaments being incompletely formed and suggesting the end of summer, was used by her to deck her hair. [30]

(*Observing*). I will now request the antelope squatting yonder to give me some intelligence of my love.

That one, seen yonder, of black and variegated hue, looks as if it is a glance cast by the sylvan deity to observe the beauty of the forest [31]

(*Seeing*). How, disregarding me, he has turned his face in another direction? (*Seeing*).

A doe approaching him was obstructed by her suckling fawn. So with a bent neck he is intently looking at her. [32]

O Lord of the herd,

Have you seen my beloved in this forest? I will give you her marks, listen. Even as your broad-eyed mate looks charmingly even so does she cast beautiful glances. [33]

कथमनादृत्य मद्वचनं कलत्राभिमुखं स्थितः। उपपद्यते।
परिभवास्पदं दशाविपर्ययः। इतो वयम्–[परिक्रामितकेन
३ अवलोक्य] शिलाभेदान्तरगतं किमेतदालोक्यते ।

प्रभालेपी नायं हरिहतमृगस्यामिषलवः
स्फुलिङ्गः स्यादग्नेर्गगनमभिवृष्टं पुनरिदम् ।

[विभाव्य ।]

अये रक्ताशोकस्तबकसमरागो मणिरयं
यमुद्धर्तुं पूषा व्यवसित इवालम्बितकरः ॥ ३४ ॥

हरति मे मनः। आदास्ये तावदेनम् । अथवा

मन्दारपुष्पैरधिवासितायां यस्याः शिखायामयमर्पणीयः।
सैव प्रिया संप्रति दुर्लभा मे किमेनमस्रोपहतं करोमि ॥३५॥

[नेपथ्ये ।] वत्स गृह्यतां गृह्यताम् ।

संगमनीय इति मणिः शैलसुताचरणरागयोनिरयम् ।
आवहति धार्यमाणः संगममचिरात् प्रियजनेन ॥ ३६ ॥

राजा—[कर्णं दत्त्वा] को नु खलु मामेवमनुशास्ति ।
[दिशोऽवलोक्य।] अये अनुकम्पते मां कश्चिन्मृगचारी मुनि-
३ र्भगवान् । भगवन् अनुगृहीतोऽस्म्यहमुपदेशाद् भवतः।
[मणिमादाय] हंहो संगमनीय

तया वियुक्तस्य विलग्नमध्यया
भविष्यसि त्वं यदि संगमाय मे ।
ततः करिष्यामि भवन्तमात्मनः
शिखामणिं बालमिवेन्दुमीश्वरः ॥ ३७ ॥

[परिक्रम्य अवलोक्य च।]अये किं नु खलु कुसुमरहितामपि
लतामिमां पश्यतो मे रतिरुपलब्धा । अथवा स्थाने
३ मनोरमा ममेयम् । इयं हि

How, heedless of what I said he turns towards his mate! But that is proper; for a reverse of fortune subjects one to insults; so from here–I–(*Walking and looking*). What is this to be seen in the rift of the rock?

This could not be a piece of the flesh of deer killed by a lion, since it is covered with lustre; nor is it a spark of fire for the sky has (just) rained.

(*Looking closely*);

Ah, this is some gem gleaming like a bunch of Ashoka blossoms, and the sun seems to endeavour to clutch at it by stretching forth his rays. [34]

How it captivates my heart! I will have it. Or rather my beloved whose hair fragrant with Mandara flowers should be adorned by this (gem) is now lost to me; why should I then soil it with my tears? [35]

(*Behind the Scenes*). Child, take it, do take it. It is the Samgamaniya jewel, sprung from the dye applied to Gauri's feet; when borne, it brings about, within a short time, union with the loved one. [36]

KING—Who is this that instructs me thus? (*Looking in space*). Some holy ascetic living the life of a deer feels compassion for me. Revered sir, I am obliged to you for this advice. (*Taking the gem*). O gem of union,

If severed as I am from her of slender waist, you unite me to her, then surely I will make you my crest-gem, even as Ishvara his crescent-moon. [37]

(*Walking about and observing*). How is it that my mind is charmed even by looking at this creeper, albeit bereft of flowers? Or rather, it is proper it should charm my mind. This is

तन्वी मेघजलार्द्रपल्लवतया धौताधरेवाश्रुभिः
शून्येवाभरणैः स्वकालविरहाद् विश्रान्तपुष्पोद्गमा ।
चिन्तामौनमिवास्थिता मधुलिहां शब्दैर्विना लक्ष्यते
चण्डी मामवधूय पादपतितं जातानुतापेव सा ॥३८॥

यावदस्याः प्रियानुकारिण्याः परिष्वङ्गप्रणयी भवामि ।
३ [इति लतामालिङ्गति । ततः प्रविशति तत्स्थान एवोर्वशी ।]

राजा—[निमीलिताक्ष एव स्पर्शं रूपयित्वा] अये उर्वशीगात्रसंपर्कादिव निर्वृतं मे शरीरम् । तथापि न पुनरस्ति
६ विश्वासः । कुतः ।

समर्थये यत् प्रथमं प्रियां प्रति
क्षणेन तन्मे परिवर्ततेऽन्यथा ।
अतो विनिद्रे सहसा विलोचने
करोमि न स्पर्शविभावितप्रियः ॥ ३९ ॥

[शनैश्चक्षुरुन्मील्य ।] कथं सत्यमेव प्रियतमा ।

उर्वशी—[बाष्पं विसृज्य] जेदु जेदु महाराओ । जयतु
३ जयतु महाराजः ।

राजा—

त्वद्वियोगोद्भवे तन्वि मया तमसि मज्जता ।
दिष्ट्या प्रत्युपलब्धासि चेतनेव गतासुना ॥ ४० ॥

उर्वशी—अब्भन्तर-करणाए मए पच्चक्खी-किद-वुत्तन्तो खु महाराओ । अभ्यन्तरकरणया मया प्रत्यक्षीकृतवृत्तान्तः खलु
३ महाराजः ।

That slender one, and the tender leaves wetted by the clouds her lower lip washed by her tears; not decked with blossom, as it is past its time of flowering, it is she with her ornaments cast aside; since the bees are not humming to it, she has been silent in anxious thoughts. So it is that irascible one, who having spurned me fallen at her feet, now seems to be stung with remorse. [38]

I will therefore, press this likeness of my beloved to my heart. (*Embraces the creeper*).

(*Enter Urvashi at that very place*).

KING—(*With eyes yet closed, showing that he perceives touch*). Ah, how the fever of my body is allayed as at the touch of Urvashi's person? Still my mind misgives me, For,

Whatever I fancy as belonging to my love turns to be otherwise a moment after. So will I not open my eyes all of a sudden, (though) I recongnize my Love through touch. [39]

(*Slowly opening his eyes*) How ! my Love forsooth !

URVASHI—(*Shedding tears*). Glory to my Lord !

KING—O slender one, while I was sinking in the darkness caused by your loss, I have fortunately recovered you, as a person dead might recover life.[40]

URVASHI—With my senses lying hidden in me, I witnessed the plight of my Lord.

राजा—अभ्यन्तरकरणयेति न खलु ते वचनार्थमवैमि।

उर्वशी—कहइस्सं । इमं दाव पसीददु महाराओ जं मए कोववसं गदाए एदं अवत्थन्तरं पाविदो महाराओ। कथयिष्यामि । एतत् तावत् प्रसीदतु महाराजो यन्मया कोपवशं गतया एतदवस्थान्तरं प्रापितो महाराजः ।

राजा—कल्याणि न तावदहं प्रसादयितव्यः । त्वद्दर्शनादेव प्रसन्नः सबाह्यान्तःकरणो ममान्तरात्मा । कथय कथमियन्तं कालमवस्थिता मया विना भवती ।

उर्वशी—सुणादु महाराओ । भअवदा कुमारेण सासदं कुमारवदं गेण्हिअ अकलुसो णाम गन्धमादण-कच्छो अज्झासिदो किदो अ एस विही । शृणोतु महाराजः । भगवता कुमारेण शाश्वतं कुमारव्रतं गृहीत्वा अकलुषो नाम गन्धमादनकच्छोध्यासितः कृतश्चैष विधिः ।

राजा—क इव ।

उर्वशी—जा इमं पदेसं इत्थिआ पविसदि सा लदाभावेण परिणमिस्सदि। गोरी-चरण-संभवं मणिं विणा तदो ण मुच्चिस्सदि त्ति । साहं गुरु-साव-संमूढ-हिअआ देवदा-समअं विसुमरिअ अगहिदाणुणआ कुमारवणं पविट्ठा । पवेसाणन्तरं एव्व वासन्ती लदा संवुत्ता। या एतं प्रदेशं स्त्री प्रवेक्ष्यति सा लताभावेन परिणंस्यति । गौरीचरणसंभवं मणिं विना ततो न मोक्ष्यत इति। साहं गुरुशापसंमूढहृदया दवतासमयं विस्मृत्य अगृहातानुनया कुमारवन प्रविष्टा। प्रवेशानन्तरमेव वासन्ती लता संवृत्ता ।

KING—I really do not understand what you mean by " the senses lying hidden."

URVASHI—I will explain. But let my Lord forgive that yielding to anger I wrought so sad a change in my Lord.

KING—Fair one, you have not to beg my forgiveness For your very sight has brought gratification to my soul together with the external and internal senses. Tell me, how you could live without me so long.

URVASHI—Let my Lord hear. The warrior God, vowing eternal celibacy, dwelt in the region bordering on the Gandhamadana, called Akalusha ; and he made this rule.

KING—What is it ?

UARVASHI—Whatever woman entered this region, would be transformed into a creeper ; and she would not be restored to her form in the absence of the gem sprung from the feet of Gauri. So, as my memory was obliterated by the curse of the preceptor, I forgot the rule prescribed by the deity, and not accepting your entreaties, entered the forest sacred to Kumara. And the moment I became a Vasanti creeper.

राजा—सर्वमुपपन्नम् ।

रतिखेदसुप्तमपि मां शयने या मन्यसे प्रवासगतम्
सा त्वं प्रिये सहेथाः कथं मदीयं चिरवियोगम् ॥४१॥

इदं तद् यथाकथितं त्वत्संगमनिमित्तं मुनेरुपलभ्य मणि-प्रभावादासादिता त्वमस्माभिः । [मणिं दर्शयति]

उर्वशी—अम्मो संगमणीआ । अदो खु महाराएण आलिङ्गिदमेत्तव्व पकिदित्थ म्हि संवुत्ता [मणिमादाय मूर्धनि वहति] अहो संगमनीयः । अतः खलु महाराजेन आलिङ्गितमात्रैव प्रकृतिस्थास्मि संवृत्ता ।

राजा—एवमेव सुन्दरि क्षणमात्रं स्थीयताम् ।

स्फुरता विच्छुरितमिदं रागेण मणेर्ललाटनिहितस्य ।
श्रियमुद्वहति मुखं ते बालातपरक्तकमलस्य ॥ ४२ ॥

उर्वशी—महन्तो खु कालो तुह पइट्ठाणादो णिग्गदस्स । असूअन्ति मं पकिदीओ । ता एहि णिवुत्तम्ह । महान् खलु कालस्तव प्रतिष्ठानात् निर्गतस्य । असूयन्ति मयं प्रकृतयः । तदेहि निवर्तावहे ।

राजा—यदाज्ञापयति भवती ।

उर्वशी—कहं महाराओ गन्तुं इच्छदि । कथं महाराजो गन्तुमिच्छति ।

राजा—

अचिरप्रभाविलसितैः पताकिना
सुरकार्मुकाभिनवचित्रशोभिना ।
गमितेन खेलगमन विमानतां
नय मां नवेन वसतिं पयोमुचा ॥ ४३ ॥

[इति निष्क्रान्ताः सर्वे ।]

विक्रमोर्वशीये चतुर्थोऽङ्कः समाप्तः ॥

KING—Everything is explained.

You who would regard me as gone away on a journey, when I would be merely sleeping, overcome by fatigue of love-dalliance, how could you (otherwise) bear long severance from me? (41)

Here then having learnt from the sage, as already narrated, this gem to be the cause of my reunion with you, through the power of this gem I recovered you. (*Shows the gem*)

URVASHI—Oh, the gem of union! that is why I was restored to myself the moment my Lord embraced me. (*Takes the gem and holds it on her head*).

KING—Hold yourself, O fair one, hold a moment thus.

Irradiated by the glow of this gem placed upon your brow, your face looks as splendid as a lotus red-gleaming in the morning light. (42)

URVASHI—It is a long time that you left Pratishthana; surely the subjects must have been incensed against me. So come, let us return.

KING—As you command, Lady.

URVASHI—How will it please my Lord to travel?

KING—Take me, O stately of gait, to my place on a cloud turned into an aerial car, with the flashes of the evanescent lightning for its banner and the bow of Indra for the fresh paintings that beautify it. [43]

(*Exeunt Omnes*)

END OF ACT IV

पञ्चमोऽङ्कः ।

[ततः प्रविशति परितुष्टो विदूषकः ।]

विदूषकः—दिट्ठिआ चिरस्स कालस्स उव्वसी-सहाओ णन्दण-वण-प्पमुहेसु देवदा-रण्णेसु विहरिअ पडिणिवुत्तो पिअ-वअस्सो । दाणिं ससक्कारोवआरेहिं पकिदीहिं अणुरज्जन्तो रज्जं करेदि । असंताणत्तणं वज्जिअ ण किं वि से हीणं । अज्ज तिहि-विसेसो त्ति भअवदीणं गङ्गा-जउँणाणं संगमे देवीहिं सह किदाहिसेओ संपदं उवआरिअं पविट्ठो । ता जाव तत्तभवदो अलंकरीअमाणस्स अणुलेवण-मल्ले अग्ग-भागी होमि [इति परिक्रामति] दिष्ट्या चिरस्य कालस्य उर्वशीसहायो नन्दनवनप्रमुखेषु देवातरण्येषु विहृत्य प्रतिनिवृत्तः प्रियवयस्यः । इदानीं ससत्कारोपचारैः प्रकृतिभिरनुरज्यमानो राज्यं करोति । असंतानत्वं वर्जयित्वा न किमपि अस्य हीनम् । अद्य तिथिविशेष इति भगवत्योर्गङ्गायमुनयोः संगमे देवीभिः सह कृताभिषेकः सांप्रतमुपकार्यां प्रविष्टः । तद् यावत् तत्रभवतः अलंक्रियमाणस्य अनुलेपनमाल्ये अग्रभागी भवामि ।

[नेपथ्ये ।] हद्धी हद्धी । दुऊलुत्तरच्छदे ताल-वेण्टाधारे णिक्खिविअ णीअमाणो मए भट्टिणो अब्भन्तर-विलासिणी-मोलि-रअण-जोग्गो मणी आमिस-सङ्किणा गिद्धेण अक्खित्तो । हा धिक् हा धिक् । दुकूलोत्तरच्छदे तालवृन्ताधारे निक्षिप्य नीयमानो मया भर्तुरभ्यन्तरविलासिनीमौलिरत्नयोग्यो मणिरामिषशङ्किना गृध्रेणाक्षिप्तः ।

विदूषकः—[कर्णं दत्वा] अच्चाहिदं । परं बहु-मदो क्खु

ACT V.

(*Enter Vidushaka who seems satisfied*).

VIDUSHAKA—Fourtunately, my dear friend has now come back, after spending a long time enjoying with Urvashi in the gardens of the gods, Nandanavana and others. Now he rules, well pleased with his subjects who treat him with honour and respect. With the exception of his childless state, there is nothing wanting to make his happiness complete. To-day being an auspicious day, he has bathed at the confluence of the Ganges and the Yamuna along with his queens and has just now entered his tent. So while he adorns himself let me partake of the first portion of the flowers and perfumes. (*Walks about*)

(*Behind the scenes*)

Alas! Alas! Here has a hawk borne away the ruby, taking it for a piece of flesh, the ruby which well would adorn the crown of our Lord's dearest Queen, when I was taking it along in a silk-covered box of palm-leaf.

VIDUSHAKA—(*Listening*). What a mischance! That was the crest-gem of reunion highly prized by my friend.

सो वअस्सस्स संगमणीओ णाम चूडा-मणी । अदो खु असमत्त-णेवच्छो तत्तभवं आसणादो उट्ठिअ इदो एव्व आअच्छदि । जाव णं उवसप्पामि । अत्याहितम् । परं बहुमतः खलु स वयस्यस्य संगमनीयो नाम चूडामणिः । अतः खलु असमाप्तनेपथ्यस्तत्रभवानासनादुत्थाय इत एवागच्छति । यावदेनमुपसर्पामि ।

[ततः प्रविशति सावेगपरिजनो राजा ।]

राजा—

आत्मनो वधमाहर्ता क्वासौ विहगतस्करः ।
येन तत्प्रथमं स्तेयं गोप्तुरेव गृहे कृतम् ॥ १ ॥

किराती—एसो एसो खु मुह-कोडि-लग्ग-हेम-सुत्तेण मणिणा आलिहन्तो विअ आआसं पडिब्भमदि । एष एष खलु मुखकोटिलग्नहेमसूत्रेण मणिना आलिखन्निव आकाशं परिभ्रमति ।

राजा—पश्याम्येनम् ।

असौ मुखालम्बितहेमसूत्रं बिभ्रन्मणिं मण्डलचारशीघ्रः ।
अलातचक्रप्रतिमं विहंगस्तद्रागरेखावलयं तनोति ॥२॥

किं नु खलु कर्तव्यम् ।

विदूषकः—[उपेत्य] अलं एत्थ घिणाए । अवराही सासणीओ । अलमत्र घृणया । अपराधी शासनीयः ।

राजा—सम्यगाह भवान् । धनुर्धनुस्तावत् ।

[निष्क्रान्ता धनुर्ग्राहिणी यवनी ।]

राजा—वयस्य न दृश्यते विहंगः ।

विदूषकः—इदो दक्खिणन्तेण अवगदो सासणीओ कुणवभोअणो । इतो दक्षिणान्तेन अपगतः शासनीयः कुणपभोजनः ।

That is why, before finishing his attire, my friend leaves his seat and comes here. So I will approach him.

(Then enter King with attendants in flurry).

KING—Where is the winged thief that courts his own death and presumes to violate for the first time the dwelling of his own protector? (1)

A forest-woman—There is he hovering in the sky, and scratching it, as it were, with the gem, the golden thread whereof he holds in his beak.

KING—Yes I see him.

As quick he flies in swift circles, with the gem the golden chain of which is in his beak, the bird seems to be hemmed in a fiery ring, by the circle of its flashing lustre. (2)

What indeed, is to be done?

VIDUSAKA—Banish compassion in the present case. A culprit deserves to be punished.

KING—You counsel wisely. A bow, a bow.

(Exit a Yavani—a bow-bearer to the King)

KING—Friend, the bird is not to be seen,

VIDUSAKA—He has flown away in the south, this carrion-feeder that ought to be punished.

१ राजा—[परिवृत्य अवलोक्य] दृष्ट इदानीम् ।

प्रभापल्लवितेनासौ करोति मणिना खगः ।
अशोकस्तबकेनेव दिङ्मुखस्यावतंसकम् ॥ ३ ॥

[प्रविश्य चापहस्ता यवनी ।]

यवनी—भट्टा एदं हत्थावाव-सहिदं सरासणं । भर्तः
३ एतद्धस्तावापसहितं शरासनम् ।

राजा—किमिदानीं धनुषा । बाणपथमतीतः क्रव्य-भोजनः । तथा हि ।

आभाति मणिविशेषो दूरमिदानीं पतत्रिणा नीतः ।
नक्तमिव लोहिताङ्गः परुषघनच्छेदसंयुक्तः ॥ ४ ॥

[कञ्चुकिनं विलोक्य ।] लातव्य मद्वचनादुच्यतां नागरिकः सायं निवासवृक्षाश्रया विचीयतां विहगदस्युरिति ।

३ कञ्चुकी—यदाज्ञापयति देवः ।

[इति निष्क्रान्तः]

विदूषकः—उववसदु भवं संपदं । कहिं गदो रअण-
६ कुम्भीलओ भवदो सासणादो मुच्चिस्सदि । उपविशतु
भवान् सांप्रतम् । क्व गतो रत्नकुम्भीरको भवतः शासनाद् मोक्ष्यते ।

राजा—[विदूषकेण सहोपविश्य ।]

रत्नमिति न मम तस्मिन् मणौ प्रियत्वं विहंगमाक्षिप्ते ।
प्रियया तेनास्मि सखे संगमनीयेन संगमितः ॥ ५ ॥

विदूषकः—णं परिगदत्थो म्हि किदो भवदा । ननु परि-गतार्थोऽस्मि कृतो भवता ।

[ततः प्रविशति सशरं मणिमादाय कञ्चुकी ।]

कञ्चुकी—जयतु देवः ।

KING—(*Turning and looking*) Now I see.

With the gem looking large owing to its flashing lustre the bird seems to adorn the face of the quarter as with an ear-ornament made of a bunch of Asoka flowers. [3]

(*Enter a Yavani, with a bow in her hand*)

YAVANI—My Lord, here is a bow with an arm-guard.

KING—What use is the bow, now? The vulture has flown beyond the arrow's reach. For

That excellent gem, as it is carried further by the bird looks like Mars clinging to a strip of a thick cloudlet. [4]

(*Looking towards the chamberlain*) Latavya, say to the prefect in my name, 'Do you track this thief of a bird at night to his tree of perch.'

CHAMBERLAIN—As my lord commands.

VIDUSHAKA—Rest you my friend now. Wheresoever gone, this thief of the gem cannot escape your punishment.

KING—(*Sitting along with the Vidushaka*).

Merely as a gem I have very little regard for the precious stone snatched by the bird; but to this gem of union, I owe reunion with my love. [5]

VIDUSHAKA—Well, you have already told me so.

(*Enter Chamberlain bringing with him the gem and an arrow*).

CHAMBERLAIN—Victory to my Lord!

अनेन निर्भिन्नतनुः स वध्यो
रोषेण ते मार्गणतां गतेन ।
प्राप्यापराधोचितमन्तरिक्षात्
समौलिरत्नः पतितः पतत्री ॥ ६ ॥

[सर्वे विस्मयं रूपयन्ति ।]

कञ्चुकी—अद्भिः प्रक्षालितो मणिः कस्मै प्रदीयताम् ।

राजा—किराति अग्निशुद्धमेनं कृत्वा पेटकं प्रवेशय ।

किराती—जं भट्टा आणवेदि [इति मणिं गृहीत्वा निष्क्रान्ता ।]
यद् भर्ता आज्ञापयति ।

राजा—लातव्य अपि जानीते भवान् कस्यायं बाण इति ।

कञ्चुकी—नामाङ्कितो दृश्यते न तु मे वर्णविचारक्षमा दृष्टिः ।

राजा—तेन ह्युपनय शरम् ।

[कञ्चुकी तथा करोति ।]

[राजा नामाक्षराण्यनुवाच्य । सापत्यतां रूपयति ।]

कञ्चुकी—यावन्नियोगमशून्यं करोमि ।

[इति निष्क्रान्तः

विदूषकः—किं भवं विआरेदि । किं भवान् विचारयति ।

राजा—शृणु तावत् प्रहर्तुर्नामाक्षराणि [वाचयति]

उर्वशीसंभवस्यायमैलसूनोर्धनुर्भृतः
कुमारस्यायुषो बाणः प्रहर्तुर्द्विषदायुषाम् ॥ ७ ॥

विदूषकः—[सपरितोषम्] दिट्ठिआ संताणेण वड्ढदि भवं । दिष्ट्या संतानेन वर्धते भवान् ।

राजा—सखे कथमेतत् । अन्यत्र नैमिषेयसत्रादवियुक्तोऽहमुर्वश्या । न च मया गर्भव्यक्तिरालक्षिता । कुत एव प्रसूतिः । किं तु

Pierced by your anger turned into an arrow, the bird that deserved death, having thus met adequate punishment, has fallen from the sky together with the crest-gem. [6]

(*All express wonder*).

CHAMBERLAIN—To whom shall this gem, cleaned with water, be given ?

KING—Ho, forester, purify it in fire and keep it in its box.

Forestwoman—As my Lord commands.

(*Takes the gem and departs*).

KING—Latavya, know you to whom the shaft belongs ?

CHAMBERLAIN—There is some name inscribed upon it, but my eye-sight cannot distinguish the characters.

KING—Well, then, bring the arrow to me.

(*The Chamberlain does as bidden; the King reads the letters of the name and he is a father.*)

CHAMBERLAIN—In the meanwhile, I will attend to my business.

(*Exit*).

VIDUSHAKA—What are you thinking ?

KING—Hear the name of the striker.

"The arrow of Ayus, the archer who strikes at the life of his enemies, the son of Urvashi and Pururavas." [7]

VIDUSHAKA—(*With satisfaction*). I congratulate you upon your having a son.

KING—Friend, how is this ? I have never been away from Urvashi, but for the interval of the sacrifice performed in the Naimisha forest. And I never marked that she was carrying. Whence then this child ? But,

आविलपयोधराग्रं लवलीदलपाण्डुराननच्छायम् ।
तानि दिनानि वपुरभूत् केवलमलसेक्षणं तस्याः ॥ ८ ॥

विदूषकः--मा भवं सव्वं माणुसी-धम्मं दिव्वासु संभावेदु । पहावणिगूढाइं ताणं चरिदाइं । मा भवान् सर्वं मानुषीधर्मं दिव्यासु संभावयतु । प्रभावनिगूढानि तासां चरितानि ।

राजा—अस्तु तावदेवं यथा भवानाह । पुत्रसंवरणे किमिव कारणं तत्रभवत्याः ।

विदूषकः--को देवदा-रहस्साइं तक्कइस्सदि । को देवता-रहस्यानि तर्कयिष्यति ।

[प्रविश्य कञ्चुकी ।]

कञ्चुकी--जयतु जयतु देवः । देव च्यवनाश्रमात् कुमारं गृहीत्वा तापसी संप्राप्ता देवं द्रष्टुमिच्छति ।

राजा--उभयमपि अविलम्बितं प्रवेशय ।

कञ्चुकी--यदाज्ञापयति देवः ।

[इति निष्क्रम्य चापहस्तेन कुमारेण तापस्या च सह प्रविष्टः ।]

कञ्चुकी--इत इतो भगवती । [सर्वे परिक्रामन्ति ।]

विदूषकः--[विलोक्य] किं ण खु सो एसो तत्तभवं खत्तिअ-कुमारओ जस्स णामङ्किदो गिद्ध-लक्ख-वेधी अद्ध-णाराओ । तह बहुअरं भवन्तं अणुकरेदि । किं न खलु स एष तत्रभवान् क्षत्रियकुमारको यस्य नामाङ्कितो गृध्रलक्षवेधी अर्धनाराचः । तथा बहुतरं भवन्तमनुकरोति ।

राजा— स्यादेवम् । अतः खलु

बाष्पायते निपतिता मम दृष्टिरस्मिन्
वात्सल्यबन्धि हृदयं मनसः प्रसादः ।

During those days, her breasts had their nipples darkened, and her cheeks grew pale as the Lavali leaf, and her eyes were full of lassitude. [8]

VIDUSHAKA—You must not suppose that the heavenly nymphs betray the qualities of mortals. They can keep their doings hidden through their power.

KING—It may be as you say. But why should she have concealed her son?

VIDUSHAKA—Who can fathom the mystery of the celestial beings?

(*Enter chamberlain*).

CHAMBERLAIN—Glory to our Lord! a hermit-woman has come from the religious domicile of the sage Chyavana, with a boy, and desires to see Your Majesty.

KING—Usher both of them without delay.

CHAMBERLAIN—As my Lord commands.

(*Departs, and then enters leading the boy with a bow in his hand, and the hermit woman*).

CHAMBERLAIN—This way, madam, this way.

(*All move about*)

VIDUSHAKA—(*Observing*). Could this be the Kshatriya lad, to whom belongs the arrow that hit the vulture? To be sure, he looks your image to a great extent.

KING—That is possible. And hence?

My eyes are dimmed with tears as they rest on him, my heart is filled with tenderness, and my mind

संजातवेपथुभिरुज्झितधैर्यवृत्ति-
रिच्छामि चैनमदयं परिरब्धुमङ्गैः ॥ ९ ॥

कञ्चुकी—भगवति एवं स्थीयताम् ।

[तापसीकुमारौ स्थितौ ।]

राजा—अम्ब अभिवादये ।

तापसी—महा-भाअ सोम-वंस-वित्थारइत्तओ होहि । [आत्मगतम्] अम्हो अणाचक्खिदोवि विण्णादो इमस्स राएसिणो अउसो अ ओरसो संबन्धो । [प्रकाशम्] जाद पणम दे गुरुं । महाभाग सोमवंशविस्तारयिता भव । अहो अनाख्यातोपि विज्ञातः अस्य राजर्षेरायुषश्चौरसः संबन्धः । जात प्रणम ते गुरुम् ।

[कुमारश्चापगर्भमञ्जलिं करोति ।]

राजा—आयुष्मान् भव ।

कुमारः—[आत्मगतम्]

यदि हार्दमिदं श्रुत्वा पिता ममायं सुतोऽहमस्येति ।
उत्सङ्गवर्धितानां गुरुषु भवेत् कीदृशः स्नेहः ॥ १० ॥

राजा—भगवति किमागमनप्रयोजनम् ।

तापसी—सुणादु महाराओ । एसो दीहाऊ आऊ जाद-मेत्तो एव्व उव्वसीए किंवि णिमित्तं अवेक्खिअ मम हत्थे णासी-किदो । जं खत्तिअ-कुमारअस्स जाद-कम्मादि विहाणं तं से भअवदा चवणेण असेसं अणुचिट्ठिदं । गहिद-विज्जो धणुव्वेदे अहिविणीदो । शृणोतु महाराजः । एष दीर्घायुरायुर्जातमात्र एव उर्वश्या किमपि निमित्तमवेक्ष्य मम हस्ते न्यासीकृतः । यत् क्षत्रियकुमारस्य जातकर्मादि विधानं तदस्य

becomes serene. Seized by a tremor, and my equanimity gone, I desire to clasp him close with my limbs. [9]

CHAMBERLAIN—Revered lady, here pause.

(*The hermit woman and the boy stand*).

KING—Hail, holy dame!

HERMIT-WOMAN—Fortunate one, may you continue the line of Soma. (*To herself*) Ah, without being told, one may tell that the royal sage and Ayus are bound by ties of blood. (*Aloud*) Boy, pay your homage to your father.

(*Joins his hands in reverence, still holding the bow in them*).

KING—May your years be many!

BOY—(*To himself*). If such my love on hearing that he is my father and I his son, how great must be the love of those who grew up fondled in the laps by their fathers? [10]

KING--Revered lady, what brings you here?

HERMIT-WOMAN—Let my lord hear. This long-lived child was for some cause confided to my care by Urvashi, the moment he was born. The rites of birth and other rites proper to the warrior-lad have been duly performed by the sage Chyavana. After having learned the sciences, he has been trained to archery.

भगवता च्यवनेन अशेषमनुष्ठितम् । गृहीतविद्यो धनुर्वेदेऽभिविनीतः ।

राजा—सनाथः खलु संवृत्तः ।

तापसी—अज्ज पुप्फ-समिदत्थं इसि-कुमारएहिं सह-गदेण इमिणा अस्सम-विरुद्धं आअरिदं । अद्य पुष्पसमिदर्थमृषिकुमारकैः सह गतेन अनेन आश्रमविरुद्धमाचरितम् ।

विदूषकः—[सावेगम्] **किं विअ ।** किमिव ।

तापसी—गहिदामिसो किल गिद्धो पादव-सिहरे णिलीअमाणो अणेण लक्खी-किदो बाणस्स । गृहीतामिषः किल गृध्रः पादपशिखरे निलीयमानोऽनेन लक्ष्यीकृतो बाणस्य

[विदूषको राजानमवलोकयति ।]

राजा—ततस्ततः ।

तापसी—तदो उवलद्ध-उत्तन्तेण भअवदा चवणेण अहं समादिट्ठा । णिज्जादेहि हत्थ-णासंति । ता इच्छामि देविं उव्वसिं पेक्खिदुं । तत उपलब्धवृत्तान्तेन भगवता च्यवनेन अहं समादिष्टा । निर्यातय हस्तन्यासमिति । तदिच्छामि देवीमुर्वशीं प्रेक्षितुम् ।

राजा—तेन हि आसनमनुगृह्णातु भगवती ।

(तापसी उपनीत आसने उपविशति ।)

राजा—लातव्य आहूयतामुर्वशी ।

कञ्चुकी—यदाज्ञापयति देवः ।

[इति निष्क्रान्तः]

राजा—[कुमारमवलोक्य] **एह्येहि वत्स ।**

सर्वाङ्गीणः स्पर्शः सुतस्य किल तेन मामुपगतेन ।
आह्लादयस्व तावच्चन्द्रकरश्चन्द्रकान्तमिव ॥ ११ ॥

KING—So he had a protector indeed.

HERMIT-WOMAN—Today while he had gone out to fetch flowers and wood with the boys of the ascetics, he acted in a way to violate (the sanctity of,) the hermitage.

VIDUSHAKA—(*Hurriedly*) How?

HERMIT-WOMAN—They say that he aimed an arrow at a vulture that carried a bit of flesh and was perched on a tree-top.

(*Vidushaka looks at the King*).

KING—What next?

HERMIT-WOMAN—Then the revered Chyavana who learnt about it, bade me return your deposit. So I wish to see Queen Urvashi.

KING—Well, please, holy dame, take a seat.

(*The Hermit-Woman occupies a seat brought for her*).

KING—Latavya, call Urvashi.

CHAMBERLAIN—As my Lord commands.

(*Exit*).

KING—(*Looking at the prince*). Come, child, come.

The touch of a son's person, they say shoots ecstasy through the whole body: therefore come and gladden me, as the moon's ray, the moonstone. [11]

तापसी—जाद आणन्देहि पितरं । जात आनन्दय पितरम् ।

[कुमारः राजानमुपगम्य पादग्रहणं करोति ।]

राजा—[कुमारं परिष्वज्य पादपीठे चोपवेश्य] **वत्स इतस्तव पितुः प्रियसखं ब्राह्मणमशङ्कितो वन्दस्व ।**

विदूषकः—किं ति सङ्किस्सदि । अस्सम-वास-परिचिदो एव्व साहामिओ । किमिति शङ्क्यते । आश्रमवासपरिचित एव शाखामृगः ।

कुमारः—[सस्मितम्] **तात वन्दे ।**

विदूषकः—सत्थि भवदो । स्वस्ति भवते ।

[ततः प्रविशति उर्वशी कञ्चुकी च ।]

कञ्चुकी—इत इतो देवी ।

उर्वशी—[कुमारमवलोक्य] **को णु खु एसो स्स-बाणासणो पादपीठे सअं महाराएण संजमीअमाण-सिहण्डओ चिट्ठदि** [तापसीं दृष्ट्वा] **अम्मो सच्चवदी-सूइदो मे पुत्तओ आऊ । महन्तो खु संवुत्तो ।** [परिक्रामति] को नु खल्वेष सबाणासनः पादपीठे स्वयं महाराजेन संयम्यमानशिखण्डकस्तिष्ठति । अहो सत्यवतीसूचितो मम पुत्रक आयुः । महान् खलु संवृत्तः ।

राजाः—[उर्वशीं दृष्ट्वा]

इयं ते जननी प्राप्ता त्वदालोकनतत्परा ।
स्नेहप्रस्रवनिर्भिन्नमुद्वहन्ती स्तनांशुकम् ॥ १२ ॥

तापसी—जाद एहि पच्चुग्गच्छ मादरं । जात एहि प्रत्युद्गच्छ मातरम् ।

[कुमार उर्वशीं प्रत्युद्गच्छति ।]

उर्वशी—अम्ब पाद-पणामं करेमि । अम्ब पादप्रणामं करोमि ।

HERMIT-WOMAN—Child, gladden your father.

(The prince approaches the King and touches his feet).

KING—*(Embracing the prince and placing him on the foot-stool)*. Child, here is this Brahmin, your father's dear friend. Bow to him without fear.

VIDUSHKA—Why should he fear ? He has been familiar enough with monkeys during his stay in the hermitage.

PRINCE—Father, I bow.

VIDUSHAKA—Fortune attend thee.

(Enter Urvashi and the Chamberlain).

CHAMBERLAIN—This way, Queen, this way.

URVASHI—*(Looking at the prince)*. Who is this, armed with the bow and seated on footstool, whose crest-knot is being tied by my Lord himself ? *(Looking at the hermit-woman)*. Oh, it must be my son Ayus, as Satyavati's presence makes clear. *(Walks about)*.

KING—*(Seeing Urvashi)*.

Here comes your mother boy, her gaze intently fixed upon you; and her breast-scarf all wetted with the milk distilled through a mother's love. [12]

HERMIT-WOMAN—Child, come, meet your mother.

(The prince goes to meet Urvashi).

URVASHI—Mother, I reverence your feet.

तापसी—वच्छे भत्तुणो बहु-मदा होहि। वत्से भर्तुर्बहुमता भव ।

कुमारः—अम्ब अभिवादये ।

उर्वशी—[कुमारमुन्नमितमुखं परिष्वज्य] **वच्छ पिदरं आराधइत्तओ होहि।** [राजानमुपेत्य] **जेदु जेदु महाराओ ।** वत्स पितरमाराधयिता भव । जयतु जयतु महाराजः ।

राजा—स्वागतं पुत्रवत्यै। इत आस्यताम् [अर्धासनं ददाति]

[उर्वशी उपविशति ।]

तापसी—एसो गहिद-विज्जो आऊ संपदं कवअ-हरो संवुत्तो । एदस्स दे भत्तुणो समक्खं णिज्जादिदो हत्थणिक्खेवो । ता विसज्जेदुं इच्छामि । उवरुज्झइ मे अस्समधम्मो । एष गृहीतविद्य आयुः सांप्रतं कवचहरः संवृत्तः । तदेतस्य ते भर्तुः समक्षं निर्यातितो हस्तनिक्षेपः । तद् विसर्जयितुमिच्छामि । उपरुध्यते ममाश्रमधर्मः ।

उर्वशी—चिरस्स अज्जं देक्खिअ अहिअदरं अवितिण्हम्हि । ण सक्कुणोमि विसज्जिदुं । अण्णय्यं उवरोहिदुं । गच्छदु अज्जा पुणो-दंसणाअ । चिरस्यार्यां दृष्ट्वा अधिकतरमवितृष्णास्मि । न शक्नोमि विस्रष्टुम् । अन्याय्यमुपरोद्धुम् । गच्छत्वार्या पुनर्दर्शनाय ।

राजा—अम्ब भगवते च्यवनाय मां प्रणिपातय ।

तापसी—एव्वं भोदु । एवं भवतु ।

कुमारः—आर्ये सत्यं यदि निवर्तसे मामपि आश्रमं नेतुमर्हसि ।

राजा—अयि वत्स उषितं त्वया पूर्वस्मिन्नाश्रमे। द्वितीयमध्यासितुं तव समयः ।

HERMIT-WOMAN—Child, ever may you retain your Lord's highest regard!

PRINCE—Mother, accept my salutations.

URVASHI—(*Embracing the prince, whose face is upturned*). Child, may you ever please your father. (*Approaching the King*). Glory to my Lord!

KING—To the matron, honour! Please to sit here. (*Gives her half his seat*).

(*Urvashi sits; all take their proper seats*)

HERMIT-WOMAN—This Ayus, who has been taught the sciences, is now old enough to wear the armour. So I have returned this deposit in the presence of your husband. So I wish to take my leave of you. For, my duties in the hermitage suffer.

URVASHI—Having seen you after such a long time, I feel particularly eager (to see you). I am not able to give you leave to go. But it would be on the other hand unjust to detain you. So may you go now to meet again.

KING—Mother, bear my reverence to the holy Chyavana.

HERMIT-WOMAN—It would be so.

PRINCE—Noble lady, if you are really going, will you not take me to the hermitage?

KING—Well, child, you have already lived the life of a student. It is now time you enter the second order (the life of a householder)

तापसी—जाद गुरुणो वअणं अणुचिट्ठ । जात गुरोर्वचनमनुतिष्ठ ।

कुमार—तेन हि

यः सुप्तवान् मदङ्के शिखण्डकण्डूयनोपलब्धसुखः ।
तं मे जातकलापं प्रेषय मणिकण्ठकं शिखिनम् ॥ १३ ॥

तापसी—[विहस्य] एव्वं करेमि । सत्थि भोदु तुम्हाणं । एवं करोमि । स्वस्ति भवतु युष्मभ्यम् ।
३
[इति निष्क्रान्ता ।

राजा—कल्याणि

अद्याहं पुत्रिणामग्र्यः सत्पुत्रेणामुना तव ।
पौलोमीसंभवेनेव जयन्तेन पुरंदरः ॥ १४ ॥

[उर्वशी स्मृत्वा रोदिति ।]

विदूषकः—किं णु खु तत्तहोदी एक्क-पदे अस्सु-मुही
३ संवुत्ता । किं नु खलु तत्रभवती एकपदेऽश्रुमुखी संवृत्ता ।

राजा—[सावेगम्]

किं सुन्दरि प्ररुदितासि ममोपपन्ने
वंशस्थितेरधिगमान्महति प्रमोदे ।
पीनोन्नतस्तनविसर्पिभिरानयन्तो
मुक्तावलीविरचनापुनरुक्तिमस्रैः ॥ १५ ॥

[बाष्पमस्याः प्रमार्ष्टि ।]

उर्वशी—सुणादु महाराओ पढमं उण पुत्त-दंसणेण
३ विसुमरिद म्हि । दाणिं महिन्द-संकित्तणेण समओ मह हिअअं आआसेदि । शृणोतु महाराजः प्रथमं पुनः पुत्रदर्शनेन विस्मृतास्मि । इदानीं महेन्द्रसंकीर्तनेन समयो मम हृदयमायासयति ।

HERMIT-WOMAN—Child, follow the bidding of your father.

PRINCE—Well then.

Send me the peacock Manikanthaka when he will have grown his plumage. the peacock that feeling happy at my scratching him about the crest would go to sleep in my lap. [13]

HERMIT-WOMAN—(*Smiling*). That I will do. Peace unto all. (*Exit*).

KING—Fair one,

By this excellent son of yours, I think myself the first among fathers like Indra by Jayanta, the son of Paulomi. [14]

(*Urvashi remembers and weeps*).

VIDUSHAKA—How all of a sudden the face of my lady is veiled with tea s ?

KING—(*Hurriedly*).

When great joy has come to me through the perpetuation of my race why should you, my dearest, weep, thus rendering superfluous the pearl-string by your tears that roll upon your heaving breast? [15]

(*Wipes away her tears*).

URVASHI—Listen, my Lord. I forgot awhile at the sight of this boy; but now the name of the great Indra brings to my mind the decree that pains my heart.

राजा कथ्यतां समयः ।

उर्वशी--अहं पुरा महाराअ-गहिद-हिअआ महिन्देण आणत्ता-अहं पुरा महाराजगृहीतहृदया मन्हेन्द्रेण आज्ञापिता-

राजा--किमिति ।

उर्वशी--जदा एसो मम पिअ-सहो राएसी तुइ समुप्पण्णस्स वंस-करस्स मुहं पेक्खिस्सदि तदा तुए भूओ वि मम समीवं आअन्तव्वं ति । तदो मए महाराअ-विओअ-भीरुदाए जादमेत्तो एव्व विज्जागम-णिमित्तं भअवदो चवणस्स अस्सम-पदे अज्जाए सच्चवदीए हत्थे अप्पआसं णिक्खित्तो। अज्ज पिदुणो आराहण-समत्थो संवुत्तो त्ति कलअन्तीए णिज्जादिदो मे दीहाऊ । ता एत्तिओ मे महाराएण संवासो । यदैष मम प्रियसखो राजर्षिस्त्वयि समुत्पन्नस्य वंशकरस्य मुखं प्रेक्षिष्यते तदा त्वया भूयोपि मम समीपमागन्तव्यमिति । ततो मया महाराजवियोगभीरुतया जातमात्र एव विद्यागमनिमित्तं भगवतश्च्यवनस्याश्रमपदे आर्यायाः सत्यवत्या हस्ते अप्रकाशं निक्षिप्तः अद्य पितुराराधनसमर्थः संवृत्त इति कलयन्त्या निर्यातितो मे दीर्घायु । तदेतावान् मे महाराजेन संवासः।

[सर्वे विषादं रूपयन्ति ।

राजा—[सनिःश्वासम्] अहो सुखप्रत्यर्थिता दैवस्य ।

आश्वासितस्य मम नाम सुतोपलब्ध्या
सद्यस्त्वया सह कृशोदरि विप्रयोगः ।
व्यावर्तिताातपरुजः प्रथमाभ्रवृष्ट्या
वृक्षस्य वैद्युत इवाग्निरुपस्थितोऽयम् ॥ १६ ॥

विदूषकः—अअं सो अत्थो अणत्थाणुबन्धो संवुत्तो संपदं

KING—Tell me what decree.

URVASHI—Formerly when my heart was lost to my Lord, I was bidden by the great Indra—

KING—What was it?

URVASHI—"When this my dear friend, the royal sage, sees the face of a son that you will bear him, who will perpetuate his family, then will you again come back to me." So afraid of severance from my Lord, I secretly put him, the moment he was born, in charge of the holy dame Satyavati in the hermitage of the sage Chyavana, that he may be initiated into the sciences. Thinking that this day he is of an age when he might give joy to his father, she has brought him back— this my long-lived boy. So my stay with my dear Lord extends no further.

(*All gesticulate sorrow*).

KING—(*Sighing*). How hostile to man's happiness is fate!

Scarce have I known the blessing of a son, when my fair one is snatched away from me, as though the blasting lightning should fall on a tree just when it revives from languishment in the blaze of heat, as the young rain descends upon it. [16

VIDUSHAKA—So this is how good fortune is followed by a series of misfortunes. I should think now that my

तक्केमि तत्तभवदा वक्कलं गेण्हिअ तवो-वणं गन्दव्वं ति ।
अयं सोर्थः अनर्थानुबन्धः संवृत्तः । सांप्रतं तर्कयामि तत्रभवता वल्कलं गृहीत्वा तपोवनं गन्तव्यमिति ।

उर्वशी—मं पि मन्द-भाइणिं किद-विणअस्स पुत्तस्स लाभाणन्तरं सग्गारोहणेण अवसिद-कज्जं महाराओ समत्थेदि । मामपि मन्दभागिनीं कृतविनयस्य पुत्रस्य लाभानन्तरं स्वर्गारोहणेन अवसितकार्यां महाराजः समर्थयते ।

राजा—मा मैवम्

न हि सुलभवियोगा कर्तुमात्मप्रियाणि
प्रभवति परवत्ता शासने तिष्ठ भर्तुः ।
अहमपि तव सूनावायुषि न्यस्तराज्यो
विचरितमृगयूथान्याश्रयिष्ये वनानि ॥ १७ ॥

कुमारः—नार्हति तातः पुंगवधारितायां धुरि दम्यं नियोजयितुम् ।

राजा—अयि वत्स

शमयति गजानन्यान् गन्धद्विपः कलभोऽपि सन्
भवति सुतरां वेगोदग्रं भुजंगशिशोर्विषम् ।
भुवमधिपतिर्बालावस्थोऽप्यलं परिरक्षितुं
न खलु वयसा जात्यैवायं स्वकार्यसहो भरः ॥ १८ ॥

लातव्य मद्वचनादमात्यपरिषदं ब्रूहि संभ्रियतामायुषो राज्याभिषेक इति ।

कञ्चुकी—यदाज्ञापयति देवः । [इति दुःखितो निष्क्रान्तः]

[सर्वे दृष्टिप्रतिघातं रूपयन्ति ।]

राजा—[आकाशमवलोक्य] किं नु खलु निरभ्रे विद्युत्संपातः ।

friend should wear barks and betake himself to some holy forest retreat.

URVASHI—Will the King regard me—unfortunate that I am—as one who has done her task, when I shall be gone to Svarga, now that I have got back my child who has finished his education !

KING—No. not so.

It is dependence, which, making severance only too natural. does not allow a person to have his own way. Do you obey your Lord. For me, I will resign my throne to your son Ayus and retire into the forest where herds of deer freely move [17]

PRINCE—It is scarcely meet that father should put an inexperienced bull to a yoke borne by a veteran.

KING—Ah, child

Even the cub of an excellent elephant soon subdues other elephants; the infant snake produces deadliest poison; a king even in his childhood is endowed with power to protect the earth. It is nature, therefore, and not age that gives each this fitness to bear his responsibility. [18]

Latavya, bid, in my name, our ministers to prepare for the coronation of Ayus.

CHAMBERLAIN—As my lord commands.

(*Departs in sadness*).

(*All show as if their eyes are dazed*).

KING—(*Looking to the sky*). How, a lightning-flash in a fair sky !

६ उर्वशी—[विलोक्य] अम्मो भअवं णारदो । अहो भग-
वान् नारदः ।

राजा—अये भगवान् नारदः । य एष

गोरोचनानिकषपिङ्गजटाकलापः
संलक्ष्यते शशिकलामलवीतसूत्रः ।
मुक्तागुणातिशयसंभृतमण्डनश्री-
र्हेमप्ररोह इव जङ्गमकल्पवृक्षः ॥ १० ॥

अर्घ्यमस्मै ।

उर्वशी—[यथोक्तमादाय] इअं भअवदे अरिहणा । इयं
२ भगवतेऽर्हणा ।

[ततः प्रविशति नारदः ।]

नारदः—विजयतां मध्यमलोकपालः ।

राजा—[उर्वशीहस्तादर्घ्यमादाय आवर्ज्य] भगवन्नभिवादये ।

उर्वशी—भअवं पणमामि । भगवन् प्रणमामि ।

नारदः—अविरहितौ दंपती भूयास्ताम् ।

४ राजा—[आत्मगतम्] अपि नामैवं स्यात् [प्रकाशम् ।
कुमारमाश्लिष्य] वत्स भगवन्तमभिवादयस्व ।

कुमारः—भगवन्नौर्वशेय आयुः प्रणमति ।

नारदः—आयुष्मानेधि ।

राजा—अयं विष्टरोऽनुगृह्यताम् ।

[नारदस्तथोपविष्टः ।

सर्वे नारदमनूपविशन्ति ।]

नारदः—राजन् श्रूयतां महेन्द्रसंदेशः ।

राजा—अवहितोऽस्मि ।

URVASHI—(*Observing*). Ah, it is Narada.

KING—Ah, the holy Narada ! Who with his matted hair bright yellow like a streak of Gorochana on a touchstone, his sacred thread pure as the crescent of the moon looks like a moving tree of heaven profusely adorned with wreaths of excellent pearls, and growing shoots of gold. [19]

Bring materials of worship for him.

URVASHI—(*Bringing what is asked for*). Here is offering for the holy sage.

(*Enter Narada*)

NARADA—Hail to the Lord of this middle sphere !

KING—(*Taking the offering from Urvashi and presenting it*). Reverence to the sage !

URVASHI—My homage to the holy one.

NARADA—Never be wife and husband disunited !

KING—(*To himeelf*) Oh, might this be ! (*Aloud, embracing the prince*) Child, pay your adoration to.the holy sage.

PRINCE—Holy sir, here is Ayus, the son of Urvashi. paying his homage.

NARADA—May your days be many !

KING—Please to honour this seat.

(*Narada takes his seat. Others occupy their seats after Narada.*)

NARADA—King, listen to the message of the great Indra.

KING—I am all attention.

नारदः--प्रभावदर्शी मघवा वनगमनाय कृतबुद्धिं भवन्तमनुशास्ति

राजा--किमाज्ञापयति ।

नारदः--त्रिकालदर्शिभिर्मुनिभिरादिष्टः सुरासुरसंगरो भावी । भवांश्च सांयुगीनः सहायो नः । तेन त्वया न शस्त्रं संन्यस्तव्यम् । इयं चोर्वशी यावदायुस्तव सहधर्मचारिणी भवत्विति ।

उर्वशी--[अपवार्य] अम्महे सल्लं मे हिअआदो अवणीदं विअ । अहो शल्यं मे हृदयादपनीतमिव ।

राजा--परवानस्मि देवेश्वरेण ।

नारदः--युक्तम् ।

त्वत्कार्यं वासवः कुर्यात् त्वं च तस्येष्टमाचरेः ।
सूर्यः समेधयत्यग्निमग्निः सूर्यं च तेजसा ॥ २० ॥

[आकाशमवलोक्य ।] रम्भे उपनीयतां स्वयं महेन्द्रेण संभृतः कुमारस्यायुषो यौवराज्याभिषेकः ।

[प्रविश्य यथोक्तहस्ता अप्सरसः ।]

अप्सरसः--भअवं इमे अभिसेअ-संभारा । भगवन्नेतेऽभिषेकसंभाराः ।

नारदः--उपवेश्यतामायुष्मान् भद्रपीठे ।

रम्भा--इदो वच्छ [कुमारमुपवेशयति] इतो वत्स ।

नारदः--[कुमारस्य शिरसि कलशमावर्ज्य] रम्भे निर्वर्त्यतां शेषो विधिः ।

रम्भा--[यथोक्तं निर्वर्त्य] वच्छ पणम भअवन्तं मादापिदरे अ । वत्स प्रणम भगवन्तं मातापितरौ च ।

NARADA—Indra, who knows through his divine power, bids you who have made up your mind to retire to the forest—

KING—What are his commands?

NARADA—Sages, who can see the past, the future, and the present, have foretold hostilities between gods and demons. You are our worthy ally in the wars. Therefore, do not relinquish your arms; and this Urvashi shall be your wife as long as you live.

URVASHI—(*Aside*). A barbed arrow has been extracted from my bosom!

KING—I am subservient to the will of the King of the Gods.

NARADA—It is wisely said.

> Indra will work your good, and you too will act according to his wishes; the Sun sustains Fire with light, and Fire too with light nourishes the Sun. [20]

(*Looking to the sky*). Rambha, bring the materials for the coronation of prince Ayus as Yuvaraja, which great Indra himself has prepared.

(*Enter nymphs carrying in their hands the materials mentioned*).

NYMPHS—Holy sir, here are the materials of coronation.

NARADA—Let the prince be seated on the holy throne.

RAMBHA—Come here, child. (*Leads the prince to the seat*).

NARADA—(*Pouring water from the ewer on the head of the prince*). Rambha, complete the rite.

RAMBHA—(*Doing as bidden*) Child, pay you adoration to the holy sage and to your parents.

[कुमारः यथाक्रमं प्रणमति ।]

नारदः—स्वस्ति भवते।

राजा—कुलधुरंधरो भव ।

उर्वशी—पिदुणो आराधइत्तओ होहि। पितुराराधयिता भव।

[नेपथ्ये वैतालिकौ ।]

प्रथमः—विजयतां युवराजः ।

अमरमुनिरिवात्रिर्ब्रह्मणोऽत्रेरिवेन्दु-
बुंध इव शिशिरांशोर्बोधनस्येव देवः ।
भव पितुरनुरूपस्त्वं गुणैर्लोककान्तै-
रतिशयिनि समाप्ता वंश एवाशिषस्ते ॥ २१ ॥

द्वितीयः—

तव पितरि पुरस्तादुन्नतानां स्थितेऽस्मिन्
स्थितिमति च विभक्ता त्वय्यनाकम्प्यधैर्ये ।
अधिकतरमिदानीं राजते राज्यलक्ष्मी-
र्हिमवति जलधौ च व्यस्ततोयेव गङ्गा ॥ २२ ॥

अप्सरसः—[उर्वशीमुपेत्य] दिट्ठिआ पुत्तस्स जुव-राअ-सिराए भत्तुणो अविरहेण वड्ढसि। दिष्ट्या पुत्रस्य युवराजश्रिया भर्तुरविरहेण वर्धसे ।

उर्वशी—साहारणो एसो अब्भुदओ। [कुमारं हस्तेगृहीत्वा] एहि वच्छ जेट्ठ-मादरं अभिवन्देहि। साधारण एषोभ्युदयः। एहि वत्स ज्येष्ठमातरमभिवन्दस्व ।

[कुमारः प्रतिष्ठते ।]

राजा--तिष्ठ। सममेव तत्रभवत्याः समीपं यास्यामस्तावत्।

(*The prince bows in due order*)

NARADA—Blessing on you.

KING—Be you the foremost of your family.

URVASHI—Be obedient to your father.

(*Behind the scenes, bards*)

FIRST BARD—Glory to the young King.

Like the Divine sage Atri of Brahman, or the Moon of Atri, or Budha of the moon, and our King of Budha, so do you be worthy of your father by your qualities which are dear to the people. For in your most exalted family all blessings have indeed reached their highest pitch. [21]

SECOND BARD—

Now royal glory shines more bright divided as it is between your father, the foremost of the exalted, and yourself whose fortitude is unshakable and who are so upright, like the Ganges whose waters are divided between the Himalaya and the Ocean. [22]

NYMPHS—(*Approaching Urvashi*) We congratulate you upon your son's coronation as Yuvaraja and upon your union, without fear of separation, with your husband.

URVASHI—This happiness is common to us all.(*Holding the prince by the hand*). Come, child, pay your reverence to your elder mother.

(*The prince starts*).

KING—Wait. We shall all go together to her ladyship.

१ नारदः—

आयुषो यौवराज्यश्रीः स्मारयत्यात्मजस्य ते ।
अभिषिक्तं महासेनं सैनापत्ये मरुत्वता ॥ २३ ॥

राजा—एवमनुगृहीतो भगवता कथं न योग्यो भविष्यति ।

नारदः—किं ते भूयः पाकशासनः प्रियं करोतु ।

३ राजा—यदि मे मघवा प्रसन्नः किमतः परमिच्छामि । तथापीदमस्तु ।

[भरतवाक्यम् ।]

परस्परविरोधिन्योरेकसंश्रयदुर्लभम् ।
संगतं श्रीसरस्वत्योर्भूतयेऽस्तु सदा सताम् ॥ २४ ॥

[इति निष्क्रान्ताः सर्वे ।]

॥ इति विक्रमोर्वशीये नाटके पञ्चमोऽङ्कः ॥

॥ समाप्तमिदं विक्रमोर्वशीयं नाटकम् ॥

NARADA—This installation as Yuvaraja of your son Ayus reminds me of the coronation of Mahasena by Indra, as chief of the heavenly host. [23]

KING—When so favoured by the holy sage, how could he fail to prove worthy?

NARADA—What further favour would you ask of Indra?

KING—If Lord Indra is pleased with me, what more can I desire? Still let this be my prayer.

(*Benediction*).

May learning and wealth, that oppose each other, unite in one common abode, which is ever so rare, to bring prosperity to the good. [24]

(*Exeunt Omnes*).

END.

Appendix—A.

श्लोकसूची ।

Appendix B—Metrical Table.

Number of syllables per quarter.	Name of the Metre.	Where employed.	Total	Measure.
8	अनुष्टुप्	I. 12,13, 14;II4, 5, 15,17,19;III.9,II,1८, 21; IV.9,14,17, 18, 19,21,27,31,40;V.1, 3,7,12,14,20,23,24.	29	पञ्चमं लघु सर्वत्र सप्तमं द्विचतुर्थयोः । गुरु षष्ठं च पादानां चतुर्णां स्यादनुष्टुभि ॥
11	उपजाति	1.17,18;IV 35; V. 2, 6.	5	{ स्यादिन्द्रवज्रा यदि तौ जगौ गः । उपेन्द्रवज्रा प्रथमे लघौ सा । (इत्यनयोरुपजातिः ।)
12	द्रुतविलम्बित	II. 9;III.6;IV 26,29.	4	द्रुतविलम्बितमाह नभौ भरौ ।
12	वंशस्थ	I. 5, 9; III. 12, 13;	7	जतौ तु वंशस्थमुदीरितं जरौ ।
		IV. 7, 37, 39.	2	
13	मञ्जुभाषिणी	IV. 33, 43.		सजसा जगौ च यदि मञ्जुभाषिणी ।
14	वसंततिलका	I. 3;II,14,16;III. 19 20;IV.6, 11,15;V.9 15, 16, 19.	12	ज्ञेया वसंततिलका तभजा जगौ गः ।
15	मालिनी	II. 6, IV; 10,13,22; V. 17, 21, 22.	7	ननमयययुतेयं मालिनी भोगिलोकैः ।

(Continued on next page)

17	पृथ्वी	II. 11.	1	जसौ जसयला वसुग्रहयतिश्च पृथ्वी गुरुः ।
17	मन्दाक्रान्ता	I.7;II.1;III.1;IV.4.	4	मन्दाक्रान्ताम्बुधिरसनगैर्मो भनौ तौ गयुग्मम् ।
17	शिखरिणी	IV. 28, 34.	2	रसै रुद्रैश्छिन्ना यमनसभला गः शिखरिणी ।
17	हरिणी	II.10;III.10;IV.20; V. 18.	5	नसमरसला गः षड्वेदैर्हयैर्हरिणी मता ।
19	शार्दूलविक्रीडित	I.1,4,8;II.7,20,23; III.2,15;IV.2,25,38.	11	सूर्याश्वैर्यदि मः सजौ सततगाः शार्दूलविक्रीडितम् ।
10/11	वैतालीय (त्रियोगिनी)	IV. 12.	1	विषमे ससजा गुरुः समे सभरा लोऽथ गुरुर्वियोगिनी ।
11/12	अपरवक्त्र	II. 22.	1	अयुजि ननरला गुरुः समे तदपर-वक्त्रमिदं नजौ जरौ ।
11/12	औपच्छन्दसिक	I.15,16;II,18;III.7; IV. 3, 16.	6	पर्यन्ते यौ तथैव शेषमौपच्छन्दसिकं सुधीभिरुक्तम् ।
12/13	पुष्पिताग्रा	III. 3, 22.	2	अयुजि नयुगरेफतो यकारो युजि तु नजौ जरगाश्च पुष्पिताग्रा ।
	आर्या	I.2,6.10,11;II.2,3, 8,21;III.4,5,8,14, 16,17;IV.5,8,23,24, 30,32,36,41,42;V.4, 5, 8, 10, 11, 13.	29	यस्याः पादे प्रथमे द्वादश मात्रास्तथा तृतीयेऽपि । अष्टादश द्वितीये चतुर्थके पञ्चदश सार्या ॥

N. B.—Verses 12 and 13 of act II are Prakrit Gathas.

Appendix C.

Text of Act IV according to the Northern Recension.

पिअ-सहि-विओअ-विमणा सहिं हंसी वाउला समुल्लवइ।
सूर-कर-फंस-विअसिअ-तामरसे सरवरूसङ्गे ॥ 1 ॥

प्रियसखीवियोगविमनाः सखी हंसी व्याकुला समुल्लपति ।
सूर्यकरस्पर्शविकसिततामरसे सरोवरोत्सङ्गे ॥ 1 ॥

[इति चित्रलेखासहजन्ययोः प्रावेशिक्याक्षिप्तिका । ततः प्रविशति विमनस्का चित्रलेखा सहजन्या च । चित्रलेखाप्रवेशान्तरे द्विपदिकया दिशोऽवलोक्य ।]

सहअरि-दुक्खालिद्धअं। सरवरअम्मि सिणिद्धअं ॥
वाहोवग्गिअ-णअणअं। तम्मइ हंसी-जुअलअं ॥ 2 ॥

सहचरीदुःखालीढं सरोवरे स्निग्धम् ।
बाष्पाववल्गितनयनं ताम्यति हंसीयुगलम् ॥ 2 ॥

सहजन्या—[चित्रलेखां विलोक्य] **सहि मिलाअमाण-सद-वत्तस्स विअ दे मुहस्स छाआ हिअअस्स अस्सत्थदं सूएदि। ता कहेहि णिव्वेद-कारणं। सम-दुक्खा भविदुं इच्छामि।**

सखि म्लायमानशतपत्रस्येव ते मुखस्य छाया हृदयस्य अस्वस्थतां सूचयति । तत् कथय निर्वेदकारणम् । समदुःखा भवितुमिच्छामि ।

चित्रलेखा—**अच्छरा-वार-पज्जाएण इह भअवदो सुज्जस्स पादमूलोवट्ठाणं वट्टदि त्ति बलिअं खु उव्वसीए**

उक्कण्ठिद म्हि । अप्सरोवारपर्यायेण इह भगवतः सूर्यस्य पादमूलोपस्थानं वर्तत इति बलवत् खलूर्वश्यामुत्कण्ठितास्मि ।

सहजन्या—जाणे वो अण्णोण्ण-सिणेहं । तदो तदो । जाने युवयोरन्योन्यस्नेहम् । ततस्ततः ।

चित्रलेखा—तदो इमाइं दिवसाइं को णु खु वुत्तन्तो त्ति पणिधाणट्ठिदाए मए अच्चाहिदं उवलद्धं । तत एतेषु दिवसेषु को नु खलु वृत्तान्त इति प्रणिधानस्थितया मया अत्याहितमुपलब्धम् ।

सहजन्या—[सावेगम्] **कीरिसं विअ ।** कीदृशमिव ।

चित्रलेखा—उव्वसी किल तं रदि-सहाअं राएसिं अमच्चेसु णिवेसिद-रज्ज-धुरं गेण्हिअ गन्धमादण-वणं विहरिदुं गदा । उर्वशी किल तं रतिसहायं राजर्षिममात्येषु निवेशितराज्यधुरं गृहीत्वा गन्धमादनवनं विहर्तुं गता ।

सहजन्या—सो णाम संभोओ जो तारिसेसु पदेसेसु । तदो तदो । स नाम संभोगो यस्तादृशेषु प्रदेशेषु । ततस्ततः ।

चित्रलेखा—तहिं खु मन्दाइणीए पुलिणेसु गदा सिअदापव्वदकेलीहिं कीलमाणा विज्जाधर-दारिआ उदयवदी णाम तेण राएसिणा णिज्झाइद त्ति कुविदा उव्वसी । तत्र खलु मन्दाकिन्याः पुलिनेषु गता सिकतापर्वतकेलीभिः क्रीडन्ती विद्याधरदारिका उदयवती नाम तेन राजर्षिणा निध्यातेति कुपिता उर्वशी ।

सहजन्या—होदव्वं । दूरारूढो खु पणओ असहणो । तदो तदो । भवितव्यम् । दूरारूढः खलु प्रणयः असहनः । ततस्ततः ।

चित्रलेखा—तदो भट्टिणो अणुणअं अपडिवज्जमाणा गुरु-साव-संमूढ-हिअआ इत्थिआ-जण-परिहरणिज्जं कुमार-वणं पइट्ठा । पवेसाणन्तरं च काणणोवन्तवत्तिलदाभा-

वेण परिणदं से रूवं । ततो भर्तुरनुनयमप्रतिपद्यमाना गुरुशापसंमूढहृदया स्त्रीजनपरिहरणीयं कुमारवनं प्रविष्टा । प्रवेशानन्तरं च काननोपान्तवर्तिलताभावेन परिणतमस्या रूपम् ।

सहजन्या—णत्थि विहिणो अलङ्घणिज्जं । तस्स अणुराअस्स अअं णाम एक्कवदे ईरिसो अणत्थो । अह किमवत्थो सो राएसी । नास्ति विधेरलङ्घनीयम् । तस्यानुरागस्य अयं नाम एकपद ईदृशोनर्थः । अथ किमवस्थः स राजर्षिः ।

चित्रलेखा—तस्सिं एव्व काणणे पिअदमं विचिण्णन्तो अहोरत्ते अदिवाहेदि । इमिणा उण णिव्वुदाणं पि उक्कण्ठाकारिणा मेहोदएण अणत्थाहीणो हविस्सदि । तस्मिन्नेव कानने प्रियतमां विचिन्वन्नहोरात्रानतिवाहयति । एतेन पुनर्निर्वृतानामपि उत्कण्ठाकारिणा मेघादयेन अनर्थाधीनो भविष्यति ।

[अनन्तरे जम्भालिका ।]

सहअरि-दुक्खालिद्धअं सरवरअम्मि सिणिद्धअं ।
अविरल-वाह-जलोल्लुअं तम्मइ हंसी-जुअलअं ॥3॥

सहचरीदुःखालीढं सरोवरे स्निग्धम् ।
अविरलबाष्पजलार्द्रं ताम्यति हंसीयुगलम् ॥ 3 ॥

सहजन्या—सहि तारिसा आकिदि-विसेसा चिरं दुक्खभाइणो ण होन्ति । अवस्सं किंपि अणुग्गह-णिमित्तं भूओ वि समाअम-कारणं हविस्सदि । ता एहि उदअम्मुहस्स भअवदो सुज्जस्स उवट्ठाणं करेम्ह । सखि तादृशा आकृतिविशेषाश्चिरं दुःखभागिनो न भवन्ति । अवश्यं किमपि अनुग्रहनिमित्तं भूयोपि समागमकारणं भविष्यति । तदेहि उदयोन्मुखस्य भगवतः सूर्यस्य उपस्थानं कुर्वः ।

[अनन्तरे खण्डधारा ।]

चिन्ता-दुम्मिअ-माणसिआ। सहअरि-दंसण-लालसिआ॥
विअसिअ-कमल-मणोहरए। विहरइ हंसी सरवरए ॥4॥

चिन्तादूनमानसिका । सहचरीदर्शनलालसिका ॥
विकसितकमलमनोहरे । विहरति हंसी सरोवरे ॥ 4 ॥

[इति निष्क्रान्ते ।]

प्रवेशकः ॥

गहणं गइन्द-णाहो पिअ-विरहुम्माअ-पअलिअ-विआरो।
विसइ तरु-कुसुम-किसलअ-भूसिअ-णिअ-देह-पब्भारो॥5॥

गहनं गजेन्द्रनाथः प्रियाविरहोन्मादप्रकटितविकारः ।
विशति तरुकुसुमकिसलयभूषितनिजदेहप्राग्भारः ॥ 5 ॥

[इति पुरूरवसः प्रावेशिकी आक्षिप्तिका। ततः प्रविशति उन्मत्तवेषो राजा।]

राजा—आः दुरात्मन् रक्षस्तिष्ठ तिष्ठ। क्व मे प्रियतमामादाय गच्छसि। हन्त शैलशिखराद् गगनमुत्पत्य बाणैर्मामभिवर्षति। [लोष्टं गृहीत्वा हन्तुं धावन्। अनन्तरे द्विपदिकया दिशोऽवलोक्य।]

हिअआहिअ-पिअ-दुक्खओ। सरवरए धुद-पक्खओ ॥
वाहोवग्गिअ-णअणओ। तम्मइ हंस-जुआणओ ॥ 6 ॥

हृदयाहितप्रियादुःखः। सरोवरे धुतपक्षः ॥
बाष्पाववल्गितनयनः। ताम्यति हंसयुवा ॥ 6 ॥

[पुनर्विभाव्य।]

नवजलधरः संनद्धोऽयं न दृप्तनिशाचरः
सुरधनुरिदं दूराकृष्टं न नाम शरासनम्।
अयमपि पटुर्धारासारो न बाणपरंपरा
कनकनिकषस्निग्धा विद्युत् प्रिया न ममोर्वशी॥१॥

[इति मूर्छितः पतति। द्विपदिकया उत्थाय निःश्वस्य।]

मइँ जाणिअ मिअ-लोअणि णिसअरु को इ हरेइ ।
जाव ण णव-तलि-सामलो धाराहरु वरिसेइ ॥ 7 ॥

मया ज्ञातं मृगलोचनीं निशाचरः कोपि हरति ।
यावन्नु नवतडिच्छयामलो धाराधरो वर्षति ॥ 7 ॥

विचिन्त्य । क्व नु खलु रम्भोरूर्गता स्यात् ।

तिष्ठेत् कोपवशात् प्रभावपिहिता दीर्घं न सा कुप्यति
स्वर्गायोत्पतिता भवेन्मयि पुनर्भावार्द्रमस्या मनः ।
तां हर्तुं विबुधद्विषोऽपि न च मे शक्ताः पुरोवर्तिनीं
सा चात्यन्तमदर्शनं नयनयोर्यातेति कोऽयं विधिः ॥२॥

इति द्विपदिकया दिशोऽवलोक्य । सनिःश्वासम् । सास्रम् । अये परावृत्तभागधेयानां दुःखं दुःखानुबन्धि । कुतः ।

अयमेकपदे तया वियोगः प्रियया चोपनतः सुदुःसहो मे ।
नववारिधरोदयादहोभिर्भवितव्यं च निरातपत्वरम्यैः ॥३॥

[अनन्तरे चर्चरी ।]

जलहर संहरु एहु, को पइँ आढत्तओ
अविरल-धारासार-दिसा-मुह-कन्तओ ।
ए मइँ पुहवि भमन्तेँ जइ पिअ पेक्खीहि
तव्वे जं जु करीहिसि तंतु सहीहिमि ॥ 8 ॥

जलधर संहरैतत्, कस्त्वामाज्ञापितवान्
अविरलधारासारदिङ्मुखक्रान्तम् ।
ए मया पृथ्वीं भ्रमता यदि प्रिया प्रेक्षिष्यते
तदा यद्यत् करिष्यसि तत्तत् सहिष्ये ॥ 8 ॥

[विहस्य ।] मुधैव खलु मनसः परितापवृद्धिरुपेक्ष्यते । यथा मुनयोऽपि व्याहरन्ति राजा कालस्य कारणमिति । तत् किमहं जलदसमयं न प्रत्यादिशामि ।

[अनन्तरे चर्चरी ।]

गन्धुम्माइअ-महुअरवरगीएहिं
वज्जन्तेहिं परहुअरव-तूरेहिं ।
पसरिअ-पवणुव्वेल्लिर-पल्लव-णिअरु
सुललिअ-विविह-पआरेँ णच्चइ कप्प-अरु ॥9॥

गन्धोन्मादितमधुकरवरगीतै-
र्वाद्यमानैः परभृतरवतूर्यैः ।
प्रसृतपवनोद्वेल्लनशीलपल्लवनिकरः
सुललितविविधप्रकारेण नृत्यति कल्पतरुः ॥ 9 ॥

[इति नर्तित्वा ।] अथवा प्रावृषेण्यैरेव लिङ्गैर्मम राजोपचारः संप्रति ! कथमिव ।

विद्युल्लेखाकनकरुचिरं श्रीवितानं ममाभ्रं
व्याधूयन्ते निचुलतरुभिर्मञ्जरीचामराणि ।
घर्मच्छेदात् पटुतरगिरो बन्दिनो नीलकण्ठा
धारासारोपनयनपरा नैगमाश्चाम्बुवाहाः ॥ ४ ॥

भवतु । किमेवं परिच्छदश्लाघया । यावदस्मिन् कानने तां प्रियामन्वेषयामि [पुनश्चर्चरीपाठस्यान्ते भिन्नकः ।]

दइआ-रहिओ अहिअं दुहिओ विरहाणुगओ परिमन्थरओ ॥
गिरि-काणणए कुसुमुज्जलए गज-जूह-वई बहु झीण-गई ॥10॥

दयितारहितोधिकं दुःखितो विरहानुगतः परिमन्थरः ॥
गिरिकानने कुसुमोज्ज्वले गजयूथपतिर्बहु क्षीणगतिः ॥ 10 ॥

[विलोक्य ।] हन्त व्यवसितस्य मे संदीपनमिव संवृत्तम् । कुतः ।

आरक्तराजिभिरियं कुसुमैर्नवकन्दली सलिलगर्भैः ।
कोपादन्तर्बाष्पे स्मरयति मां लोचने तस्याः ॥ ६ ॥

इतो गतेति कथं नु तत्रभवती मया सूचयितव्या ।

पद्भ्यां स्पृशेद् वसुमतीं यदि सा सुगात्री
मेघाभिवृष्टसिकतासु वनस्थलीषु ।
पश्चान्नता गुरुनितम्बतया ततोऽस्या
दृश्येत चारुपदपङ्क्तिरलक्तकाङ्का ॥ ६ ॥

[द्विपदिकया परिक्रम्य अवलोक्य च सहर्षम् ।] उपलब्धमुपलक्षणं येन तस्याः कोपनाया मार्गोऽनुमीयते ।

हृतोष्ठरागैर्नयनोदबिन्दुभिर्निमग्ननाभेर्निपतद्भिरङ्कितम् ।
च्युतं रुषा भिन्नगतेरसंशयं शुकोदरश्याममिदं स्तनांशुकम् ॥७

[विभाव्य ।] कथम् । सेन्द्रगोपं नवशाद्वलमिदम् । कुतो नु खलु निर्जने वने प्रियाप्रवृत्तिरवगमयितव्या । [दृष्ट्वा] अये आसारोच्छ्वसितशैलेयस्थलीपाषाणमारूढः

आलोकयति पयोदान् प्रबलपुरोवातनर्तितशिखण्डः ।
केकागर्भेण शिखी दूरोन्नमितेन कण्ठेन ॥ ८ ॥

[उपेत्य ।] यावदेनं पृच्छामि । [अनन्तरे खण्डकः ।]

संपत्त-विसूरणओ । तुरिअं पर-वारणओ ॥
पिअदम-दंसण-लालसओ गअ-वरु विम्हिअ-माणसओ ॥11॥

[तेना खण्डकान्ते चर्चरी ।]

बंहिण पइँ अब्भत्थेमि आअक्खहि मं ता ।
एत्थु रण्णेँ भमन्तेँ जइ पइँ दिट्ठी सा महु कन्ता ॥
णिसम्महि मिअङ्क-सरिसँ वअणेँ हंस-गइँ ।
एँ चिण्हेँ जाणिहिसि आअक्खिउ तुज्झु मइँ ॥ 12 ॥

संप्राप्तविसूरणः त्वरितं परवारणः ॥
प्रियतमादर्शनलालसः गजवरो विस्मितमानसः ॥ 11 ॥

बर्हिण त्वामभ्यर्थये आचक्ष्व मे तत् ।
अत्र अरण्ये भ्रमता यदि त्वया दृष्टा सा मम कान्ता ॥
निशामय मृगाङ्कसदृशवदनेन हंसगत्या ।
अनेन चिह्नेन ज्ञास्यस्याख्यातं तव मया ॥ १२ ॥

[चर्चरिकया उपविश्य अञ्जलिं बद्ध्वा ।]

नीलकण्ठ ममोत्कण्ठा वनेऽस्मिन् वनिता त्वया ।
दीर्घापाङ्गा सितापाङ्ग दृष्टा दृष्टिक्षमा भवेत् ॥ ९ ॥

[चर्चरिकया अवलोक्य ।] कथमदत्त्वा प्रतिवचनं नर्तितुं प्रवृत्तः । किं नु खलु हर्षकारणमस्य । [विचिन्त्य] भवतु ! विदितमेतत् ।

मृदुपवनविभिन्नो मत्प्रियाया विनाशाद्
घनरुचिरकलापो निःसपत्नोस्य जातः ।
रतिविगलितबन्धे केशहस्ते सुकेश्याः
सति कुसुमसनाथे किं करोत्येष बर्ही ॥ १० ॥

भवतु । परव्यसननिर्वृत्तं न खल्वेनं पृच्छामि [अनन्तरे खुरकः]

विज्जज्झर-काणण-लीनओ ।
दुक्ख-विणिग्गअ-बाहुप्पीडओ ॥
दूरोसारिअ-हिअआणन्दओ ।
अम्बर-माणे भमइ गइन्दओ ॥ 13 ॥

[खुरकान्ते चर्चरी ।] हेले हेले

परहुअ महुर-पलाविणि कन्ति ।
णन्दण-वण सच्छन्द भमन्ति ॥
जइ पइँ पिअअम सा महु दिट्ठी ।
ता आअक्खहि महु परपुट्ठि ॥ 14 ॥

विद्याधरकाननलीनो दुःखविनिर्गतबाष्पोत्पीडः ॥
दूरोत्सारितहृदयानन्दः अम्बरमानेन भ्रमति गजेन्द्रः ॥13॥
परभृते मधुरप्रलापिनि कान्ते नन्दनवने स्वच्छन्दं भ्रमन्ति ॥
यदि त्वया प्रियतमा सा मम दृष्टा तदाचक्ष्व मम परपुष्टे ॥14॥

[एतदेव नर्तित्वा । वलन्तिकया उपसृत्य जानुभ्यां स्थित्वा]

इयमातपान्तसंधुक्षितमदा जम्बूविटपमध्यास्ते परभृता। विहंगमेषु पण्डिता जातिरेषा। यावदेनामभ्यर्थये। भवति

त्वां कामिनो मदनदूतिमुदाहरन्ति
मानावभङ्गनिपुणं त्वममोघमस्त्रम् ।
तामानय प्रियतमां मम वा समीपं
मां वा नयाशु कलभाषिणि यत्र कान्ता ॥ ११ ॥

[वामकेन किंचिद् वलित्वा । आकाशे ।] किमाह भवती। कथं त्वामेवमनुरक्तं विहाय गतेति । शृणोतु भवती ।

कुपिता न तु कोपकारणं
सकृदप्यात्मगतं स्मराम्यहम् ।
प्रभुता रमणेषु योषितां
न हि भावस्खलितान्यपेक्षते ॥ १२ ॥

कथं कथाच्छेदकारिणी स्वकार्य एव सक्ता ।

महदपि परदुःखं शीतलं सम्यगाहुः
प्रणयमगणयित्वा यन्ममापद्गतस्य ।
अधरमिव मदान्धा पातुमेषा प्रवृत्ता
फलमभिमुखपाकं राजजम्बूद्रुमस्य ॥ १३ ॥

एवंगतेऽपि प्रियेव मे मञ्जुस्वनेति न कोपोऽस्याम् । इतो वयम्-[द्विपदिकया परिक्रामितकेन कर्णं दत्त्वा] अये

दक्षिणेन प्रियाचरणनिक्षेपशंसी नूपुररवः । यावदत्र गच्छामि ।

[परिक्रम्य ।]

पिअअम-विरह-किलामिअ-वअणओ ।
अविरल-वाह-जलाउल-णअणओ ॥
दूसह-दुक्ख-विसंठुल-गमणओ ।
पसरिअ-उरु-ताव-दीविअ-अङ्गओ ॥
अहिअं दुम्मिअ-माणसओ ।
काणणं भमइ गइन्दओ ॥ 15 ॥

प्रियतमाविरहक्लान्तवदनः अविरलबाष्पजलाकुलनयनः ॥
दुःसहदुःखविसंष्ठुलगमनः प्रसृतगुरुतापदीप्ताङ्गः ॥
अधिकं दूनमानसः काननं भ्रमति गजेन्द्रः ॥ 15 ॥

[इति ककुभेन षड्डुपभङ्गाः । अनन्तरे द्विपदिकया दिशोऽवलोक्य ।]

पिअ-करिणी-विच्छोइअओ गुरु-सोआणल-दीविअओ ।
वाह जलाउल-लोअणओ करि-वरु भमइ समाउलओ ॥16॥

प्रियकरिणीवियुक्तो गुरुशोकानलदीप्तः ।
बाष्पजलाकुललोचनः करिवरो भ्रमति समाकुलः ॥ 16 ॥

अहो धिक् धिक् ।

मेघश्यामा दिशो दृष्ट्वा मानसोत्सुकचेतसाम् ।
कूजितं राजहंसानां नेदं नूपुरशिञ्जितम् ॥ १४ ॥

भवतु । यावदेते मानसोत्सुकाः पतत्रिणः सरसो नोत्पतन्ति तावदेतेभ्यः प्रियाप्रवृत्तिरवगमयितव्या । [वलन्तिकया उपेत्य] भो भो जलविहंगमराज

पश्चात् सरः प्रति गमिष्यसि मानसं तत्
पाथेयमुत्सृज बिसं ग्रहणाय भूयः ।

मां तावदुद्धर शुचो दयिताप्रवृत्त्या
स्वार्थात् सतां गुरुतरा प्रणयिक्रियैव ॥ १५ ॥

यथोन्मुखो विलोकयति मानसोत्सुकेन मया न लक्षिते-त्येवं वचनमाह [उपविश्य चर्चरी]

रेरे हंसा किं गोइज्जइ
रेरे हंस किं गोप्यते ।

[इति नर्तित्वोत्थाय ।]

यदि हंस गता न ते नतभ्रूः
सरसो रोधसि दर्शनं प्रिया मे ॥
मदखेलपदं कथं नु तस्याः
सकलं चोर गतं त्वया गृहीतम् ॥ १६ ॥

गइ-अणुसारेँ मइँ लक्खिज्जइ ॥
गत्यनुसारेण मया लक्ष्यते ॥

[चर्चरिकया उपसृत्य अञ्जलिं बद्ध्वा] अतश्च

हंस प्रयच्छ मे कान्तां गतिरस्यास्त्वया हृता
विभावितैकदेशेन देयं यदभियुज्यते ॥ १७ ॥

[पुनश्चर्चरी ।]

कइँ पइँ सिक्खिअ ए गइलालस ।
सा पइँ दिट्ठी जहण-भरालस ॥ 17 ॥

कुतस्त्वया शिक्षिता एषा गतिलालसा ।
सा त्वया दृष्टा जघनभरालसा ॥ 17 ॥

[पुनश्चर्चरी । हंस प्रयच्छेत्यादि पठित्वा द्विपदिकया निरूप्य विहस्य ।]
एष चोरानुशासी राजेति भयादुत्पतितः [परिक्रम्य]
अयमिदानीं प्रियासहायश्चक्रवाकः । तावदेनं पृच्छामि ।
[अनन्तरे कुटिलिका ।]

मम्मर-रणिअ-मणोहरए।
[मल्लघटी।] कुसुमिअ-तरु-वर पल्लवए।
[चर्चरी।] दइआ-विरहुम्माइअओ।
काणणं भमइ गइन्दओ ॥ 18 ॥
मर्मररणितमनोहरे।
कुसुमिततरुवरपल्लवे।
दयिताविरहोन्मादितः।
काननं भ्रमति गजेन्द्रः ॥ 18 ॥

[द्विलयान्ते चर्चरी।] गोरोअण-वण्णा चक्का भण्णइ मइँ।
महु-वासर कीलन्ती धणिअ ण दिट्ठी पइँ ॥19॥
गोरोचनवर्ण चक्र भण्यते मया।
मधुवासरे क्रीडन्ती धन्या न दृष्टा त्वया ॥ 19 ॥

[चर्चरिकया उपसृत्य जानुभ्यां स्थित्वा।]

रथाङ्गनामन् वियुतो रथाङ्गश्रोणिबिम्बया।
अयं त्वां पृच्छति रथी मनोरथशतैर्वृतः ॥ १८ ॥

कथं कः क इत्याह। मा तावत्। न खलु विदितोऽहमस्य।

सूर्याचन्द्रमसौ यस्य मातामहपितामहौ।
स्वयं वृतः पतिर्द्वाभ्यामुर्वश्या च भुवा च यः ॥१९॥

कथम् तूष्णीं स्थितः। भवतु। उपालप्स्ये तावदेनम्।

सरसि नलिनीपत्रेणापि त्वमावृतविग्रहां
ननु सहचरीं दूरे मत्वा विरौषि समुत्सुकः।
इति च भवतो जायास्नेहात् पृथक्स्थितिभीरुता
मयि च विधुरे भावः कान्ताप्रवृत्तिपराङ्मुखः ॥२०॥

सर्वथा मदीयानां भाग्यविपर्ययाणामयं प्रभावः। यावदन्यमवकाशमवगाहे [पदान्तरे स्थित्वा] भवतु न तावद् गच्छामि [द्विपदिकया परिक्रम्य अवलोक्य च]

इदं रुणद्धि मां पद्ममन्तःकूजितषट्पदम् ।
मया दष्टाधरं तस्याः ससीत्कारमिवाननम् ॥ २१ ॥

भवतु । अस्मिन्नेव कमलाध्यासिनि मधुकरे प्रणयित्वं करिष्ये । इतो गतस्यानुशयो मा भूदिति [अस्यान्तरे अर्धद्विचतुरस्रकः]

एक्केक्कम-वड्ढिअ-गुरुअर-पेम्म-रसे ।
सरे हंस-जुआणओ कीलइ काम-रसें ॥ 20 ॥

एकैकवर्धितगुरुतरप्रेमरसे ।
सरसि हंसयुवा क्रीडति कामरसेन ॥ 20 ॥

[चतुरस्रकेण उपेत्य अञ्जलिं बद्ध्वा ।]

मधुकर मदिराक्ष्याः शंस तस्याः प्रवृत्तिं–

[विभाव्य ।]

वरतनुरथवासौ नैव दृष्टा त्वया मे ।
यदि सुरभिमपास्यस्तन्मुखोच्छ्वासगन्धं
तव रतिरभविष्यत् पुण्डरीके किमस्मिन् ॥ २२ ॥

साधयामस्तावत् [द्विपदिकया परिक्रामितकेन] एष नीपस्कन्धनिषण्णहस्तः करिणीसहायो नागराजस्तिष्ठति । अस्मात् प्रियोदन्तमुपलप्स्ये [कुटिलिकया]

करिणी-विरह-संताविओ ॥

[मल्लघटी ।]

काणणे गन्धुद्धअ-महुअरओ ॥ 21 ॥

करिणीविरहसंतापितः
कानने गन्धोद्धतमधुकरः ॥ 21 ॥

[अतोऽन्तरे विलोक्य ।] भवतु न त्वरा कार्या ।

अयमचिरोद्गतपल्लवमुपनीतं प्रियकरेणुहस्तेन ।
अभिलषतु तावदासवसुरभिरसं सल्लकीभङ्गम् ॥ २३ ॥

[क्षणमात्रं स्थित्वा । स्थानकेन अवलोक्य] हन्त कृताह्निकः संवृत्तः । भवतु पृच्छामि ।

हउँ पइँ पुच्छिमि अक्खहि गअ-वरु
ललिअ-पहारेँ णासिअ-तरु-वरु ।
दूर-विणिज्जिअ-ससहर-कन्ती
दिट्ठी पिअ पइँ संमुह जन्ती ॥ 22 ॥

अहं त्वां पृच्छामि आचक्ष्व गजवर
ललितप्रहारेण नाशिततरुवर ।
दूरविनिर्जितशशधरकान्तिः
दृष्टा प्रिया त्वया संमुखं यान्ती ॥ 22 ॥

[पदद्वयं पुरत उपसृत्य ।]

मदकल युवतिशशिकला
गजयूथप यूथिकाशबलकेशी ।
स्थिरयौवना स्थिता ते
दूरालोके सुखालोका ॥ २४ ॥

[सहर्षम् ।] अनेन स्निग्धमन्द्रेण गर्जितेन प्रियोपलम्भशंसिना समाश्वासितोऽस्मि। साधर्म्याच्च त्वयि मे भूयसी प्रीतिः।

मामाहुः पृथिवीभृतामधिपतिं नगाधिराजो भवान्
अव्युच्छिन्नपृथुप्रवृत्ति भवतो दानं ममाप्यर्थिषु ।
स्त्रीरत्नेषु ममोर्वशी प्रियतमा यूथे तवेयं वशा
सर्वं मामनु ते प्रियाविरहजां त्वं तु व्यथां मानुभूः ॥२५॥

सुखमास्तां भवान् । साधयामस्तावत् [पार्श्वतो दृष्टिं दत्त्वा] अये सुरभिकन्दरो नाम विशेषरमणीयः सानु-

मानालोक्यते । प्रियश्चायमप्सरसाम् । अपि नाम सुत नुरस्योपत्यकायामुपलभ्येत [परिक्रम्य अवलोक्य च] कथमन्धकारः । भवतु । विद्युत्प्रकाशेनावलोकयामि ' हन्त मदीयैर्दुरितपरिणामैर्मेघोऽपि शतह्रदाशून्यः संवृत्तः । तथापि शिलोच्चयमेतमपृष्ट्वा न निवर्तिष्ये [अनन्तरे खण्डिका]

पसरिअ-खर-खुर दारिअ-मेइणिओ वण-गहणे अविचाल्लु ।
परिसक्कइ पेच्छहु लीणो णिअ-कज्जुज्जुअ कोलु ॥ 23 ॥

प्रसृतखरखुरदारितमेदिनीको वनगहनेऽविचलः ।
परिष्वक्कते पश्यत लीनो निजकार्योद्युक्तः कोलः ॥ 23 ॥

अपि वनान्तरमल्पकुचान्तरा श्रयति पर्वत पर्वसु संनता ।
इदमनङ्गपरिग्रहमङ्गना पृथुनितम्ब नितम्बवती तव ॥२६॥

कथं तूष्णीमास्ते । शङ्के विप्रकृष्टो न शृणोतीति । समीपेऽस्य गत्वा पुनरेनं पृच्छामि [अनन्तरे चर्चरी]

फलिह-सिला-अल-णिम्मल-णिज्झरु ।
बहु-विह-कुसुमे विरइअ-सेहरु ॥
किण्णर-महुरुग्गीअ-मणोहरु ।
देक्खावहि महु पिअअम महिहरु ॥ 24 ॥

स्फटिकशिलातलनिर्मलनिर्झर ।
बहुविधकुसुमैर्विरचितशेखर ॥
किंनरमधुरोद्गीतमनोहर ।
दर्शय मम प्रियतमां महीधर ॥ 24 ॥

[इति परिक्रम्य अञ्जलिं बद्ध्वा ।]

सर्वक्षितिभृतां नाथ दृष्टा सर्वाङ्गसुन्दरी ।
रामा रम्ये वनान्तेऽस्मिन् मया विरहिता त्वया ॥२७॥

[आकर्ण्य । सहर्षम् ।] कथं यथाक्रमं दृष्टेत्याह । भवानपि अतः प्रियतरं गृणोतु । क्व तर्हि मम प्रियतमा [नेपथ्ये तदेवाकर्ण्य] हा धिक् । ममैवायं कन्दरमुखविसर्पी प्रतिशब्दः । [विषादं रूपयित्वा] श्रान्तोऽस्मि । अस्यास्तावद् गिरिनद्यास्तीरे स्थितस्तरङ्गवातमासेविष्ये । इमां नवाम्बुकलुषामपि स्रोतोवहां पश्यतो मे रमते मनः ।

तरङ्गभ्रूभङ्गा क्षुभितविहगश्रेणिरसना
विकर्षन्ती फेनं वसनमिव संरम्भशिथिलम् ।
यथाविद्धं याति स्खलितमभिसंधाय बहुशो
नदीभावेनेयं ध्रुवमसहना सा परिणता ॥ २८ ॥

भवतु । याचिष्ये तावदेनाम् [अनन्तरे कुटिलिका]

पसिअ पिअअम सुन्दरि एणए ।
खुहिअकरुण-विहङ्गमए णए ॥
सुर-सरि-तीर-समूसुअएणए ।
अलि-उल-झङ्कारिअए णए ॥ 25 ॥

[कुटिलिकान्तरे चर्चरी ।]

पुव्व-दिसा-पवणाहअ-कल्लोलुग्गअ-बाहओ
मेहअङ्गे णच्चइ सललिअ जलणिहि-णाहओ ।
हंस-रहङ्ग-कुङ्कुम-सङ्ख-कआभरणु
करि-मअराउल-कसण-कमल-कआवरणु ॥
वेला-सलिलुव्वेल्लिअ-हत्थ-दिण्ण-तालु
ओत्थरइ दस दिस रुन्धेविणु णव-मेहआलु ॥26॥

प्रसीद प्रियतमे सुन्दरि एनया ।
क्षुभितकरुणविहंगमे नत्या ॥

सुरसरित्तीरसमुत्सुकेणके ।
अलिकुलझङ्कारिते नदि ॥ 25 ॥

पूर्वदिक्पवनाहतकल्लोलोद्गतबाहुः
मेघाङ्केन नृत्यति सललितं जलनिधिनाथः ।
हंसरथाङ्ककुङ्कुमशङ्खकृताभरणः
करिमकराकुलकृष्णकमलकृतावरणः ॥
वेलासलिलोद्वेल्लितदत्तहस्ततालः
अवस्तृणाति दश दिशो रुद्ध्वा नवमेघकालः ॥ 26 ॥

[इत्युपसृत्य अञ्जलिं कृत्वा ।]

त्वयि निबद्धरतेः प्रियवादिनः
प्रणयभङ्गपराङ्मुखचेतसः ।
कमपराधलवं मम पश्यसि
त्यजसि मानिनि दासजनं यतः ॥ २९ ॥

अथवा परमार्थसरिदेवैषा । न खलूर्वशी पुरूरवसमपहाय समुद्राभिसारिणी भविष्यति । भवतु । अनिर्वेदप्राप्याणि श्रेयांसि । यावदमुमेव प्रदेशं गच्छामि यत्र मे नयनयोः सुनयना तिरोभूता । [परिक्रम्य अवलोक्य] हन्त दृष्टमुपलक्षणं तस्या मार्गस्य ।

रक्तकदम्बः सोऽयं प्रियया घर्मान्तशंसि यस्यैकम् ।
कुसुममसमग्रकेसर-विषममपि कृतं शिखाभरणम् ॥३०॥

[विलोक्य] । इमं तावत् प्रियाप्रवृत्तिनिमित्तं सारङ्गमासीनमभ्यर्थये ।

अभिनवकुसुमस्तबकिततरुवरस्य परिसरे
मदकलकोकिलकूजितरवझङ्कारमनोहरे ।

नन्दनविपिने निजकरिणीविरहानलेन संतप्तो
विचरति गजाधिपतिरैरावतनामा ॥ 27 ॥

[गलितकः । जानुभ्यां स्थित्वा ।]

कृष्णशारच्छविर्योऽसौ दृश्यते काननश्रिया ।
वनशोभावलोकाय कटाक्ष इव पातितः ॥ ३१ ॥

[विलोक्य] । किं नु खलु मामवधीरयन्निव अन्यतोमुखः संवृत्तः । [दृष्ट्वा ।]

अस्यान्तिकमायान्ती शिशुना स्तनपायिना मृगी रुद्धा ।
तामयमनन्यदृष्टिर्भुग्नग्रीवो विलोकयति ॥ ३२ ॥

[इति नर्तित्वा चर्चरी ।]

सुर-सुन्दरि जहण-भरालस पीणुत्तुङ्ग-घण-त्थणि
थिर-जोव्वण तणुअ-सरीहि हंस-गइ ।
गअणुज्जल-काणणे मिअ-लोअणि भमन्तें दिट्ठा पइँ
तह विरह-समुद्दन्तरें उत्तारहि मइँ ॥ 28 ॥

सुरसुन्दरी जघनभरालसा पीनोत्तुङ्गघनस्तनी
स्थिरयौवना तनुशरीरा हंसगतिः ।
गगनोज्ज्वलकानने मृगलोचना भ्रमता दृष्टा त्वया
तर्हि विरहसमुद्रान्तरादुत्तारय माम् ॥ 28 ॥

[उपसृत्य अञ्जलिं बद्ध्वा ।] हंहो यूथपते

अपि दृष्टवानसि मम प्रियां वने
कथयामि ते तदुपलक्षणं शृणु ।
पृथुलोचना सहचरी यथैव ते
सुभगं तथैव खलु सापि वीक्षते ॥ ३३ ॥

कथमनादृत्य मद्वचनं कलत्राभिमुखः स्थितः । उपपद्यते ।

परिभवास्पदं दशाविपर्ययः । इतो वयम्–[परिक्रामितकेन अवलोक्य] शिलाभेदान्तरगतं किमेतदालोक्यते ।

प्रभालेपी नायं हरिहतमृगस्यामिषलवः
स्फुलिङ्गः स्यादग्नेर्गगनमभिवृष्टं पुनरिदम् ।

[विभाव्य ।]

अये रक्ताशोकस्तबकसमरागो मणिरयं
यमुद्धर्तुं पूषा व्यवसित इवालम्बितकरः ॥ ३४ ।

हरति मे मनः । आदास्ये तावदेनम् ।

पणइणि–बद्धासाइअओ वाहाउल–णिअ–णअणओ
गअ–वइ गहणे दूहिअओ भमइ क्खामिअ–वअणओ ॥29॥

प्रणयिनीबद्धाशाको बाष्पाकुलनिजनयनः ।
गजपतिर्गहने दुःखितः भ्रमति क्षामितवदनः ॥ 29 ॥

[द्विपदिकया उपसृत्य । ग्रहणं नाटयति ।] अथवा

मन्दारपुष्पैरधिवासितायां यस्याः शिखायामयमर्पणीयः ।
सव प्रिया संप्रति दुर्लभा मे किमेनमस्त्रोपहतं करोमि ॥३५॥

[नेपथ्ये ।] वत्स गृह्यतां गृह्यताम् ।

संगमनीय इति मणिः शैलसुताचरणरागयोनिरयम् ।
आवहति धार्यमाणः संगममचिरात् प्रियजनेन ॥ ३६ ॥

राजा—[कर्णं दत्त्वा] को नु खलु मामेवमनुशास्ति । [दिशोऽवलोक्य ।] अये अनुकम्पते मां कश्चिन्मृगचारी मुनिर्भगवान् । भगवन् अनुगृहीतोऽस्म्यहमुपदेशाद् भवतः । [मणिमादाय] हंहो संगमनीय

तया वियुक्तस्य विलग्नमध्यया
भविष्यसि त्वं यदि संगमाय मे ।

ततः करिष्यामि भवन्तमात्मनः
शिखामणिं बालमिवेन्दुमीश्वरः ॥ ३७ ॥

[परिक्रम्य अवलोक्य च ।] अये किं नु खलु कुसुमरहितामपि लतामिमां पश्यतो मे रतिरुपलब्धा । अथवा स्थाने मनोरमा ममेयम । इयं हि

तन्वी मेघजलार्द्रपल्लवतया धौताधरेवाश्रुभिः
शून्येवाभरणैः स्वकालविरहाद् विश्रान्तपुष्पोद्गमा ।
चिन्तामौनमिवास्थिता मधुलिहां शब्दैर्विना लक्ष्यते
चण्डी मामवधूय पादपतितं जातानुतापेव सा ॥ ३८ ॥

यावदस्याः प्रियानुकारिण्याः परिष्वङ्गप्रणयी भवामि ।

लए पेक्खु विणु हिअएँ भमामि ।
अइ विहि-जोएँ पुणि तहिं पाविमि ॥
ता रण्णेँ विणुकरमि णिब्भन्ती ।
पुणु णइ मेलइ ताह कअन्ती ॥ 30 ॥

लते प्रेक्षस्व विना हृदयेन भ्रमामि
यदि विधियोगेन पुनस्तां प्राप्नोमि ।
तदरण्येन विनाकरोमि निर्भ्रान्ति
पुनर्न वियोजयति तस्याः कृतान्तः ॥30॥

[इति चर्चरिकया उपसृत्य लतामालिङ्गति ।]

[ततः प्रविशति तत्स्थान एवोर्वशी ।]

राजा—[निमीलिताक्ष एव स्पर्शं रूपयित्वा ।] अये उर्वशीगात्र-संपर्कादिव निर्वृतं मे शरीरम् । तथापि न पुनरस्ति विश्वासः । कुतः ।

समर्थये यत् प्रथमं प्रियां प्रति
क्षणेन तन्मे परिवर्ततेऽन्यथा ।

अतो विनिद्रे सहसा विलोचने
करोमि न स्पर्शविभावितप्रियः ॥ ३९ ॥

[शनैश्चक्षुरुन्मील्य ।] कथं सत्यमेव प्रियतमा। [इति मूर्छितः पतति ।]

उर्वशी--[बाष्पं विसृज्य] जेदु जेदु महाराओ । जयतु जयतु महाराजः ।

राजा—

त्वद्वियोगोद्भवे तन्वि मया तमसि मज्जता ।
दिष्ट्या प्रत्युपलब्धासि चेतनेव गतासुना ॥ ४० ॥

उर्वशी—अब्भन्तर-करणाए मए पच्चक्खी-किद-वुत्तन्तो खु महाराओ । अभ्यन्तरकरणया मया प्रत्यक्षीकृतवृत्तान्तः खलु महाराजः ।

राजा—अभ्यन्तरकरणयेति न खलु ते वचनार्थमवैमि ।

उर्वशी—कहइस्सं । इमं दाव पसीददु महाराओ जं मए कोववसं गदाए एदं अवत्थन्तरं पाविदो महाराओ। कथयिष्यामि । एतत् तावत् प्रसीदतु महाराजो यन्मया कोपवशं गतया एतदवस्थान्तरं प्रापितो महाराजः ।

राजा—कल्याणि न तावदहं प्रसादयितव्यः । त्वद्दर्शनादेव प्रसन्नः सबाह्यान्तःकरणो ममान्तरात्मा । कथय कथमियन्तं कालमवस्थिता मया विना भवती।

[अनन्तरे चर्चरी ।]

मोरो परहुअ हंस रहङ्गम
अलि गअ पव्वअ सरिअ कुरङ्गम ।
तुज्झह कारणेँ रण्णे भमन्ते
को ण हु पुच्छिउ मइँ रोअन्ते ॥ 31 ॥

मयूरः परभृतो हंसो रथाङ्गः ।
अलिर्गजः पर्वतः सरित् कुरङ्गमः ॥
तव कारणेनारण्ये भ्रमता ।
को न खलु पृष्टो मया रुदता ॥ 31 ॥

उर्वशी—एव्वं अन्तक्करण-पच्चक्खी-किद-वुत्तन्तो महाराओ । एवमन्तःकरणप्रत्यक्षीकृतवृत्तान्तो महाराजः ।

राजा—प्रिये अन्तःकरणमिति न खल्ववगच्छामि ।

उर्वशी—सुणादु महाराओ । भअवदा कुमारेण सासदं कुमारवदं गेण्हिअ अकलुसो णाम गन्धमादण-कच्छो अज्झासिदो किदो अ एस विही । श्रृणोतु महाराजः । भगवता कुमारेण शाश्वतं कुमारव्रतं गृहीत्वा अकलुषो नाम गन्धमादनकच्छोऽध्यासितः कृतश्चैष विधिः ।

राजा—क इव ।

उर्वशी—जा इमं पदेसं इत्थिआ पविसदि सा लदाभावेण परिणमिस्सदि । गोरी-चरण-संभवं मणिं विणा तदो ण मुच्चिस्सदि त्ति । साहं गुरु-साव-संमूढ-हिअआ देवदा-समअं विसुमरिअ अगहिदाणुणआ कुमार-वणं पविट्ठा । पवेसाणन्तरं एव्व वासन्ती लदा संवुत्ता । या एतं प्रदेशं स्त्री प्रविशति सा लताभावेन परिणंस्यति । गौरीचरणसंभवं मणिं विना ततो न मोक्ष्यत इति । साहं गुरुशापसंमूढहृदया देवतासमयं विस्मृत्य अगृहीतानुनया कुमारवनं प्रविष्टा । प्रवेशानन्तरमेव वासन्ती लता संवृत्ता ।

राजा—सर्वमुपपन्नम् ।

रतिखेदसुप्तमपि मां शयने या मन्यसे प्रवासगतम् ।
सा त्वं प्रिये सहेथाः कथं मदीयं चिरवियोगम् ॥४१॥

इदं तद् यथाकथितं त्वत्संगमनिमित्तं मुनेरुपलभ्य मणिप्रभावादासादिता त्वमस्माभिः । [मणिं दर्शयति ।]

उर्वशी—अम्मो संगमणीओ । अदो खु महाराएण आलिङ्गिदमेत्तव्व पकिदित्थ म्हि संवुत्ता [मणिमादाय मूर्धनि वहति ।] अहो संगमनीयः । अतः खलु महाराजेन आलिङ्गितमात्रैव प्रकृतिस्थास्मि संवृत्ता ।

राजा—एवमेव सुन्दरि क्षणमात्रं स्थीयताम् ।

स्फुरता विच्छुरितमिदं रागेण मणेर्ललाटनिहितस्य ॥
श्रियमुद्वहति मुखं ते बालातपरक्तकमलस्य ॥ ४२ ॥

उर्वशी—महन्तो खु कालो तुह पइट्ठाणादो णिग्गदस्स । असुअन्ति मं पकिदीओ । ता एहि णिवुत्तम्ह । महान् खलु कालस्तव प्रतिष्ठानाद् निर्गतस्य । असूयन्ति मह्यं प्रकृतयः । तदेहि निवर्तावहे ।

राजा—यदाज्ञापयति भवती ।

उर्वशी—कहं महाराओ गन्तुं इच्छदि । कथं महाराजो गन्तुमिच्छति ।

राजा—

अचिरप्रभाविलसितैः पताकिना
सुरकार्मुकाभिनवचित्रशोभिना ।
गमितेन खेलगमने विमानतां
नय मां नवेन वसतिं पयोमुचा ॥ ४३ ॥

[चर्चरी ।]

पाविअ-सहअरि-संगमओ पुलअ-पसाहिअ-अङ्गअओ ।
सेच्छा-पत्त-विमाणओ विहरइ हंस-जुआणओ ॥ 32 ॥

प्राप्तसहचरीसंगमः पुलकप्रसाधिताङ्गकः ।
स्वेच्छाप्राप्तविमानो विहरति हंसयुवाः ॥ 32 ॥

[इति खण्डधारया निष्क्रान्तौ]

विक्रमोर्वशीये चतुर्थोऽङ्कः समाप्तः ॥

NOTES

ACT 1.

The prologue.

[The play is introduced with the Prastavana or prologue which opens with the usual benedictory stanza called Nandi, after which the Sutradhara or manager makes his appearance on the stage. He then calls his assistant and tells him that as he is going to stage the new play of Kalidasa called विक्रमोर्वशीय, the actors should be advised to attend carefully to their respective parts. The Sutradhara then requests the audience to hear and witness attentively the play of Kalidasa about to be staged. Just then the screams of heavenly nymphs crying for help are heard from behind the scenes. The Sutradhara concludes that the heavenly nymphs must be screaming and crying for help as their friend Urvashi has been abducted by the demons. Thereafter he makes his exit.]

In consonance with the time-honoured practice of Indian writers, Kalidasa opens his play with a benedictory stanza (the so-called नान्दी), invoking the grace of Shiva. According to the science of Indian Dramaturgy, an elaborate series of preliminaries (called the पूर्वरङ्ग) had to be performed before the actual commencement of a drama The last of these preliminaries was called the नान्दी, which consisted of a stanza or stanzas in glorification of some deity. The नान्दी was regarded as the most important part of the पूर्वरङ्ग, so that although in the course of time the other preliminaries were conveniently omitted in practice, the नान्दी was always attended to and religiously carried out (cf. Bharata: यद्यप्यंगानि भूयांसि पूर्वरंगस्य नाटके । तथाप्यवश्यं कर्तव्या नान्दी विघ्नप्रशान्तये ।). The two other plays of Kalidasa open with similar benedictory stanzas in praise of Shiva. The Raghuvamsha too opens with a salutation to Shiva. In the Meghaduta and Kumarasambhava also, we come across several appreciative references to the same deity. All this would make it seem probable that Kalidasa was a votary of Shiva. But it must not be forgotten that although Kalidasa had a particularly soft corner in his heart for Shiva, he was still by no means a bigot in his religious views. If we read Raghuvamsha X and Kumarasambhava II, we find that his admiration for Vishnu and Brahmadeva was as great as for Shiva. Altogether he was a man thoroughly catholic in his religious persuasions and by no means a bigoted fanatic. Vide Introduction p. V–VI.

I. 1. Construe: यं वेदान्तेषु रोदसी व्याप्य स्थितम् एकपुरुषम् आहुः। यस्मिन् ईश्वरः इति अनन्यविषयः शब्दः यथार्थाक्षरः (भवति) । यः च नियमितप्राणादिभिः मुमुक्षुभिः अन्तः मृग्यते । सः स्थिरभक्तियोगसुलभः स्थाणुः वः निःश्रेयसाय अस्तु । वेदान्तेषु—In the Upanishads. The Upanishads are called वेदान्त, because they form the concluding portion of each Veda, which consists of four parts, संहिता, ब्राह्मण, आरण्यक and उपनिषद्. Chronologically, too, the Upanishads are the last compositions in the literature coming under each Veda. Doctrinally again they represent the culminating phase of Vedic thought. एकपुरुषम् — The Supreme Spirit, or Being, which is the one without a second (एकमेवाद्वितीयम्) as the Upanishads put it. रोदसी व्याप्य स्थितम् — who completely pervades the two worlds viz. heaven and earth.

For this use of the root स्था along with the absolutive form of another root cf. Shakuntala I. 1 श्रुतिविषयगुणा या स्थिता व्याप्य विश्वम्। cf. also the Purushasukta (Rigveda X. 90), stanza 1: स भूमिं विश्वतो वृत्वा अत्यतिष्ठत् दशांगुलम्। ईश्वरः The Lord or Ruler. The word is derived from the root ईश् (II. A.) to rule + the suffix वर, which we find also in such words as नश्वर, इत्वर, सृत्वर etc. अनन्यविषयः—न विद्यते अन्यः विषयः (वाच्यत्वेन यस्य सः। not signifying anything else, exclusively applicable to Him alone and none else. Other gods are called ईश्वर only by sufferance and courtesy, but Shiva alone is called ईश्वर with the fullest justification, as he possesses all the qualities signified and implied by that epithet. यथार्थाक्षरः—यथार्थानि (अर्थम् अनतिक्रान्तानि) अक्षराणि यस्य सः (शब्दः) literally true, significant to the letter. cf. II. 17 *infra*: जयशब्दः सहस्राक्षादगतः पुरुषान्तरम्, where अगतः पुरुषान्तरम्=अनन्यविषयः। नियमितप्राणादिभिः मुमुक्षुभिः— by spiritual aspirants (literally, those who are desirous of salvation) who have restrained the five vital airs. प्राण, and others. In Yogic physiology the vital functions of the body are analysed into the five vital breaths or airs प्राण, अपान, व्यान, उदान and समान, and the spiritual aspirant is recommended to hold these under control and to regulate their movements while practising abstract contemplation. मुमुक्षु is a desiderative adjective from the root मुच्, used in the sense of a substantive. अन्तः within i.e. in the mind or heart (हृदये, मनसि वा). स्थिरभक्तियोगसुलभः— This compound may be variously explained: (1) स्थिरः भक्तियोगः येषां ते स्थिरभक्तियोगाः, तैः सुलभः। (2) स्थिरौ भक्तियोगौ येषां ते स्थिरभक्तियोगाः, तैः सुलभः। (3) स्थिरेण भक्तियोगेन सुलभः। (4) स्थिरा भक्तिः, योगः (ध्यानं) च ताभ्यां सुलभः। भक्तियोग means the same as भक्तिमार्ग – the path or way of devotion. योग

by itself means abstract meditation. स्थाणुः from the root स्था. It literally means that which stands, that which is stationary. Hence, immovable, eternal, abiding. As an epithet of Shiva it means the Eternal One. निःश्रेयसाय अस्तु— May he conduce to your highest good i.e. salvation. निःश्रेयसम् means that which has nothing superior to it, hence the highest welfare or spiritual well-being in the form of मोक्ष. निर्गतं (i.e. अविद्यमानं) श्रेयः यस्मात् तत् निःश्रेयसम् or according to the सिद्धान्तकौमुदी, निश्चितं श्रेयः निःश्रेयसम् । The final अ in this word is laid down by Panini V. 4. 77.

I.1.1. नान्द्यन्ते—At the end of the benedictory stanza. नान्दी is defined as आशीर्नमस्क्रियारूपः श्लोकः काव्यार्थसूचकः *i. e.* a stanza of the form of a salutation or benediction which is suggestive of the story of the drama. It is called नान्दी because it is a source of delight to the gods. cf. नन्दन्ति देवता ह्यस्यां तस्मान्नान्दीति कीर्तिता. The commentators काटयवेम and others take special pains to show how the नान्दी stanza of our play hints indirectly at the subject-matter. एकपुरुष refers to Pururavas, the hero of the play; व्याप्य स्थितं रोदसी hints at his world-wide reputation. The second line of the stanza suggests that Pururavas alone deserves the title ईश्वर, on account of his unique prowess. The words अन्तः मृग्यते in the third line are supposed to hint at the fact of Urvashi having of her own accord decided to seek his company. The commentators proceed in the same strain to show that the remaining expressions in the stanza are suggestive more or less indirectly of the subject-matter of the play. But it must be said that such attempts on the part of the commentators are purely fantastic, and one wonders if the author of the play ever intended the नान्दी stanza to express such a deeper meaning as the commentators try to read into it.

I. 1. 2. नेपथ्याभिमुखम्—In the direction of the tiring or green room. The word नेपथ्य means here जवनिकान्तर्भूमिः वेषपरिग्रहस्थलम्—the space behind the scenes. where the actors dress themselves and do their toilet. मारिष—This is a term of polite address used by the Sutradhara in addressing his assistant. cf. भावो मान्यः समुद्दिष्टः किंचिदूनस्तु मारिषः । and also सूत्रधारं वदेद् भाव इति वै पारिपार्श्वकः । सूत्रधारो मारिषेति पारिपार्श्वकमादिशेत् ।

I. 1. 3. पारिपार्श्वक: (or according to काटयवेम, पारिपार्श्विकः) —the assistant of the Sutradhara. The word is derived from परिपार्श्व + the suffix अण् (in the sense of तत्र भवः) + क (स्वार्थे) परिपार्श्वे भवः पारिपार्श्वः । स एव पारिपार्श्वकः । If, however we adopt the form पारिपार्श्विक, we shall have to derive it from परिपार्श्व+ठक्(इक). Vide Panini IV. 4. 29. and सिद्धान्तकौमुदी. He is characterized as follows by भरत in his नाट्यशास्त्र– सूत्रधारस्य पार्श्वे यः प्रवदन् कुरुतेऽर्थनाम् । काव्यार्थसूचनालापं स भवेत् पारिपार्श्वकः

I. 1. 4. भाव—Exalted sir. When an inferior person addresses his superior, he uses the word भाव; cf. the quotations given above under मारिष. I. 1. 6. प्रयोगबंध dramatic composition, play. प्रयुज्यते इति प्रयोगः, तस्य बंधः The singular is used here for the plural. We have a variant reading : दृष्टप्रयोगाः प्रबंधाः । Here प्रबंध would mean a dramatic composition and प्रयोग would mean theatrical representation. The Nirnayasagara Ed. reads परिषदेषा पूर्वेषां कवीनां दृष्टरसप्रबंधा. In this case रसप्रबंध would mean a dramatic composition abounding in emotional flavour. रसप्रधानः प्रबंध रसप्रबंधः । All these readings are good in their own way and it is difficult to say which is the best परिषद्—Assembly *i. e.* the audience or spectators. पूर्वेषां कवीनाम् We know from the मालविकाग्निमित्र, that भास, सौमिल्ल, कविपुत्र etc., were among the predecessors of Kalidasa. सोऽहं......प्रयोक्ष्ये । This is virtually equal to तस्मादहं......प्रयोक्ष्ये 'Therefore shall I exhibit on the stage. 'Therefore' *i. e.* because the audience have many a time witnessed the plays of former poets. विक्रमोर्वशीयम्—The title of our play is explained in two ways: (1) विक्रमं (पुरूरवसं) च उर्वशीं च अधिकृत्य कृतं नाटकम् (काटयवेम). Here विक्रम is taken as a name of पुरूरवस् (विक्रमशब्दः पुरूरवसः संज्ञा इति संप्रदायः । काटयवेम), although there is no authority for taking the word in that sense, beyond the संप्रदाय (tradition or convention) referred to by काटयवेम. The form is explained on the analogy of such formations as किरातार्जुनीयम्, राघवपाण्डवीयम् etc. Vide Panini IV. 3. 38 (2) विक्रमेण (पराक्रमेण) लब्धा या उर्वशी ताम् अधिकृत्य कृतं नाटकम् । on the analogy of अभिज्ञानशाकुन्तलम्. In the former case the title would mean 'The drama of Pururavas and Urvashi,' while in the latter case it would mean 'The drama of Urvashi won by valour.' The latter way of explaining the title is open to the objection that the rescue of Urvashi by Pururavas, although it starts the action of the play, is by no means its central theme so as to justify its giving the name to the play after itself. Whatever the way in which we explain the title of the play, the hidden allusion to the patron of the poet is unmistakable. cf. I. 13. 5 (विक्रममहिम्ना वर्धते भवान्) and I, 15. 1 (अनुत्सेकः खलु विक्रमालंकारः), where also there is a similar secret allusion to the patron of the poet. अपूर्वम्—न विद्यते पूर्वं यस्य तत् । which has not been staged here-to-fore. For नाटकं we get in the Northern Recension the reading त्रोटकं. त्रोटक is only a variety of नाटक. For the technical meaning of the term, see Introduction, Technical Names, *p*. XXVI. I. 1. 11. आर्यमिश्रान्—the noble audience. The word आर्य in itself means noble or honourable. मिश्र is simply an honorific addition. cf. Ranganatha : पूज्ये मिश्रवचनं नित्य-बहुवचनान्तम् ।

I. 2. प्रणयिषु–प्रणयः विद्यते यस्य सः प्रणयी । प्रणय means an humble request, a petition, प्रणयिन् means a servant, a supplicant. दाक्षिण्य courtesy, regard, generosity of disposition. सद्वस्तुपुरुषबहुमानात्–वस्तुनः पुरुषः वस्तुपुरुषः । सन् (शोभनः) वस्तुपुरुषः सद्वस्तुपुरुषः । तस्मिन् बहुमानः । वस्तु means इतिवृत्त or the plot of the play. वस्तुपुरुष means कथानायक. क्रिया–work, dramatic composition.

I. 2. 1. नेपथ्ये–Behind the scenes. Here नेपथ्य means curtain or scene. पक्षपातिन् – a friend, one who is favourably disposed, a sympathiser. गतिः unimpeded movement. अंबरतले – Through the sky – along the surface of the sky. I. 2.6. कुररी an osprey–what is called *Titavi* in Marathi. It is a bird often found in the vicinity of rivers and lakes and is only too well-known for its shrill and yet plaintive tone. cf. रघुवंश XIV. सा मुक्तकण्ठं व्यसनातिभाराच्चक्रन्द विग्ना कुररीव भूयः ।; also मालतीमाधव V.20 नादस्ताव-द्विकलकुररीकूजितस्निग्धतारः । After I. 2.6, the Nirnayasagara Ed. gives an additional stanza: मत्तानां कुसुमरसेन षट्पदाना शब्दोऽयं परभृतनाद एष धीरः । आकाशे सुरगणसेविते समन्तात् किं नार्यः कलमधुराक्षरं प्रगीताः । Vide Introduction. p. XII. Ranganatha comments upon it. Katayavema passes over it in silence. The stanza contains three guesses put forward by the Sutradhara in the process of identifying the mournful sounds, which he has only recently heard. It is only after these probable guesses that he comes to the definite knowledge that the sounds in question are the wailings of the Apsarases. That the stanza is an interpolation is quite evident from the improbability of the Sutradhara indulging in three guesses one after another especially when he has heard a shrill and plaintive cry (as of an osprey) indicative of some one in distress. Further the wording of the stanza is very faulty, especially because in the first two lines, the particle किं has got to be supplied. I. 3. Construe: नरसखस्य मुनेः ऊरूद्भवा सुरस्त्री कैलासनाथमुपसृत्य निवर्तमाना विबुधशत्रुभिः अर्धमार्गे बंदीकृता, अतः अवम् अप्सरसां गणः शरणं क्रन्दति । सुरस्त्री means not "The wife of a god," but "A divine or heavenly woman or a nymph". cf. सुरांगना used in this very sense in I. 18. ऊरूद्भवा–ऊरुः उद्भवः (source) यस्याः or ऊरोः उद्भवः (birth, springing into existence) यस्याः । नरसखस्य—of the friend of Nara. नरस्य सखा नरसखः, according to राजाहःसखिभ्यः टच् । Panini V. 4. 91. नरसख means नारायण. नर and नारायण were two great sages of yore, who used to practise penance together and were great friends of each other. In later mythology नर came to be identified with Arjuna and नारायण with कृष्ण or विष्णु. नर and नारायण figure amongst the ऋषिs or poets of the Rigveda. In regard to the sage नारायण, it is said that while he was practising austere penance, Indra, alarmed at his penance, sent a band of Apsarases to him in order to entice and seduce him. The Apsarases came to him and tried their best to allure him by their seductive charms. नारायण, however, was not to be lured away by these, and he put them all to shame by producing from his thigh (ऊरु) a damsel of surpassing beauty, whom he sent as a present to Indra. cf. I. 14. *infra*. This damsel was none else but

उर्वशी, and she is therefore called here नरसखस्य मुनेः करूइवा. cf. I. 7. 12. *infra.* कैलासनाथ—Kubera and not Shiva as Ranganatha wrongly takes it. cf. I. 3. 21. below, where it is expressly said. कुबेरभवनात् प्रतिनिवर्तमाना । उपसृत्य=सेवित्वा having approached him *i. e.* having paid him a visit in order to wait upon him. बंदीकृता (predicate) was taken prisoner; a च्वि formation from बन्दि m. a prisoner or captive. अर्धमार्गे while half on her way. मार्गस्य अर्धम् अर्धमार्गः। विबुधशत्रुभिः by the enemies of the gods *i. e.* the demons. अप्सरसां गणः Band or company of Apsarases. The Apsarases are so called because they are believed to have sprung from the water of the ocean when it was churned by the gods and demons (अप् water+सरस् from सृ to move, to start). शरणं क्रन्दति cries for help or protection. This reading is to be preferred to करुणं क्रन्दति, since it directly tells us what it was that the Apsarases were crying for-करुणं क्रन्दति would mean "Cries in a piteous manner" and would be therefore very vague and uncertain.

I. 3, 2. प्रस्तावना—The prelude or prologue. It is also called आमुख or Introduction. The प्रस्तावना is of several kinds. The one that we have here in our play is called प्रयोगातिशय, since the Sutradhara introduces the Apsarases with the words अप्सरसां गणोऽयम्. For details, vide Introduction, under Technical Names, *p.* XXV.

THE MAIN SCENE.

The first Act is easily divisible into six scenes as follows :—

(1) FIRST SCENE IN THE SKY.

The Apsarases रंभा, मेनका and सहजन्या who are crying for help against the violenee done to them by the demon Keshin in kidnapping उर्वशी along with चित्रलेखा, accidentally meet पुरूरवस् and inform him of the nature of the outrage. Pururavas at once sets out in pursuit of the demon.

(2) **SECOND SCENE** : On a peak of the Hemakuta Mountain:

The Apsarases in the meanwhile descend from the sky on to a peak of the Hemakuta Mountain and rest there for sometime awaiting the King's return, speculating about the chances of his success in rescuing Urvashi from the demon when they see in the distance the returning chariot of the King in the sky.

(3) **THIRD SCENE** : In the sky, near the peak of the Hemakuta; the king moving in his chariot.

The King makes his appearance in his chariot along with उर्वशी and चित्रलेखा. The King and चित्रलेखा try to comfort and cheer up उर्वशी, who has fainted away on account of the outrage done to her. After some time उर्वशी regains her consciousness and learns from her friend चित्रलेखा that she must thank King Pururavas for their deliverance from the demon. The King and Urvashi exchange mutual glances and straightway fall in love with one another.

(4) **FOURTH SCENE** : Peak of the Hemakuta.

रंभा, मेनका and सहजन्या are very much delighted to see the King return triumphant and unhurt along with उर्वशी and चित्रलेखा.

(5) **FIFTH SCENE** : In the sky and then on the ground; the king's chariot still in motion.

At the command of the King, his charioteer lands the chariot on the peak of the Hemakuta and drives over the uneven regions of the mountain to where the Apsarases are waiting for the King.

(6) **SIXTH SCENE**: ON THE PEAK OF THE HEMAKUTA.

While the Apsarases and the King are rejoicing at the rescue of उर्वशी and are congratulating one another, चित्ररथ, the chief of the Gandharvas, who was sent by Indra with an army to rescue Urvashi on learning about her abduction by Keshin from Narada, descends upon the peak of Hemakuta, having learnt on his way about the deliverance of Urvashi by Pururavas. He offers his congratulations to the King and requests him to see Indra. The King, however, declines the request, whereupon चित्ररथ leaves with the Apsarases. Urvashi departs slowly, with a parting glance at Pururavas. The latter also makes his exit in a sad and depressed manner.

I. 3. 8 सूर्योपस्थानात् प्रतिनिवृत्तम्—Just returned from (*i. e.* after performing) attendance upon the Sun. उपस्थान—Attendance upon, service. It appears to have been the practice of King Pururavas to pay visits to the Sun—his great grand-father on the mother's side—from time to time and to wait upon him. King Pururavas, although a mortal, had access to heaven and his assistance was called upon even by Indra whenever a war with the demons arose; cf. I. 4. 7. and V. 19. 20*ff. infra*. The reason why he mentions his own name and speaks of himself as having just returned after waiting upon the Sun, is to inspire confidence in the minds of the frightened Apsarases. They already know the fame and the might of Pururavas arms. cf. I. 4. 7–9 and I. 4. 15 below. I. 3. 11—अवलेप violence, outrage. I. 3. 12 किं पुनः......अपराद्धम् । 'But say in what way (किम्=केन प्रकारेण) have your ladyships suffered from the demon's violence?' Pururavas wants to know the exact nature of the outrage committed by the demon or demons, before he can dart off in his pursuit of the same. किं....अपराद्धम् is an impersonal construction, meaning कः अपराधः कृतः । I. 3. 19. तपोविशेषपरिशंकितस्य सुकुमारं प्रहरणं महेन्द्रस्य—Indra, the lord of the gods, is always represented in classical mythology as being jealous or intolerant of an excess of penance practised by any one on earth. He at once sends down a band of nymphs in order to entice the person practising penance into vice and immorality. This is a trait in Indra's character often referred to in the works of Kalidasa. cf. Shakuntalà I. अस्ति एतद् अन्यसमाधिभीरुत्वं देवानाम् । and Raghuvamsha VIII. 79 चरतः किल दुश्चरं तपः तृणबिन्दोः परिशंकितः पुरा । प्रजिघाय समाधिभेदिनी हरिरस्मै हरिणीं सुरांगनाम् । सुकुमारं प्रहरणम्—a weapon delicate enough in appearance but dangerous in its consequences. Indra's usual weapon is his वज्र or bolt. But is is extremely hard, while उर्वशी is a very tender weapon in the armoury of Indra. प्रत्यादेशः 'One that obscures or eclipses, puts to shame or throws into shade,' 'Obscurer.' श्रियः—of Laxmi the goddess of wealth and beauty. I. 3. 21. समापत्तिदृष्टेन—seen by accident or chance *i. e.* seen all of a sudden, unexpectedly. cf. मालविका III.19.32 समापत्तिदृष्टेन देव्याः परिजनेन संकथा ।; also Raghu. VII. 23 and Kumara VII. 75. चित्रलेखाद्वितीया—Having चित्रलेखा for her second *i. e.* together with चित्रलेखा. अर्धपथे एव । cf. अर्धमार्गे above (I. 3). पथः अर्धम् अर्धपथः । पथिन् (m) path, becomes पथ at the end of a compound according to Panini V. 4. 74 (ऋक्पूरब्धूःपथामानक्षे)–बन्दिग्राहं गृहीता । 'Was taken captive.' बन्दिग्राहं is a gerundial formation from बन्दि (m. captive) and the root ग्रह to seize + the suffix णमुल् (अम्), according to Panini III, 4. 45–46 (उपमाने कर्मणि च । कषादिषु यथाविध्यनुप्रयोगः।) The meaning is the same as बन्दीकृता (stanza 3 above). बन्दिमिव गृहीत्वा गृहीता–बन्दिग्राहं गृहीता । I. 3. 23. जाल्मः Villain, wretch, miscreant. I. 3. 24 पूर्वोत्तरेण In the North-eastern direction. पूर्वस्याः उत्तरस्याः च दिशः अन्तरालभूतः दिग्विभागः पूर्वोत्तरः। Vide Panini II. 2. 26. I. 3. 25 विषादः Distress, fear. I. 3, 27 सदृशं—Worthy of, becoming=उचितं,योग्यम्। सोमादेकान्तरस्य—Removed from Soma (the Moon) only by one degree. Pururavas was the son of Budha and the grandson of Soma (the Moon). Cf. III. 7. 2. and V. 21 below. एकः बुधः अन्तरं व्यवधानं यस्य सः एकान्तरः। The Nirnayasagara Ed. reads सोमवंशसंभवस्य, which is evidently secondary since it simplifies the sense of सोमादेकान्तरस्य. Moreover our reading is supported by काटयवेम.

I. 3. 31. ऐशानी दिक् The direction presided over by ईशान *i. e.* Shiva, the North-east. Cf. पूर्वोत्तर above, I. 3. 24. I. 3. 32 आयुष्मन् literally "Oh long-lived one!" The word is used much in the sense of "My lord, my dear sir." I. 3. 33. The stage direction रथवेगं निरूपयन् (gesticulating speed of the chariot) is used because actual speed such as is described in the following stanza is impossible on the stage, and has therefore only to be gesticulated. वैनतेय–विनतायाः अपत्यं पुमान् वैनतेयः The son of Vinata, wife of Kashyapa, *i. e.* Garuda, who is regarded as the king of birds and is perhaps the fastest member of its class. आसादयेयम्–I shall approach *i. e.* overtake. पूर्वप्रस्थितम् started in advance of me *i. e.* having the start of me. अपकारिणं मघोनः The offender against Maghavan *i. e.* Indra. This refers to the demon Keshin who had kidnapped Urvashi and thus offended against Indra.

I. 4. construe: अमी चूर्णीभवन्तो घनाः रेणुवद् रथस्य अग्रे यान्ति। चक्रभ्रान्तिः अरान्तरेषु अन्याम् अरावलिं जनयतीव। वेगानिलात् हयशिरसि आयामवत् चामरं चित्रन्यस्तमिव अचलं (भाति or दृश्यते)

(वेगानिलात्) ध्वजपटःयष्ट्यग्रे च प्रान्ते च समं स्थितः। चूर्णीभवन्तो घनाः The heavy clouds (घन as an adjective means, solid or heavy) that are being reduced to powder under the ponderous tread of the horses. रेणुवत् like the particles of dust. रथस्य अग्रे यान्ति rise or are rising before the chariot. चक्रभ्रान्तिः=चक्रयोः भ्रमणम्–the rapid revolutions of the wheels. अरान्तरेषु in the intervals of the spokes. अर m. means the spoke of a wheel. अन्तर *n.* means space between or interval. अरान्तराणि means, therefore, the interstices between the spokes. अन्याम् अरावलिं जनयतीव–produces as it were another series or set of spokes. Any one who has observed a revolving wheel will remember that the space between the spokes becomes less and less as the rapidity of the revolutions increases, so that at last the number of spokes appears to be doubled or trebled. Hence it is said here that another series of intermediate spokes is produced as it were, by the revolutions of the wheels. आयामवत् चामरम्–The long (tall) chowries (fixed on the heads of the horses as ornaments). The singular चामरं is used for the plural. चामर means a mass of the bushy tail of the चमर deer, used as an ornamental fan, a chowri. हयशिरसि (singular) is used for the plural हयशिरःसु चित्रन्यस्तमिवाचलम् 'Motionless as if they were painted in a picture.' The idea is that on account of the wind produced by the high speed of the horses, their tall ornamental chowries were held erect and motionless. Cf. शाकुंतल I. 8 निष्कंपचामरशिखा निभृतोर्ध्वकर्णाः। ध्वजपटः the banner-cloth. समं स्थितः stands straight, even, level, without a single fold upon it. यष्ट्यग्रे च प्रान्ते च between the top of the flagstaff (यष्टि) and its own skirt (प्रान्त). But for the powerful wind produced by the high speed, the banner-cloth would have fallen down parallel to the flag-staff. Here, however, it is held in an out-stretched and horizontal position on account of the wind produced by the high speed. We get a various reading रेणुपदवीं for रेणुवदमी in the first line. Ranganath explains it as follows: रेणुपदवीं यान्ति–रेणुमार्गम् अनुसरन्ति। जलगुरवोपि जलदाः चक्रधारया पिष्टीकृताः मत्स्यंदनाग्रतः पांसुवद् उत्सर्पन्ति । रेणुपदवीं यान्ति means "Behave like particles of dust" (रेणुवद् आचरन्ति, रेणुत्वं यान्ति वा।) Kalidasa is very fond of giving realistic descriptions of rapidly moving objects. Cf. शाकुन्तल I.7 (the high speed of a deer), I.8 and 9 (the speed of a chariot), VII.8 (an aerial car making a rapid descent to the ground). I. 4.2. यथानिर्दिष्टं प्रदेशं– To the spot pointed out (by us to the King) i.e. the हेमकूटशिखर. I. 4.4. The nymphs were all this while in the air and hence the stage-direction that they gesticulate descending to the mountain-peak.

I. 4.7. उपस्थितसंपरायः "Whenever hostilities are imminent." उपस्थितः (approached) संपरायः (युद्धं) यस्य । Like Pururavas, Dushyanta also was called upon to help the Gods in their hostilities against the demons. Cf. Shakuntala II. 15, VI 29, 30. विजयसेनामुखे—"At the head of his victorious or conquering forces."

I. 4.14. उच्चलितहरिणकेतनः। "Having its deer-emblazoned flag proudly lifted on high." केतन (*n*) means "A flag." हरिणकेतन "A flag having the figure of a deer upon its cloth." The flag is proudly lifted up उच्चलित or उल्लसित (v. l.), because the king is returning victorious.

I. 5. भीरु. "Oh timid one," त्रिलोकरक्षी महिमा हि वज्रिणः। Mark the humility of the King in attributing the deliverance of Urvashi to the all-saving prowess of Indra. Vide I. 15 below. चक्षुः आयतम्–"Large eye." Singular again for the dual. प्रत्युषस् (*n*), "Morning", "Dawn", "Day-break." पद्मिनी "Lotus plant". The Nirnayasagara Ed. reads "निशावसाने नलिनीव पङ्कजम् ।" This reading has the advantage that निशावसाने exactly corresponds to गतं भयं सुरारिसंभवम्. The night is to the lotus plant what the demon's violence is to Urvashi. But then, as Mr. Pandit points out, पंकजम् by itself does not match well with चक्षुरायतम्. As each of the two readings has one point of advantage, it is not possible to decide which is the better.

I. 5.1. उच्छ्वसितमात्रजीविता—"Whose vital activity (जीवित) consists only in her hard breathing" "Alive only because she is breathing out." उच्छ्वसित means "Breathing or respiration." Ranganath reads: उच्छ्वसितमात्रसंभावितजीविता "Who is supposed or believed to be living only on account of her hard breathing." संज्ञा "Consciousness". संज्ञां प्रतिपद्—"To recover consciousness, to come to one's self."

I. 5.4. बलवत् Adverb, "Powerfully", "Exceedingly", Cf. शाकुन्तल I. 2 बलवदपि शिक्षितानाम् । and *ibid* III बलवदस्वस्थशरीरा शकुन्तला । The Northern Recension adds here the stanza मन्दारकुसुमदाम्ना etc., which we have given in our Introduction p. XII. It contains almost the same idea as that of stanza 6.

I. 6. Construe : पश्य । अस्याः कुसुमसमबन्धनं हृदयं (कर्तृ) स्तनमध्योच्छ्वासिना हरिचन्दनेन कथितं (सूचितम्) कम्पं (कर्म) न तावद् (अद्यापि) मुञ्चति ।

कुसुमसमबन्धनं हृदयम् "Her heart tender like a flower." This is the subject and कम्प (tremor) is the object

कुसुमसमं बन्धनं यस्य—"Whose stem is delicate like that of a flower." बन्धन seems to mean here "Structure, construction." "Whose structure is as delicate as that of a flower." Cf. Meghaduta I 9. "कुसुमसदृशम्.....अंगनानाम्...... हृदयम् ।" हरिचन्दन (*n*) "Yellow sandal." Here "Paste or smearing of yellow sandle." स्तनमध्योच्छ्वासिना "Heaving up and down between her breasts." The Nirnayasagara Ed. reads this stanza as follows :—

मुञ्चति न तावदस्या भयकम्पः कुसुमकोमलं हृदयम् ।
सिचयान्तेन कथंचित् स्तनमध्योच्छ्वासिना कथितः ॥

Although the expression कुसुमकोमलं is more direct than कुसुमसमबन्धनं, the word कथंचित् spoils the whole sense and so the reading has to be rejected.

I. 6. 1. पर्यवस्थापय—"Compose yourself."

अनप्सरा इव मम प्रतिभासि—"You strike me as if you were not a nymph, although you are really one." चित्रलेखा means to say that in being so much overpowered by fear Urvashi behaves like a human being rather than like an Apsaras, who in her nature must be above fear.

प्रत्यागच्छति—"Comes to herself, regains consciousness."

I. 6. 4. प्रकृतिम् आपद्—"To recover consciousness."

1. 7. Construe : शशिनि आविर्भूते तमसा मुच्यमाना रात्रिः इव, नैशस्य हुतभुजः छिन्नभूयिष्ठधूमा अर्चि इव,: रोधःपतनकलुषा प्रसादं गृह्णती गंगा इव, इयं वरतनुःअन्तः मोहेन मुक्तकल्पा (सती) लक्ष्यते ।

नैशस्य हुतभुजः अर्चिः इव "Like the flame of a nocturnal fire." छिन्नभूयिष्ठधूमा—छिन्नः भूयिष्ठः (बहुलः) धूमः यस्याः सा । "From which the smoke has been mostly removed or or from which most of the smoke has been removed." रोधःपतनकलुषा—"Turbid on account of the tumbling in of the banks." प्रसादं गृह्णती—"Regaining her natural clearness or purity." अन्तः (=हृदये) मोहेन मुक्तकल्पा "Almost relieved of her mental stupor." The suffix कल्प has the sense of "Almost, for the most part." Cf. Panini V. 3. 67. ईषदसमाप्तौ कल्पब्देश्यदेशीयरः। Thus : ईषदूना मुक्ता=मुक्तकल्पा *i. e.* मुक्तप्राया. We get a v. l. मुच्यमाना which conveys the same sense as मुक्तकल्पा.

I. 7. 1. विश्रब्धा "Of good cheer, cheerful." हताशाः "Wretched, vile, accursed." त्रिदशपरिपन्थिनः "The opponents or enemies of the Gods." त्रिदश literally "The thrice ten" is a name of the Gods collectively. Mallinatha on Kumar III. 1. explains the word as : त्रिः आवृत्ताः दश परिमाणम् एषाम् इति त्रिदशाः "Whose number is thrice ten."

I. 7. 4. किं प्रभावदर्शिना महेन्द्रेण। Mark the naturalness and extreme innocence of Urvashi's question. As soon as she hears that the demons have been defeated, she most naturally thinks that Indra and none else must have been the cause of their overthrow. प्रभावदर्शिना महेन्द्रेण "By the great Indra who saw (the whole thing *i. e.* the outrage committed by the demons) by means of his divine power (प्रभाव)." प्रभावेण द्रष्टुं शीलम् अस्य इति प्रभावदर्शी।

I. 7. 9. उपकृतं खलु दानवैः—Urvashi thinks that in committing an outrage upon her, the demons have obliged her, for how could she otherwise have had the privilege of seeing the King, and coming in such intimate contact with him?

I. 7. 11. प्रकृतिस्था "Completely recovered," "Come to herself." स्थाने खलु etc. Vide notes on अनुद्भवा नरसरवस्य etc. above p. 7.

I. 8. कान्तप्रभः "Of lovely light." सर्गविधौ—निर्माणकर्मणि "In creating." प्रजापतिः अभूत् "Acted the part of the creator" नु expresses the sense of guess or conjecture.

(Cf. नु: वितर्के). शृंगारैकरसः मदनः "Cupid, who excels in the graces of love, or who joys or revels in love and love alone." शृंगारः एकः एव रसः यस्य। पुष्पाकरः मासः "The month which is a repertory of flowers *i. e.* the vernal season-spring." पुष्पोद्भवस्थानरूपः वसन्तः। पुराणो मुनिः "The ancient ascetic, the ascetic of yore" referring to the sage नारायण, who is supposed to have produced Urvashi from his thigh. वेदाभ्यासजडः "Made blunt or dull by his constant lucubrations over the Vedas." विषयव्यावृत्तकौतूहलः "Whose curiosity has been weaned away from the pleasures of the senses." विषयेभ्यः व्यावृत्तं कौतूहलं यस्य सः। The idea is : Urvashi, being a damsel of surpassing beauty, presupposes a creator equally beautiful and charming, so in her case either the Moon or the Vernal season or the God of love himself must have been the creator, and *definitely not* that old sage नारायण, who has lost all zest for sensual pleasures on account of his constant application to the study of Vedas. Cf. मालतीमाधव I. 21. तस्याः सखे नियतमिन्दुसुधामृणालज्योत्स्नादि कारणमभूत् मदनश्च वेधाः ॥

I. 8. 3. अभयदायी—"Who has given us protection from danger." अभय (*n*) means "Security or protection."

I. 9. Construe :- हे सुन्दरि, त्वं यस्य अवन्ध्ययोः नेत्रयोः पथि यदृच्छया सकृदपि स्थिता, सः अपि त्वया विना समुत्सुकः भवेत्। आर्द्रसौहृदः ते सखीजनः किमुत। यदृच्छया "By chance, accidentally" अवन्ध्य—"Firuitful, fortunate, lucky :" it is the opposite of वन्ध्य "barren" (Cf. वांझ in Marathi and Gujarati.) नेत्रयोः पथि स्थिता "Stood within the Sange of the eyes." समुत्सुकः "Full of deep longing." आर्द्रसौहृदः—आर्द्रं सौहृदं यस्य. "Whose affection for you is ever fresh." सौहृद (*n*) "Friendship or affection" from सुहृद् "A friend."

I. 9.1. अभिजातम्—"Noble, dignified." वचनम्—"Speech, manner of address." चन्द्राद् अमृतम्—The Moon is believed to be a repository of nectar or ambrosia. मे हृदयं त्वरते—"My heart hastens or grows impatient."

I. 10. उपप्लवात् मुक्तम् —"Released from eclipse." प्रत्यागतप्रसादम्–प्रत्यागतः प्रसादः यं सः प्रत्यागतप्रसादः। "Who has regained his clearness."

I. 10.1. Chitralekha wants to direct Urvashi's attention to Rambha and Sahajanya who are standing on the summit of Hemakuta. Urvashi obviously understands her meaning, but all the same she continues looking at the King with steadfast gaze and says " समदुःखः पिबतीवमां नयनाभ्याम् ।" These words apply to the friends of Urvashi as well as to the king. Urvashi does this in order to draw the attention of चित्रलेखा to her own feelings as regards the King, and she succeeds in calling her friend's attention to that fact. For in I.10.4 चित्रलेखा asks her "अयि कः" Showing thereby that she has become aware of Urvashi's state of mind.

I. 10.7. विशाखासमीपगतः (to be construed with चन्द्रः) "Standing in the vicinity of the constellation विशाखा." विशाखा is the sixteenth lunar mansion consisting of two stars. Pururavas who is accompanied by उर्वशी and चित्रलेखा is compared to the Moon accompanied by the two stars of the विशाखा constellation. Cf. शाकुन्तल III. "किमत्र चित्रं यदि विशाखे शशांकलेखामनुवर्तेते ।"

I. 10.12. प्रत्यानीता—" Brought back or restored to us."

I. 10.15. Sahajanya means that the demons are really so powerful that there is every reason why they should rejoice at the victory and safe return of the King.

I. 10. 18. चक्रोद्घातं रूपयित्वा—"Acting as if he received a jolting of the chariot-wheels." विषमावतार: "Descent upon an uneven (rugged) surface." दत्तफल:—दत्तं फलं येन—"Not vain, not futile." हन्त is a particle expressing joy. I. 11. Construe: यद् रथसंक्षोभाद् अयं (मम) अंसः रथापमश्रोण्याः अंसेन सरोमविक्रियं स्पृष्टः (तत्) मनसिजेन अंकुरितमिव । रथसंक्षोभ—"Jolting of the chariot". रथोपमश्रोणी seems to be elliptical for रथचक्रापमश्रोणी "Whose hips are round like the wheel of a chariot", "Fair, beautiful." Cf. IV. 18. रथांगश्रोणिबिंबया. सरोमविक्रियम्—रोमविक्रियया (रोमांचेन) सहितं यथा स्यात् तथा—"So as to cause horripilation on the body." We have to supply तत् before अंकुरितं मनसिजेनेव । The construction is : यद् अयं अंसः......स्पृष्टः, तत् मनसिजेन अंकुरितमिव । "That my shoulder was touched by hers so as to cause horripilation upon the body seems like the sprouting of love." The fact is that at the thrilling touch of Urvashi's shoulder, Pururavas felt a horripilation upon his body. This horripilation is fancied by the poet to be the sprouting of the future tree of love. Cf. for this representation of the emergence of love as the sprouting of the tree of love, मालविकाग्निमित्र IV. 1. The Nirnayasagara Ed. reads : " यदिदं रथसंक्षोभादंगेनागं रथोपश्रोण्याः । स्पृष्टं सरोमविक्रियमंकुरितं मनसिजेनेव ॥ Katayavema reads : अंकुरितमनोभवेनेव for अकुरितं मनसिजेनेव. In this case अंकुरितमनोभवेन would be an adjective qualifying अंसेन. This reading gives a simpler grammatical construction.

I. 11.2. किमपि परतः अपसर "Move a little further" Urvashi says this because she feels rather ashamed that her shoulder should have brushed against that of Pururavas.

I. 11.5. संभावयामः—"Let us honour or greet or pay our congratulations to."

I. 12. यावत् "So that." सुभ्रूः "Having beautiful eye-brows", "Fair". सखीभिः संपर्कं याति—"May join her friends." आर्तवी श्रीः "Vernal beauty" आर्तवी (ऋतोः इयम् आर्तवी) "Of the season (viz. Spring)" i. e. "Vernal".

I. 12.7. पीडितम् used adverbially—"Hard, powerfully, closely."

I. 12.10. कल्पशतानि "For hundreds of Kalpas." कल्प is a fabulous period of time equal to 1000 Yugas or 432 millions of human years. पृथिवीं पालयिता भवतु—One would naturally expect here पृथिव्याः पालयिता; but that is prohibited by Panini II. 3. 69. न लोकाव्ययनिष्ठाखलर्थतृनाम् ।

I. 13.3-4. महेन्द्रोपकारपर्याप्त—"Sufficient to oblige the great Indra", "Capable of laying the great Indra under obligations." विक्रममहिमा—"The greatness or excess of valour."

परस्परं हस्तौ स्पृशतः "Touch each other's hands." Touching or shaking or holding by the hand was a mode of greeting among Hindus of ancient times. Mr. Pandit gives the following quotation from the भागवतपुराण X. 65.5: समुपेत्याथ गोपालान् हास्यहस्तग्रहादिभिः । विश्रान्तं सुखमासीनं पप्रच्छुः पर्युपागताः ॥ which mentions the practice of हस्तग्रह.

I. 13.10. अन्तरा "In the mean-while." चारण "A bard, minstrel or panegyrist." जयोदाहरणम्—"A panegyric in verse beginning with some such word as जयति, ornamented with alliterations and containing all the eight cases of Nominal Declension." To give the reader an idea of what a जयोदाहरण is like, we quote in full the following stanza from the रामरक्षा of बुधकौशिक—रामो दाशरथिः सदा विजयते, रामं रमेशं भजे । रामेणाभिहता निशाचरचमू रामाय तस्मै नमः ॥ रामान्नास्ति परायणं परतरं रामस्य दासोऽस्म्यहम् । रामे चित्तलयः सदा भवतु मे, भो राम मामुद्धर ॥ Cf. Raghu. IV 78.

where Mallinatha explains the word as follows: जयख्यापकः प्रबन्धविशेषः I. 14. पुरा नारायणेनेयम् etc. vide Notes on I. 3 above. मरुत्वते=इन्द्राय. मरुत्वान् is a title of Indra. मरुत् means a god in general, and मरुत्वत् means "Lord of the Gods". i. e. Indra. In the Rgveda, the मरुत्s are the storm-Gods, and Indra is their lord; hence he is called मरुत्वान्.

I. 15. भिनत्ति—"Shatters or puts to flight." Mark again the modesty of the King. Cf. I. 5 above, and Notes *ad. loc.*

I. 15.1. अनुत्सेकः खलु विक्रमालंकारः अनुत्सेकः means "Humility, modesty, freedom from pride or vanity." विक्रमालंकार "The ornament of valour." In choosing the word विक्रम alone of all those that express the idea of valour (e. g. वीर्य, शौर्य, पराक्रम, etc.) the poet no doubt wants to make a hidden allusion to the name of his patron. the illustrious विक्रमादित्य. Cf. also I. 13.4. and Note on the title of the play, under I. 1.4 above. For the idea Cf. नीतिशतक 82. शौर्यस्य वाक्संयमः (विभूषणम्)

I. 15.9. त्वं मे मुख भव ॥ "Be you my mouth" i. e. "Speak for me or on my behalf."

I. 15.13. इच्छामि प्रियसखीमिव महाराजस्य कीर्तिं महेन्द्रलोकं नेतुम् This is a round-about way of asking for the permission of Pururavas to depart "I wish to take your fame to the world of Indra" means "I wish to have your permission to go away."

I. 15.15 गम्यतां पुनर्दर्शनाय Mr. Pandit compares the French expression "*au revoir*.

I. 15.17. उत्पतनभङ्गं रूपयित्वा—"Acting as if her flight (उत्पतन) was suddenly obstructed. अहो लताविटपे मे एकावली लग्ना। We have a very parallel situation in Shakuntala Act I, where while Shakuntala is about to leave Dushyanta, her foot is pricked by a thorn and her bark-garment becomes entangled in the branches of a free. This is of course intended by the poet to enable the heroine to cast a parting glance at the hero. एकावली "A single string of pearls."

I. 15.20. इदं खलु लग्ना । दुर्मोचनीया इव मे प्रतिभाति ॥ Chitralekha says this smilingly (सस्मितम्). She of course intends to convey the idea that Urvashi has fallen desperately in love with Pururavas.

I. 15. 23. स्मर तावद् आत्मनः वचनम् ॥ "Remember these words of yours," referring to भवतु, यतिष्ये तावत् ॥ Urvashi asks Chitralekha not to forget her promise (expressed in the words "भवतु, यतिष्ये तावत् ।") to help her in her love for Pururavas. Cf. II. 9.6–7. below.

I. 16. अपांगनेत्रा—According to V. S. Apte this expression means "Having her eyes turned towards their corners." अपांगयोः प्रेरिते नेत्रे यया सा ॥ अपांग *m.* means "The corner of the eye." The expression would therefore ultimately mean "Casting side-glances." Ranganatha takes अपांग in the sense of Cupid (the bodiless). अपांगनेत्रा means then, मदनजनकनेत्रा "Having love-darting eyes." पुनरपि अद्य "Once again for the last time, this day."

I. 17. सुरेन्द्रस्य कृतापराधान् is an irregular expression having the sense: कृतसुरेन्द्रापराधान् ॥ We come across many such instances in Kalidasa's works. Cf. Raghu. VI. 20 ततो नृपाणां श्रुतवृत्तवंशा=ततः श्रुतनृपवृत्तवंशा ॥ Mallinatha observes: सापेक्षत्वेऽपि गमकत्वात् समासः ॥ वायव्यम् अस्त्रम्—"A missile weapon (shaft) presided over by the deity वायु." The idea is that the missile weapon is to be hurled against the enemy with a मन्त्र or incantation addressed to the God वायु.

I. 17. 1. उपश्लेषय " Bring here."

I. 17. 4. दुर्लभाभिनिवेशी ॥ दुर्लभे (वस्तुनि) अभिनिविशते इति दुर्लभाभिनिवेशी ॥ "Bent upon the unattainable" *i. e.* "Causing one to long for an unattainable object."

I. 18. पितुः मध्यमं पदम् "The middle footstep of her father" *i. e.* the sky. We have seen above that the sage नारायण was the father of Urvashi. In latter mythology this नारायण was indentified with विष्णु. Here पितुः मध्यमं पदम् means विष्णोः मध्यमं पदम् ॥ "The middle footstep of Vishnu." In the Rgveda विष्णु appears as a personification of the sun who is said to traverse the whole world in three steps. These three steps refer to the three stages of the sun in his daily march from the East to the West. The first step corresponds to the rise of the sun on the eastern horizon; the second to the zenith position of the sun at midday; and the third to his setting behind the western horizon. Thus the second or middle step of विष्णु means the sky. In classical Mythology also the sky is regarded as the second (or middle) of the three steps that विष्णु took in the वामनावतार. The sky is, therefore, often called विष्णुपद in sanskrit. Cf. Raghuvansha XIII. 1. अथात्मनः शब्दगुणं गुणज्ञः पदं विमानेन विगाहमानः ॥ एषा सुरांगना—"This heavenly damsel". सूत्रम्—"The fibre or filament in a lotus-stalk".

ACT II.

[The Second Act opens with an introductory scene-technically called प्रवेशक, followed by the main scene.

Introductory Scene : Precincts of the विमानोत्संग palace of the King.

Vidushaka, the boon companion of Pururavas, has learnt from the latter about his amour for Urvashi.

The King has however charged him to keep the matter to himself. Vidushaka is carrying on a heroic flight with his extremely communicative nature. Nipunika, the maid-servant of the Queen makes her entry and in the course of a soliloquy tells us that the Queen (काशिराजपुत्री alias औशीनरी) has noticed a great change in Pururavas, ever since his return from his सूर्योपस्थान and that she is considerably worried over it. At the Queen's instance, Nipunika wants to know from Vidushaka what the matter is with the King. She approaches him and by using a very ingenious trick succeeds in screwing out of him the secret of the King's passion for Urvashi. A bard announces the hour of midday, which is the time for the King to leave his council-chamber for bath, meal, etc.

THE MAIN SCENE.

The main scene in Act II contains as many as 7 sub-scenes, as shown below:—

1. **FIRST SCENE** : THE PALACE.

The King enters with his friend Vidushaka. The King is suffering severely from the pangs of love for Urvashi.

2. **SECOND SCENE** THE PRAMADAVANA

To divert his mind the King goes to the प्रमदवन. He however finds that the beauty of the प्रमदवन instead of offering any relaxation to his mind, only augments his love-longing.

3. **THIRD SCENE** : THE अतिमुक्तलतामण्डप IN THE प्रमदवन.

The King and Vidushaka while wandering in the प्रमदवन reach the अतिमुक्तलतामण्डप, enter it and take their seats within. At the request of the King, Vidushaka begins to meditate and think out some means of bringing about a meeting between the king and Urvashi. The king has a good omen and his mind is filled with hope.

4. **FOURTH SCENE**: IN THE SKY.

Urvashi and Chitralekha, moving in the air, reach the region where the King's palace is situated. They move on in the air to the region of the प्रमदवन.

5. **FIFTH SCENE**: THE अतिमुक्तलतामण्डप AGAIN.

They get down from the sky and see the King in the garden with his friend. Urvashi approaches the King unseen in order to overhear his talk with his friend. From what she hears, she is convinced of the King's deep love for her. The King blames Urvashi for her indifference to him, whereupon Urvashi writes on a Bhurja-patra (birch leaf) two stanzas expressing her deep love for Pururavas and drops it before the King. The King is overjoyed to read Urvashi's protestation of love for him. He hands over the love-letter to Vidushaka for safe-keeping. In the meanwhile Chitralekha goes to the King and communicates to him the prayer of Urvashi that the King should take pity on her and accept her love. The King only too willingly gives his consent to the proposal. Urvashi also now reveals herself to the King and greets him with victory. The King receives her and seats her by his side. Just then a देवदूत announces that Urvashi and Chitralekha must return to heaven immediately, as their presence is required there in connection with the staging of a drama composed by the sage Bharata. Urvashi being helpless leaves the King most reluctantly. The King now wants some consolation and asks his friend for the love-letter. But Vidushaka has in the meanwhile dropped it and allowed it to be blown away by the wind. He begins to look for it here and there.

(6) **SIXTH SCENE** : BACKSIDE OF THE अतिमुक्तलतामण्डप.

Enter Queen and Nipunika. The Queen, who has learnt from Nipunika that the King has gone to the अतिमुक्तलतामण्डप along with Vidushaka wants to over-hear him and to see if she can get any confirmation for the report brought by Nipunika about the King's amour for Urvashi. As she is about to hide herself behind a bush she sees a scroll of birch-leaf blown along by the wind, which at last clings to her anklet. On further scrutiny it proves to be a love-letter from Urvashi to the King. The Queen takes hold of the letter with a view to confronting the King with that irrefutable proof of his illicit love.

(7) **SEVENTH SCENE** : THE अतिमुक्तलतामण्डप ONCE AGAIN.

Vidushaka is still looking for the love-letter but to no purpose, and the King is grievously disappointed. Just then the Queen enters, with the birch-leaf in her hand. The King is able to give only a lame excuse by saying that it is altogether a different birch-leaf that has been missing and for which he has been looking and not the one the Queen has brought with her. But this does not satisfy the Queen. Vidushaka tries to defend the King but only makes matters worse. The King begs the Queen's pardon for his crime-in-love, which he can no longer deny, and prostrates at her feet. The Queen however leaves him in a rage in utter disregard of his prostration. The King is stung with a sense of humiliation at the scant ceremony with which the Queen has treated his apology, though he still continues to hold her in loving regard.—The midday hour having now approached, the King repairs to the palace for his bath, meal etc.

II. o. 8. आकीर्णे " In the midst of a crowd ", "When in company with others." आकीर्णे=जनसंपाते. (Katayavema) कार्यासन "The seat, sitting on which he settles disputes and dispenses justice ;" " Council hall ;" " The seat of judgement." विरलजनसंपाते- विरल: जनसंपात: यत्र । "Which is but slightly frequented by people." विमानोत्संगपरिसरे—" In the precincts of the palace called विमानोत्संग " Katayavema reads विमानप्रतिच्छन्द as the name of the palace. Ranganatha reads देवच्छन्द as its name. In the Shakuntala the palace of Dushyanta is called मेघप्रतिच्छन्द. Whatever the reading that we adopt, this much is certain that it is the name of a palace.

II. o. 21. देव्या काशिराजपुत्र्या *i. e.* Aushinari, the queen of Pururavas. ब्रह्मबन्धु: " An unworthy, wicked, vile Brahmin." It is used as a contemptuous term. ब्रह्मबन्धुरधिक्षेपे—Amarakosha. It is to be explained as : ब्रह्म (ब्राह्मणजातिरेव) बन्धु: अस्य । जात्या एव ब्राह्मण:, न तु कर्मणा आचारेण वा ।

आलिखित: वानर: इव " The very picture of a monkey." The विदूषक is usually an ugly, deformed man and so निपुणिका calls him " The very picture of a monkey." Cf. V. 11. 6. below. किमपि तूष्णीं भूत: " Sitting silent for some reason or another."

आर्यमाणवक: The noble, Manavaka. माणवक is the name of the Vidushaka. He is of a short stature and hence gets the appropriate name माणवक– a dwarf, manikin. क्षुद्रो मानव:–माणवक: ।

II. o. 32. संगीतव्यापारम् " Your practice of music." Nipunika was not a mere attendant upon the Queen, but was also an accomplished woman.

II. o. 39: मयि पक्षपाती "Favourably disposed towards me, a friend of mine." अनुचितवेदनादुःखिताम्–अनुचितया वेदनया दुःखिताम् "Distressed or afflicted by an unusual suffering." It must not be forgotten by the reader that the Queen's message delivered by Nipunika to the विदूषक is nothing but an invention of her own brain.

II o. 45. आलपिता "Was addressed." नामधेयेन. The suffix धेय is added to नाम without any additional sense. Thus नामधेय means the same thing as नाम.

II. o. 51. जिह्वायन्त्रणेन By restraining my tongue."

II. o. 61. मृगतृष्णिका Mirage. Here the mirage is of course the attainment of Urvashi.

II. o. 64. वैतालिकः–"Bard, minstrel." विविधेन तालेन गायतीति वैतालिकः The duty of the वैतालिक was to announce to the King the different periods of the day, by means of suitable descriptive songs in praise of the King. The भावप्रकाश describes the वैतालिक as follows :—

तत्तत्प्रहरकयोग्यै रागैस्तत्कालवाचिभिः श्लोकैः ।
सरभसमेव वितालं गायन् वैतालिको भवति ॥

II. 1 आ लोकान्तात् etc. applies to the Sun as well as to the King. आ लोकान्तात् प्रजानां प्रतिहततमोवृत्तिः (i) "Driving to away the darkness oppressing the people, beyond the confines of the world." (ii) "Suppressing the criminal tendencies of the subjects all over the wide world." तमोवृत्ति means (i) तमोव्यापार "The obscuring and oppressing activity of darkness." (ii) तमोगुण. "Criminal or evil tendencies of the people." दिवसस्य षष्ठे भागे "In the sixth part or division of the day." According to works on politics (अर्थशास्त्र), a king is recommended to divide the day (*i. e.* from morning to evening) into eight parts, each part being thus equal to one hour and a half. Different duties are assigned to these divisions of the day. The sixth division commences at about 1–30 P. M. and lasts till 3 P.M. The King is recommended to pass this period of time according to his will *i. e.* he is not required to do any particular or set duty, but is allowed to spend that time according to his pleasure आत्मनः छन्दवर्ती तिष्ठत्येष etc. does not refer to the time of the day when the king rises from his judgment seat. It is said only in a general way to bring out the comparison between the Sun and the King. The King has to pass a very busy day in the midst of various engagements and gets rest only in the sixth part of the day. So too the Sun stands and rests for a moment when he comes to the zenith-position, and then again commences his rapid course westwards.

प्रवेशकः—For the technical meaning of this term, see Introduction, Technical Names. p. XXVI

II. 2. Construe : मकरकेतोः अवन्ध्यपातेन बाणेन कृतमार्गं मे हृदयं सा सुरलोकसुन्दरी आ दर्शनात् प्रविष्टा (अस्ति)। मकरकेतु "The dolphin-bannered God" i. e. "Cupid" whose banner is adorned with the figure of a fish (मकर). अवन्ध्यपातेन (Scil. बाणेन) "Infallible, unerring, unmissing (अवन्ध्य) in its aim" कृतमार्गम्—कृतः मार्गः यस्मिन् तत् कृतमार्गम्। "Access to which was given" "A breach in which was effected."

II. 2.2. तपस्विनी "Poor, miserable". A term of commiseration. संपीडिता "Sorely afflicted or pained at heart." Vidushaka has already promised निपुणिका, that he would try his best to dissuade the King from running after the mirage. Now from the speech of the King he sees that he has fallen over head and ears in love with Urvashi, and therefore commiserates the Queen in the words संपीडिता etc....

II. 2.3. रहस्यनिक्षेपः=निक्षिप्तं रहस्यम् "The secret entrusted to you."

II. 2.6. अभिसंहितोस्मि "I have been outwitted or overreached". दास्या "By that wench, slave girl."

II. 2.10. सहसा "Off-hand, without due consideration." Mark the presence of mind shown by the Vidushaka in answering the question of the King.

II. 2.17. पंचविधस्य अभ्यवहारस्य । Katayavema gives the following as the five varieties of articles of food. (1) भक्ष्य Things to be thoroughly chewed before they are eaten, such as bread; (2) भोज्य Things to be eaten without much chewing, such as boiled rice; (3) लेह्य Things to be licked, such as liquid condiments and soups; (4) चोष्य Things to be sucked, such as mango-pickles; (5) पेय Things to be drunk, such as milk, etc. Or the expression might refer to some five specific food-preparations, corresponding perhaps to Marathi पंच पक्वान्न. उपनतसंभारस्य "Having all the requisite articles or materials brought together." योजनाम् "Preparation". शक्यम् उत्कण्ठा विनोदयितुम् । This is a contamination of two constructions: शक्यम् उत्कण्ठां विनोदयितुम् and शक्या उत्कण्ठा विनोदयितुम् । Ranganatha justifies this irregular construction by citing a precedent for it from no less an authority than the महाभाष्यकारः—शक्यं श्वमांसादिभिरपि क्षुत् प्रतिहन्तुम् इति महाभाष्यकारप्रयोगाद् उत्कण्ठा विनोदयितुं शक्यम् इति साधु ॥ Cf. also मालविकाग्निमित्र III. 23. एवं हि प्रणयवती सा शक्यमुपेक्षितुं कुपिता ॥ विनोदय् means to remove, drive away, beguile.

II. 2.20. दुर्लभप्रार्थनः "Desiring or longing for an object difficult to be had." दुर्लभं प्रार्थनं यस्य or दुर्लभवस्तुविषयिका प्रार्थना यस्य सः । विनोदयितव्यः Here विनोदय् means to divert, amuse, entertain, please.

II. 2.20 ननु भवान् etc. The Vidushaka means to say "If Urvashi has but once seen you, she cannot help falling in love with you and making a voluntary offer of herself to you, so handsome and lovable you are."

II. 2.24. पक्षपातोयमवधार्यताम् "If you choose to pay such a compliment to me, though, as I very well know, I am unworthy of it, it is your affection for (पक्षपात:-partiality) me that is responsible for it."

II. 2.28. अहमिव विरूपतया । As remarked above the Vidushaka in the Sanskrit Drama is always represented as an ugly and deformed person. Cf. विकृतांगवचोवेषहास्यकारी विदूषकः quoted by रंगनाथ.

II. 3. आभरणस्याभरणम् । Cf. Kumara. I.42. कण्ठस्य तस्याः स्तनबन्धुरस्य मुक्ताकलापस्य च निस्तलस्य । अन्योन्यशोभाजननाद् बभूव साधारणो भूषणभूष्यभावः ॥

II 3. 2. दिव्यरसाभिलाषिणा चातकव्रतं गृहीतम् । चातकव्रतम् means 'The vow of the Chataka bird", which, it is said, does not drink water lying on the ground, however thirsty it may be, but always looks up towards the sky and cries aloud piteously until at last rain-drops fall into its mouth. Cf. नीतिशतक 121: सूक्ष्मा एव पतंति चातकमुखे द्वित्राः पयोबिन्दवः । also नीतिशतक 51 रे रे चातक सावधानमनसा etc. दिव्यरसाभिलाषिणा is used here in a double sense. With the Chataka it means "Longing for heavenly water, water coming directly from the clouds" With the King it means "Longing for heavenly love *i.e.* the love of a heavenly nymph". रस means both water and love.

II. 3.4. उत्सुक "Love-sick, love-lorn". विविक्तम् "Solitude" प्रमदवन The name of the pleasure garden attached to the King's palace. Literally "The garden of pleasure".

II. 3.6. का गतिः "What escape (*is there*) from the King's command? I must obey it against my will." चोदित "Deputed, sent forward". आगन्तुकः " A guest ". भवान् दक्षिणमारुतेन प्रत्युद्गतः "Your Honour is being received with respect by the southern wind (i.e. the Malaya breeze). Cf. मालविकाग्निमित्र III. वसन्तः किल एताभिः पवनचलिताभिः पल्लवांगुलीभिः त्वरयतीव भवन्तम्, एतत् प्रमदवनं प्रविशेति। प्राते + उद् + गम् means "To rise and go forward to meet or receive a guest".

II. 3.11. The King understands the expression दक्षिण-मारुतेन used above by the Vidushaka in a second sense also, besides that in which it was used by the Vidushaka. He says "This cool breeze here, is fit to be called दक्षिण-मारुत, not only because it proceeds from the south, but also because it is generous or considerate, solicitous to oblige, attentive to ladies" as is shown in the following stanza. दाक्षिण means "Southern" and also " Solicitous to oblige, attentive to ladies" The epithet दक्षिण is usually applied to lovers (दक्षिणाः कामिनः) who even when they really love one lady, do not fail to please others also by their kindness and solicitous attention. Cf. अनेकासु नायिकासु अवैषम्येण स्नेहानुवर्ती दक्षिणो नायकः (प्रतापरुद्रीय).

II 4. In this stanza the King compares the Malaya breeze to a lover (कामी). Like a lover, who, while really loving one lady, is solicitous to oblige others also, the Malaya breeze too, while impregenating the माधवी creeper with honey-drops (निषिञ्चन्) and thus showing its genuine love (स्नेह) for the same, makes the कौन्दी creeper dance and thus shows its kindness and solicitous attention (दाक्षिण्य) to it. The माधवी is a creeper flowering in spring. It is otherwise called वासन्ती. मधु means " Spring " or the " Vernal season " and so the creeper that flowers in spring comes to be called माधवी (or वासन्ती) "The spring creeper". कौन्दी (Also called माघी) Is a creeper flowering two months before the माधवी, in the month of Magha: By the time that Malaya breeze sets in, the कौन्दी creeper is no longer in flowers, having outlived its day. So the best attention that the Malaya breeze can show unto it is to make it dance. In this stanza the माधवी creeper is compared (suggestively though) to a young sweet-heart and the कौन्दी to an elderly sweet-heart who has already passed the pink of youthful loveliness and perfection.

II. 4. 2–3. ईदृश एव ते अभिनिवेशः भवतु । अभिनिवेश means "Determination". The Vidushaka means to say that the King must henceforth behave himself just like the Malaya breeze, i.e. while he may love Urvashi, he must not be indifferent to Queen औशीनरी, but must do his best to please and placate her. It will appear in the sequel, that the King in fact acts up to this advice of the Vidushaka. Cf. II. 22 4–5; III 4. 4.

II. 4. 6–7. मया न साधु समर्थितम् " I was not right in imagining that etc." आपत्प्रतीकारः "A remedy against distress or afflction."

II. 6. असुलभवस्तुप्रार्थनादुर्निवारम् । असुलभवस्तुप्रार्थनायाः (Ablative) दुःखेन निवार्यते इति । "Very difficult to be withdrawn from its longing for an unattainable object." प्रथममपि "Even as it is, even already." पंचबाणः–The five-arrowed or five-armed God" i. e. Cupid, who is supposed to be armed with the five arrows mentioned in the following stanza:—अरविंदमशोकं च चूतं च नवमल्लिका । नीलोत्पलं च पंचैते पंचबाणस्य सायकाः ॥ किमुत etc. Because the sight of the mango-trees with their fresh tender sprouts and the touch of the gentle Malaya breeze are very potent excitants of the passion of love and immensely intensify the torments of the already suffering, miserable victim of Love.

II. 6. 3. अविरेण इष्टसंपादयिता etc. Cf. Shakuntla III. स्मर एव तापहेतुर्निर्वापयिता स एव मे जातः । and III. 20 below.

II. 6. 4. प्रतिगृहीतं ब्राह्मणवचन् Referring to the belief that the words of a Brahmin are bound to be fulfilled although they might have been uttered casually and off-hand Cf. मालविकाग्निमित्र III. विदूषकः । प्रहरिष्यति तत्रभवती (Scil मालविका) त्वामपराद्धम् ॥ राजा । प्रतिगृहीतं वचः सिद्धिदर्शिनो ब्राह्मणस्य ॥

II. 7. उपोढरागसुलभम् । उपोढेन (प्राप्तेन, प्रवृद्धेन वा) रागेण सुभगम् ॥ भेदोन्मुखम् । " Ready to burst or bloom or open ". ईषद्बद्धरजःकणाग्रकपिशा । ईषद्बद्धैः रजःकणैः अग्रे (अग्रभागे) कपिशा । कपिश– " Yellow " मुग्धत्वस्य च यौवनस्य च मध्ये, " On the borderland between childhood and youth ".

II. 7. 4. मणिशिलापट्टकसनाथः " Furnished with a marble (मणिशिला crystal) seat " or " Furnished with a jewelled stone-seat. " कृतोपचारः । कृतः उपचारः येन । " Honouring (you)". प्रतीच्छति " Recevies " (you) ". The hovering bees dash against the delicate अतिमुक्तक flowers & cause them to fall down. The poet fancies that the अतिमुक्तक bower is as it were receiving the King with honour by making an offering of flowers.

II. 8. कुसुमित is derived from कुसुम + thetermination इतच् (इत) according to Panini V 2–36 तदस्य संजातं तारकादिभ्य इतच् ॥ कुसुमानि संजातानि अस्याःसा कुसुमिता (लता) । धृति बन्ध् " To take delight in " दुर्ललित " Fastidious, hard to please by anything else. "

II. 8. 3. अहल्याकामुकस्य महेन्द्रस्य वैद्यः " The physician to the great Indra who had fallen in love with अहल्या. " Who the physician to Indra is cannot be ascertained Perhaps the reference is not to any particular physician of Indra but only in a general way to any physician in the service of Indra whom the latter must have consulted in his wasting love-malady caused by his unfulfilled passion for Ahalya. According to the Ramayana, Ahalya was the first woman to be created by Brahma. She was given in marriage to गौतम. Indra however became enamoured of her and seduced her by assuming the form of Gautama. When Gautama came to know of this, he expelled Ahalya from his hermitage and caused her to become a stone and to remain in that condition until she should be touched by the feet of Dasharathi Rama.

उन्मत्तौ–" Mad, helpless " " At our wit's end. "

II. 8. 5. We read मा मा एवम् before अतिस्नेहः खलु कार्यदर्शी, following four of Mr. Pandit's eight Mss. We think the words are absolutely necessary to connect the preceding speech of the Vidushaka with the following remark of the King. Cf. मालविकाग्निमित्र IV. 6. कार्यसिद्धिपथः सूक्ष्मः स्नेहेनाप्युपलभ्यते

II. 8. 9. ।। निमित्तं सूचयित्वा Katayavema observes निमित्तं दक्षिणाक्षिस्पन्दनम् । " " An omen i.e. the palpitation or throbbing of the right eye." Cf. also III. 9. च...च । Such a construction shows the contrast or incompatibility between the two things described. इदम् अनंगविचेष्टितम् । Referring to the omen which he has had just now. " This (omen) inspired or produced by Cupid, " किमपि "Unaccountable" अभिमुखीष्विव etc. These two lines describe the condition of his mind immediately after the perception of the good omen.

II. 9. 6. तदा हेमकूटशिखरे etc. Cf. I. 15. 17–22. above.

II. 9. 11. अपहस्तितलज्जः व्यवसायः–" An undertaking or adventure in which I have cast aside all sense of shame."

अपहस्तित=निरस्त, परित्यक्त, दूरीकृत अपहस्तित is the past passive participle from the denominative अपहस्तय् "To take hands off a thing" hence "To abandon, give up, cast away."

II. 9. 16. संप्रधार्यतां तावत् "Think well beforehand (तावत्) whether you are right in going to him" (तावत्) first of all, beforehand.

II. 9. 18. Urvashi means to say that if she were going of her own accord then it would have been proper for her to consider whether it was right to do so. But she is going to Pururavas at the command of Madana (Cupid) and so it is not her business to consider the propriety or otherwise of what she is doing.

अपराजिता नाम शिखाबन्धनविद्या–"The mysterious lore of tying the hair, called अपराजिता 'The invincible'." It seems the preceptor of the Gods–बृहस्पति had taught the Apsarases this mysterious lore of tying the hair to the accompaniment of certain magic charms whereby they could make themselves inaccessible to the demons, the enemies of the Gods.

II. 9. 29. अहो विस्मृतं मे हृदयम्। This shows that Urvashi was so deeply engrossed with thoughts about Pururavas, that she forgot the fact that she was under the influence of the mysterious lore अपराजिता. Well indeed has Prof. Ryder said about her: "She is too much of a woman to be a nymph."

सिद्धमार्गम आसाद्य। "Coming down to the path of the Siddhas." सिद्धs are semi-divine beings possessed of supernatural powers and capable of flying in the sky at a short distance from the surface of the earth. सिद्धमार्गम् आसाद्य, then, means that the Apsarases come down and move across the sky at a short distance from the surface of the ea th.

II. 9. 34. प्रतिष्ठान—Modern Allahabad was the capital of Pururavas. It stood at the confluence of the Ganges and the Jamna, Cf. विष्णुपुराण–राज्यं स कारयामास प्रयागे पृथिवीपतिः । उत्तरे जाह्नवीतीरे प्रतिष्ठाने महायशाः ॥ शिखाभरणभूत "Being as it were the crest–ornament (of प्रतिष्ठान)."

II. 9. 40. आपन्नानुकम्पी "Friend of the distressed" आपन्नान् नुकम्पते इति । This refers to her recent deliverance by Pururavas from the power of the demon Keshin.

II. 9. 47. प्रतीक्षते "Is waiting for you, is expecting you."

II. 9. 55. तिरस्करिणीप्रतिच्छन्ना । "Hidden or concealed by means of the तिरस्करिणी विद्या". तिरस्करिणी is a magic lore by means of which a person can make himself invisible at will. तावत् "For a while, just for some time." विजने "In a retired, solitary place."

II. 9. 62. तूष्णीमास्ते–because his mind is too much occupied with thoughts about Urvashi, to allow him to hear attentively the words of the विदूषक.

II. 9. 65. आत्मानं विकत्थते । "Boasts of herself," "Remains stubborn and indifferent in her pride or haughtiness."

II. 9. 66–67. किं पुनः मानुष्यं विडम्ब्यते "But why do you act the part of a human being?" "You are not a human being, but an Apsaras. So you can, by consulting your supernatural powers, easily find out who is the subject of the King's thoughts. Why do you behave like a poor, miserable, helpless mortal?" विडम्बय् "To imitate, to act like."

II. 9. 68. But to this Urvashi says that she is afraid of knowing by means of her supernatural powers something that is most unpalatable to her. For, who knows, the King might be entertaining thoughts about some other damsel than herself? And if it were true, what a great shock would that revelation bring to her? Here again we see that Urvashi is too much of a woman to be a nymph.

II. 9. 78. हीनसत्व हृदय "Oh timid heart." सत्त्व (n) means "Courage."

II. 10. न च etc. Construe : हे सखे तां सुवदनां प्रियाम् आलेख्ये असमाप्यापि मम नयनयोः उद्बाष्पत्वं न भविष्यति इति न i. e. भविष्यत्येव ।

असमाप्यापि "Even before finishing" (*her likeness in the painting*). उद्बाष्पत्वम् "Being flooded with tears." The construction is ungrammatical, for the gerund (असमाप्य) must have the same subject as the principal verb (भविष्यति). Here, however, अहम् is the subject of असमाप्य and उद्बाष्पत्वं is the subject of भविष्यति. The correct construction would be: तां सुवदनां प्रियाम् आलेख्ये असमापितवतोऽपि मम etc. or तां सुवदनां प्रियाम् आलेख्ये असमाप्यापि अहम् उद्बाष्पनयनः न भविष्यामि (इति) न ॥ For a similar idea Cf. शाकुंतल VI. 22. प्रजागरात्खिलीभूतः तस्याः स्वप्ने समागमः। बाष्पस्तु न ददात्येनां द्रष्टुं चित्रगतामपि॥ Also मेघदूत II. 45. (त्वामालिख्य etc.) मालतीमाधव I. 35.

II. 11. प्रभाव means divine, supernatural power. अलब्धफलनीरसान्—अलब्धफलाश्च ते नीरसाश्च अलब्धफलनीरसाः तान् "Vain, because of their failing to get their object." भवतु पंचबाणः कृती. The King means to say that he is quite powerless before the all-conquering shafts of Cupid, and that if Cupid wants to regard himself as triumphant by frustrating the desires of the King, he should by all means do so and glory himself in having killed a poor victim. For the King is sure to die, if his desires are frustrated. तस्मिन् जने = उर्वश्याम् "In regard to Urvashi" कृती "Victorious," "Blessed."

II. 11. 6. प्रभावनिर्मितेन "Produced by means of divine power," because no natural one was at hand.

II. 11. 9. अविधा or अविदा An interjection showing surprise and fear at the sight of something never seen before. अविधेत्याक्रोशे (काटयवेम); अविदेत्यदृष्टाश्रुतप्राप्तौ(रंगनाथ)

II. 11. 13. अक्षरविन्यास: "A writing", literally "Arrangement of letters".

II. 11. 14. अक्षराणि विसृष्टानि भवन्ति—"Letters may have been sent (to you)." अक्षराणि "Syllables. letters."

II. 11.18. नास्ति अगति: मनोरथानाम् Cf. Kumara. V. 64. मनोरथानामगतिर्न विद्यते। "There is nothing inaccessible or too high for desires." अनुवाच्य "Reading to himself." Cf. II. 19.33. and V. 6.10. प्रसन्न "Happy, felicitous, correct."

II. 11.21. भवानिदानीं प्रसीदतु। The Vidushaka makes a pun upon the word प्रसन्न used by the King in II 11. 18. He means to say, "The guess has shown itself to be प्रसन्न i.e. correct; now be yourself प्रसन्न i.e. pleased to read out the contents of the letter."

II. 11.22. नागरिक—"Belonging to the town, urban, clever, ingenious" as opposed to जानपद "Rustic."

II. 12-13. Construe : हे स्वामिन्, यदि नाम अज्ञाता अहं यथा त्वया संभाविता तथा अनुरक्तस्य तव उपरि (स्याम्) (तर्हि) ननु मे लुलितपारिजातशयनीये शरीरके नंदनवनवाता अपि अत्युष्णा भवन्ति। अज्ञाता— "Being unknown to you", "Whose heart or feelings or sufferings are unkown to you". In stanza 11, Pururavas has made a serious allegation against Urvashi, viz. that Urvashi is indifferent to him although she very well knows how he is pining for her. To this allegation Urvashi replies in this stanza: "If I am really indifferent to you as you imagine me to be, then how is it, that even when I lie upon a bed strewn over with Parijata flowers, my body exposed to the delightful breezes of the Nandanavana, I roll about restlessly and do not find even a moment's relief from the oppressive pangs of love ?" She means to say that the King does not really know the state of her mind; hence she speaks of herself as अज्ञाता. If, on the other hand, the King knew that she is constantly pining for him, he would never make such an allegation against her. लुलितपारिजातशयनीये (Scil. शरीरके) । लुलितं पारिजातस्य शयनीयं येन तस्मिन् । Compare with this, the love-letter written by Shakuntala in Shakuntala III. 15.

तव न जाने हृदयं मम पुनः कामो दिवापि रात्रावपि ।
निर्घृण तपति बलीयस्त्वयि वृत्तमनोरथाया अंगानि ॥

II. 13.1. किं नु खलु सांप्रतं भणिष्यति । That is " Will he say that he loves me or will he say that he does not love me ?"

II. 13.4. कमलनालायमानैः अंगैः । "By means of his limbs that have become thin and flaccid like a lotus-stalk", on account of his deep yearning for you. Chitralekha means to say that it is not at all necessary that the King should say verbally that he loves Urvashi. His emaciated body itself bears eloquent testimony to his love for Urvashi.

II. स्वस्तिवाचनम्—"मंगलार्थकस्वस्तिपदस्य वाचनं पठनं स्वस्तिवाचनम् । पुण्याहवाचनमित्यर्थः । 'स्वस्ति भवन्तो ब्रुवन्तु' इति यजमानः प्रार्थयते, ततो ब्राह्मणाः 'आयुष्मते स्वस्ति' इति उक्त्वा "स्वस्ति न इन्द्र" इत्यादीन् मन्त्रान् पठन्ति । तेन पुण्याहवाचनकर्मणः स्वस्तिवाचनमिति नामधेयम् ॥" Raddi Shastri. स्वस्तिवाचन is the same as पुण्याहवाचन. It is a rite performed immediately before any solemn observance, in which the Brahmins sprinkle water over the Yajamana and invoke blessings on him by means of मन्त्रs from the scriptures. The Brahmins receive, in return for their services, sweet-meats, presents etc. Hence the importance of the स्वस्तिवाचन to the विदूषक. स्वस्तिवाचन literally means "Invocation of good fortune" by means of the repetition of sacred mantras. Mr. Pandit, however, thinks that the Sanskrit equivalent of the original Prakrit सोत्थिवाअण is स्वस्ति–उपायन and not स्वस्तिवाचन. स्वस्ति–उपायन would mean "A present offered to a Brahmin in order to secure his good wishes and blessings at the end of any religious ceremony." समाश्वासनम् "Consolation, encouragement."

II. 14. Construe: हे सखे, पत्रे निवेशितं तुल्यानुरागपिशुनं ललितार्थबन्धं प्रियाया: उदाहरणम्, उत्पक्ष्मण: मम आननेन तस्या: मदिरेक्षणाया: आननं समागतमिव। तुल्यानुरागपिशुनम्=तुल्यप्रेमसूचकम्— "Indicating a love as great as that of mine for her." ललितार्थबन्धम्. "Full of charming meaning." ललित: अर्थबन्ध: यस्मिन् तत्। उदाहरणम्—"Utterance, expression;" more correctly here "Song, piece of poetry.," पत्रे निवेशितम् "Committed to writing on the Bhurja leaf." मदिरेक्षणा "Having bewitching (मदिर = मादक) eyes." उपिक्ष्मणो मम "Of me (who am looking at it) with upturned or raised up eyelashes," i. e. "Of me (who am looking at it) with staring eyes." V. I. उत्पक्ष्मलं–Agreeing with तस्या: आननम्–means the same thing: Vide Translation. तस्या: आननं मम आननेन समागतमिव। "Her face has as it were come into contact with mine." The King means that his reading the letter of Urvashi is not simply a consolation to him but that it is as if her face came into contact with his own. For the words coming from her mouth and committed to writing on the Bhurja leaf, are devoured by the King with his eager eyes.

II. 14. 1. अत्र आवयोः प्रीतिः समविभागा—"Here i. e. now, is our love of equal shares" i. e. "Now it is proved beyond doubt that we love each other equally."

II. 14. 3. अंगुलीस्वेदेन । स्वेद—Perspiration is one of the eight involuntary manifestations of inner love. (सात्त्विकभावs as they are called). अयं प्रियायाः स्वहस्तः "This autograph of my beloved."

II. 14. 6–7. The Vidushaka thinks that the King has asked him to preserve the autograph of Urvashi, as a written evidence of her avowal of love that could be used against her in case she denies her having ever made such an avowal. Therefore he asks the King whether it is possible that Urvashi will ever disappoint him, having made such a confession of her love. The King of course wanted the Vidushaka to preserve that letter simply as a valuable hand-writing and memorial of Urvashi विसंवद्—"To fail to fulfil any promise, to disagree, to fail to produce an expected result."

II. 14. 11. Mark how human Urvashi is in her attitude towards the King. She is afraid of placing herself directly into his presence all of a sudden. So she first sends चित्रलेखा as her agent.

II. 14. 13. तिरस्करिणीम् अपनीय—"Casting aside the veil of invisibily"—"Withdrawing or removing the influence of the तिरस्करिणी spell."

II. 15. संगमे पूर्वदृष्टेव etc. "Like the Yamuna first seen in confluence with the Ganga, but then afterwards seen without the Ganga" as a person proceeds upstream along the river-bank; i.e. The Yamuna by herself is not so charming as she is when united with the Ganga.

II. 12. सुरारिसंभवे दुर्जाते—Referring to her encounter with the demon Keshin. दुर्जात (n) " Misfortune, calamity ".

II. 15. 15. भद्रमुखि " Oh sweet-faced one ! ", i. e. " My good lady ".

II. 16. प्रियदर्शना " Fair one ". तदर्थं आर्त—" Afflicted on her account, pining for her ". प्रणयः " Prayer, solicitation, humble request ". स्मरस्य = स्मरं प्रति " Unto the God of love ". घटन (n) " Joining together ". Mr. Pandit translates the third line as follows : " This prayer proceeding from love is common to us both. " But it is unwarrantable to take स्मरस्य प्रणयः in the sense of स्मरनिमित्तकः प्रणयः । We therefore propose to take स्मरस्य in the sense of स्मरं प्रति and translate : " This is our common prayer unto the God of love ". The prayer that two lovers make unto the god of love is, of course, that they should be united before long.

II. 16. 3. त्वत्तोऽपि निर्दयतरम्—" Even more merciless (to him) than to you."

II. 16. 6. लघु " Lightly, only too readily, willingly." त्वया उज्झितास्मि । Because चित्रलेखा has now become the messenger of Pururavas, she has as it were given up Urvashi.

II. 16. 9. आचारं तावत् प्रतिपद्यस्व.— " Observe first the formality (आचारं)," (of greeting the King appropriately).

II. 17. जयशब्दः सहस्राक्षाद् अगतः पुरुषान्तरम्–" The word " Victory " which proceeding from your mouth, does not greet any other being save the thousand-eyed God (Indra)." Cf. यस्मिन्नीश्वर इत्यनन्यविषयः शब्दो यथार्थाक्षरः I. 1–above.

II. 18. मुनिना भरतेन—The sage Bharata who is regarded as the founder of the drama and the originator of the histrionic art. He is credited with the authorship of that famous work on dramaturgy the भारतीयनाटयशास्त्र. अष्टरसाश्रय: प्रयोग: "The drama viz. लक्ष्मीस्वयंवर which forms the substratum for the display and development of the eight रसs or emotional flavours." The eight रसs which were to be exhibited in the drama in question, are enumerated in the following stanza: शृंगारहास्यकरुणवीररौद्रभयानका: । बीभत्साद्भुतसंज्ञौ चेत्यष्टौ नाटये रसा: स्मृता:। काव्यप्रकाश, IV. 29. The लक्ष्मीस्वयंवर appears to have been a wonderful play that afforded scope for the development of all the eight रसs. नियुक्त: "Has been assigned" (to your ladyships). ललिताभिनयम् "Abounding in beautiful acting" i. e. "Which calls into play a good deal of very fine acting." सलोकपाल: "Together with the लोकपालs i. e.(guardians of the eight quarters of the world." द्रष्टुमना: "Is desirous of witnessing."

II. 18. 4. अनुमान्यतां महाराज: "Secure the assent of His Majesty" to your departure i. e. "Take your leave of His Majesty."

II. 18. 8. अयं जन: "This humble lady here." इच्छति देवेषु अनपराद्धम् आत्मानं कर्तुम् "Wishes to avoid offending against the Gods," "Wishes to make herself blameless towards the Gods." i.e. "Wishes to go at once and thus avoid offending them by disobeying their commands."

II. 18. 13. वैयर्थ्यमिव चक्षुष: "My eyes are useless as it were," since Urvashi has gone away. Singular for the dual.

II. 18. 22. मा भवान् अंगानि मुंचतु "Do not drop your limbs through despair." i. e. "Do not give way to despair." शिथिलय—(Denominative from शिथिल "Slack, loose") "To slacken."

II. 19, हृदयं स्ववशम् "Her free heart," "Her heart of which she was mistress." The Gods were the masters of her body. But of her heart, she herself was the mistress. न्यस्तम् " Was left as it were " (with me). The King fancies that the sighs of Urvashi were due to the passage of her heart from below her breasts to himself.

II. 19. 3. इमां वेलाम् " By this time ". ग्रहीतव्यं भविष्यति= गृहीत भवेत् ।

II. 19. 8. गतम् उर्वश्याः मार्गेण " Has gone to heaven along with her ", " Has gone the way of Urvashi ".

II. 19. 9. वैधेयः " A fool or blockhead " मूर्खवैधेयबालिशाः । इति अमरः । सर्वत्र प्रमादी " Bungles everywhere. "

ततः प्रविशति etc. The following scene in which Queen औशीनरी and her attendant are shown to be in quest of Pururavas and in which the Queen happening to come by an irrefutable evidence of the King's infidelity, exposes him at last and then leaves the stage in indignation has a close parallel in मालविकाग्निमित्र Act III.

II. 19. 18. अन्यथा " Falsely ", " Incorrectly ", " Have I ever before falsely informed Your Majesty ? "

II. 19. 21. विश्रब्धामन्त्रितानि " Confidential talks "

II. 19. 26. इतोमुखम् "Hitherwards", "in this direction".

II. 19. 29. परिवर्तनविभाविताक्षरम् " Which as it turns round and round reveals some letters upon it ". कथम् । वाच्यताम् । " How ? shall I read it ? "

II. 19. 33. अनुवाचय " Read to yourself ". अविरुद्ध " Unobjectionable; not unfit for a lady's ears ".

II. 19. 37. कौलीनम् " Scandal ".

II. 19. 42. 43. अनेन एव उपायनेन i. e. " Taking this very letter of Urvashi as a present to him ".

II. 20. The King believes that the breeze has carried away the भूर्जपत्र and so addresses it. संभृतं पौष्पं रजः "The accumulated pollen of flowers ". मिथ्या = वृथा. " For no purpose, uselessly, in vain ". जानीते हि etc. Construe : हि (यतः) अञ्जनां प्रति आलक्षितप्रार्थनः भवान् एवंविधैः मनोविनोदनफलैः धारितं कामार्तं जनं जानीते। अंजनां प्रति आलक्षितप्रार्थनः भवान् " You who are known to have courted or made love to Anjana." Anjana was the mother of Maruti and the sweet-heart of वायु (wind). एवंविधैः मनोविनोदनफलैः। " By means of such things (i. e. such memorials as a love-letter received from the other party), intended to give some diversion to the mind (मनोविनोदनं " Consolation or diversion of the mind"). The King means, that the wind (वायु) having himself experienced a romantic love for अंजना, very well knows or ought to know the importance of such love-memorials to lovers.

II. 20. 5. म्लायमानकेसरच्छविना " Having the complexion or appearance of a fading *bakula* flower. ".

II. 20. 11. दुरागतम् The Vidushaka plays upon the word स्वागतम् which literally means "Well come", and says " It is no longer a "Well come", but an "Ill come" i.e. the antithesis of a welcome, meaning that the Queen would hardly appreciate the King's welcome, but on the contrary would resent it.

II. 20. 15. This remark of the Vidushaka must be supposed to be made जनान्तिकम् (" Aside, to the King "), although none of the Mss. gives the requisite stage-direction. He does not of course desire that the Queen should hear it. And further the question of the King to which the Vidushaka gives his reply here, is asked जनान्तिकम्. लोप्त्रम् " Stolen property ". लोप्त्रगृहीतः कुम्भीरकः " A thief caught together with the stolen property i. e.

caught red-handed". For the idea Cf. मालविकाग्निमित्र III. कर्मगृहीतेन कुम्भीलकेन संधिच्छेदनं शिक्षितोऽस्मीति वक्तव्यं भवति॥

II. 20. 16. परसमन्वेषणार्थम् "For the purpose of finding out another (Bhurja-leaf) altogether". The King admits that he was searching for a Bhurja-leaf, but says that it was not the one the Queen had brought.

II. 20. 19. सौभाग्यम् "Good fortune" viz. his having received a letter from Urvashi containing a fervent expression of her love for him.

II. 20. 21. The Vidushaka tries to explain away the conduct of the King by saying that the King is suffering from a bilious attack and is therefore acting incoherently like a madman. The bilious attack is due to the fact that the King has not had any food till a late hour (for it is midday now). The Vidushaka therefore suggests to the Queen to arrange for the dinner of the King in order to cure him of his bilious affection. पित्तापशमनसमर्थम् "Capable of quelling down the vitiated bile" (of the King).

II. 20. 23. शोभनं खलु ब्राह्मणेन आश्वासितः वयस्यः। "Very well indeed has the Brahmin come to his friend's help". She says this of course ironically.

II. 20. 25. आश्वासितः पिशाचोऽपि (भवति।) "Even a ghost is pacified or conciliated" by the offering of food. How much more then a bilious attack?

II. 20. 26. आपादयसि "You make me to be, you show me to be". We read so, instead of प्रतिपादयसि which appears rather hackneyed and less idiomatic. बलात् "Forcibly", "Falsely". The King does not approve of the excuse put forward by the Vidushaka. He wants to adhere to the plea that it was another Bhurja-leaf that he was looking for. So he chides him in this manner.

II. 21. रम्भोरु–रम्भे इव ऊरू यस्याः सा रम्भोरूः, तत्संबोधनं 'रम्भोरु'। Although the word ऊरु ends in a short उ, still when appearing as the final member of a compound, it lengthens that उ. Cf. उरूत्तरपदादौपम्ये। विरम संरम्भात् "Give up your anger, or wrath or rage". सेव्यो जनः etc. "Is it ever possible that the master can get angry unless his servant is in the wrong?"

II. 21. 4. मा खलु etc.. "I must not in my light heartedness be carried away by this supplication (अनुनय)." अदाक्षिण्यकृतात् पश्चात्तापात् बिभेमि "But then, I am afraid of the heart-burning or remorse that will be caused to me later on by my *hauteur* (अदाक्षिण्य) in spurning the King's supplication." अदाक्षिण्य "Unkindness, discourteousness, loftiness of manner". Later on (Vide III. 4. 11, 13 etc.), the Queen does in fact feel the bitings of her conscience for her having treated the King's prostration with scant ceremony.

II. 21. 7. अप्रसन्ना (i) "Turbid, muddy"; (ii) "Offended, angry, in a rage".

II. 21. 9. इदम् 'This' i. e. The fact that she has gone away unreconciled and angry. न अनुपपन्नम्। "Is not wrong i. e. is as it should be i. e. it is not unreasonable".

II. 22. प्रियवचनशतोऽपि "Although couched in hundreds of sweet words". रसाद् ऋते "In the absence of genuine love". हृदयं न प्रविशति "Does not appeal to their hearts". तद्विदाम् = मणिपरीक्षकाणाम्। तद्विद् "A lapidary who is expert in his craft". कृत्रिमरागयोजितः This epithet applies both to the मणि and the अनुनय. In the former case it means

" Possessed of an artificial redness i. e. not possessing a natural red colour ". In the latter case, " Accompanied only by a semblance of love (कृत्रिमप्रेम) i. e. not showing any genuine feeling of love ". तद्विदाम् could also be connected with योषिताम् " Women, who are expert in recognizing the genuineness of the supplications of their beloveds. " Cf. मालविकाग्निमित्र III.3.

उचितः प्रणयो वरं विहन्तुं बहवः खण्डनहेतवो हि दृष्टाः ।
उपचारविधिर्मनस्विनीनां न तु पूर्वाभ्यधिकोऽपि भावशून्यः ॥

II. 22. 3. अक्षिदुःखितः " With sore eyes ".

II. 22. 4. स एव " The same " i. e. as before.

प्रणिपातलंघनात् " because of her disregarding my prostration at her feet". अस्यां धैर्यमवलंबिष्ये " I shall assume an attitude of stiffness or patient indifference towards her" Cf. Katayavema " अत्र प्रणामोपाये व्यर्थेऽपि सति उपेक्षा नामोपायः प्रयुक्त इत्यनुसंधेयम् । " Or धैर्यम् may be taken in the usual sense of courage. " I shall take courage as regards her i. e. I shall no longer be afraid of her ", since she has given me an insult in spurning my prostration. Cf. मालविकाग्निमित्र III. 23. मन्ये प्रियाहृतमनाः तस्याः प्रणिपातलंघनं सेवाम् । In other words, the King wishes to use the insult given him by the Queen " As a lever to secure his own purposes".

II. 22. 8. तावत् " For some time ". अवलम्ब्य " To support, to sustain, "

II. 23. उष्णालुः " Oppressed by heat." Katayavema उष्णासहः । It is formed from the word उष्ण according to the Sutra "शीतोष्णतृप्रेभ्यस्तदसहने " इत्यालुच् । (quoted by Katayavema). The v. l. उष्णार्तः is simpler and more direct, but for that very reason, rather suspicious. उपरि निर्भिद्य " Having pierced through or forced open at the top." कर्णिकार

is, according to Mr. Pandit, the Pangara tree, which has blood-red flowers in early spring, when it is still completely shorn of its leaves. The bee is oppressed by the heat of the sun and so resorts to the कर्णिकार bud, having pierced it at the top. The singular षटपद: does not, at first sight, appear to harmonize with the plural मुकुलानि, and hence it has given rise to the v. l. आशेरते षट्पदाः। But if we consider the line a little more closely, we begin to perceive that the plural मुकुलानि is intentionally used by the poet. One and the same bee hops from bud to bud, pierces through and rests in each bud for a while and again proceeds to another. Thus one single bee visits several buds, one single bud not sufficing to give it complete relief from the intense heat of the sun.

कारण्डव: " A kind of water-duck. "

क्रीडावेश्मनि "In the pleasure house or pleasure-pavilion".

Cf. with this description of the noon मालविकाग्निमित्र II, 12.

ACT III.

[Like the Second Act, the third Act also opens with an Introductory Scene (technically called विष्कंभक), which is followed by the Main Scene.

INTRODUCTORY SCENE:—HERMITAGE OF THE SAGE BHARATA.

We learn from a dialogue between two pupils of Bharata, that the drama लक्ष्मीस्वयंवर, staged by Bharata before the heavenly audience, would have proved a complete success, but for one blemish which was due to a very unfortunate slip of the tongue on the part of Urvashi, who, while acting the part of Lakshmi, said, in her absent-mindedness, that her heart was fixed upon Pururavas, when as a matter of fact she ought to have said that it was fixed upon Purushottama. Bharata thereupon pronounced a curse upon her to the effect that she would be banished from heaven. Indra, however, took pity upon Urvashi and conferred a favour upon her by allowing her to remain with Pururavas, his friend in war, until Pururavas beholds the child that she would bear him.

THE MAIN SCENE ;—The main scene really consists of four sub-scenes as shown below :—

FIRST SCENE :—THE PALACE OF THE KING.

The King enters pining for the love of Urvashi. The Chamberlain (Latavya) communicates to him the request of the Queen that the King should be kind enough to go to the terrace of the मणिहर्म्य palace, where she would meet him, and also to pass some time there, enjoying the beauty of the moon-lit night. The King grants the request, but is surprised at such a softening of the Queen's temperament and concludes that the Queen must have been stung with remorse for her discourteous behaviour towards him. The King and Vidushaka go to the मणिहर्म्य.

SECOND SCENE :—THE TERRACE OF THE मणिहर्म्य PALACE.

The King and Vidushaka pass some time in enjoying the beauty of the moon-rise. The King's thoughts, however, return again and again to the all-engrossing theme of his unfulfilled love for Urvashi, and Vidushaka again and again comforts him with hope-inspiring words.

THIRD SCENE :—In the sky.

Urvashi dressed as an Abhisarika and Chitralekha appear in the sky and move towards the terrace of मणिहर्म्य, where the King is sitting with Vidushaka.

FOURTH SCENE :—The terrace of the मणिहर्म्य palace.

Urvashi and Chitralekha get down from the sky, and, remaining concealed by their divine power, overhear the talk of the King and Vidushaka and secretly watch everything that happens.

The King describes to Vidushaka his love-lorn condition and tries to give him an idea of the intensity of his feeling for Urvashi. Urvashi is completely satisfied about the ardour and sincerity of the King's love for her and is almost on the point of revealing herself to the King, but is cruelly disappointed by the arrival of Queen औशीनरी with her attendants.

The Queen explains to the King her object in requesting his presence there at that time, *viz.* that she wants to carry out the vow of प्रियानुप्रसादन (conciliation of the beloved) which she has been observing. In connection with that vow, she worships the Moon and the King and then gives the King an assurance that thenceforward she would treat with indulgence and toleration the King's love-affairs with other women. The Queen then departs and the King once again falls into a fit of love-longing, when he is very agreeably surprised by the sudden appearance before him of Urvashi and Chitralekha.

The King seats Urvashi by his side. Chitralekha leaves for heaven, requesting the King to take care of Urvashi. The King gives expression to his sense of joy and blessedness in being united with Urvashi, and then both of them retire for rest.]

As already remarked, this act opens with an interlude (technically called, विष्कंभ or विष्कंभक, for the meaning of which term *vide,* Introduction, Technical Names p. XXV.) between two pupils of भरत. Of these one viz. गालव speaks sanskrit, while the other called पल्लव uses Prakrit (शौरसेनी). The reason for this discrimination is, that गालव is the senior disciple of भरत, while पल्लव appears to be a novice and hence not yet possessing a facile command over the Sanskrit tongue. This becomes evident when we consider that भरत, when going to heaven entrusts the management of the अग्निशरण to गालव, while, he takes पल्लव along with him as his seat-bearer (आसनं ग्राहितः।) Compare in this connection उत्तररामचरित, Act IV, विष्कंभक.

III. o. 4. त्वम् आसनं प्रतिग्राहितः। "You were made to carry the seat." It seems, Bharata had taken पल्लव to heaven to carry his seat (व्याघ्रचर्म or कृष्णाजिन) wherever he went to serve as his seat-bearer, so to say. अग्निशरण= अग्निगृह or अग्निशाला *i. e.* "The place where the sacred fire is kept," "Fire-sanctuary." संरक्षण "Keeping watch over, looking to." स्थापित "Appointed." दिव्या परिषद् "The celestial audience." आराधित "Pleased, satisfied."

III. o. 10. सरस्वतीकृतकाव्यबन्धे सरस्वतीग्रथिते "Composed by सरस्वती." तेषु तेषु रसान्तरेषु तन्मया आसीत्। The subject is दिव्या परिषद् appearing in III. रसान्तरेषु—अन्ये रसाः रसान्तराणि। रसान्तरेषु thus stands for रसेषु. रस "A sentiment; the dramatic representationof a sentiment or emotion." तन्मया "Deeply absorbed in."

III. o. 12. ते वाक्यशेष: "The remaining part of your sentence." सदोषावकाशः (दोषस्य अवकाशः दोषावकाशः, तेन सहितः।) इव (भाति ।) "Appears to imply a fault," in the dramatic performance. "Seems to hint at a fault."

III. o. 14. वचनं प्रमादस्खलितम् आसीत् "(She) committed a blunder in her speech;" "Was guilty of a slip of the tongue."

III. o. 19. लक्ष्मीभूमिका "The character or part of लक्ष्मी." वारुणी appears to be the name of some Goddess. भावाभिनिवेश "Fixed love," "Strong inclination of the heart."

III. o. 26. भवितव्यानुविधायीनि इन्द्रियाणि "The sense-organs follow, or act according to, destiny—what is destined to happen.

III. o. 37. दिव्यं स्थानम् "Heavenly or celestial residence." प्रेक्षणावसाने "At the end of the theatrical show or dramatic representation." अत्र "Here, in this matter" *i. e.* now that you have been cursed to dwell amongst mortals. त्वयि दृष्टसंतानः भवति । "Sights or beholds the child you will bear him."

III. o. 42. सदृशम् "Befitting, becoming to." पुरुषान्तरविदः "Who knows or can read the hearts (अन्तर) of others."

III. o. 45. अपराद्धा "Has been transgressed or exceeded,"

III. o. 49. The कञ्चुकिन् or chamberlain in Indian Drama is always an old Brahmin of irreproachable character in charge of the royal harem.

III, 1. कल्ये वयसि "In the prime of life," "In vigorous youth." कल्य "Healthy, vigorous, youthful." सर्वः कुटुम्बी "Every married man." कल्पते विश्रमाय "Is able to take rest." परिणतिः "Old age." सादयन्ती शरीरम् "Wasting the body, sapping the vigour of the body." सेवाकारा (supply भवति). "Assumes the form of servitude," *i. e.* "Is passed in servitude." सेवा आकारो यस्याः सा सेवारूपा, सेवामयी वा ।

For सादयन्ती शरीरम we get a variant साधयन्ती प्रतिष्ठाम् which would mean, "Effecting stability or fixity in our position." For the older the man, the better is he qualified for the post of a कञ्चुकिन्.

Katayavema reads सेवा कारापरिणतिः and explains: सेवा कारायाः परिणतिः, बन्धनगृहस्य परिणामः । Ranganatha also has the same reading and explains: कारापरिणतिः बन्धनालयरूपा, यतो वार्द्धकेऽपि मुक्तिः सुतरां नास्तीति भावः । But this reading cannot be accepted as it fails to harmonize with the purport of the stanza. For here the कञ्चुकिन् contrasts the old age of ordinary people with the old age of the class of men to which he belongs. While the old age of others brings rest to them, his old age gives him no relief So one expects to find a word meaning "old age" to appear in a prominent position in the last two lines. This scarcely happens in the case of the reading adopted by Katayavema and Ranganatha. The कञ्चुकिन् does not in fact wish to make any statement about सेवा (service), but about "old age."

III, 1. 1. सनियमया "Who is observing the rules" in connection with the vow of प्रियानुप्रसादन "Propitiating the beloved." (See III. 12. 20) मानम् उत्सृज्य "Giving up my sense of wounded pride." मान means the indignation that a woman feels towards her husband when she finds him attached to another woman (Cf. स्त्रीणामीर्ष्याकृतो मानः कोपोऽन्यासंगिनि प्रिये ।). सन्ध्याजाप्य "Evening prayers."—वृत्तान्तः "The scene or general appearance of things."

III. 2. वासयष्टि "Perching rod." उत्कीर्णाः इव "As if sculptured out." वलभयः "The topmost parts of the palace, the turrets," or according to Mr. Pandit "The slanting wooden supports or struts jutting out from the wall close above the windows and propping up the projecting eaves of the roof." Cf. गोपानसी तु वलभी छादने वक्रदारुणि । अमरः । संदिग्धपारावताः (वलभयः) "In which the doves are confounded with" the volumes of smoke issuing from burnt incense. The doves have the same ashy colour as the smoke issuing from burnt incense. शुद्धान्तवृद्धाजनः "Old matrons of the female apartments." आचारप्रयतः "Clean or holy by or intent upon, the performance of the customary acts." सपुष्पबलिषु स्थानेषु–"In places strewn over with offerings of flowers." विभजते (subject जनः) "Arrange, place, distribute."

III. 3. गतिमान्–"In motion." अपक्षलोपात्=पक्षच्छेदाभावात्, "Because of its wings being unclipt." Mountains, so we are told in the Puranas, had formerly wings and could fly at will. But when they began to harass mankind by their wanton movements, Indra was forced to deprive them of their wings. अनुतट etc. अनुतटं पुष्पिताः कर्णिकारयष्टयः यस्मिन् । कर्णिकारयष्टि means "A thin tall. Karnikara tree." The women holding lights in their hands are compared to thin, tall Karnikara trees, which are covered with bright red flowers.

III. 4. अन्तरित "Shut out". अविनोददीर्घयामा । अविनोदेन–विनोदाभावेन दीर्घाः यामाः यस्याः । "With its hours (याम–a period of time equal to three hours) tediously long for want of diversion". Cf. मेघदूत II. 28. सव्यापारामहनि न तथा पीडयेद्द् विप्रयोगः । शंके रात्रौ गुरुतरशुचं निर्विनोदां सखीं ते ॥

III. 4. 2. मणिहर्म्यपृष्ठ The terrace of मणिहर्म्य, a palace so-called. सुदर्शनः "Well visible". यावद् रोहिणीसंयोगः (supply भवति). "Until the Moon enters the asterism of Rohini."

III. 4. 5-6. देव्याः आरम्भः "What the Queen has proposed to do, what she has set herself about."

III. 4. 12. प्रमार्ष्टुकामा "Wishes to make amends for."

III. 5. Construe : अवधूतप्रणिपाताः मनस्विन्यः पश्चात् संतप्यमानमनसोऽपि (सत्यः) दयितानुनयैः निभृतैः (= निभृतं) व्यपत्रपन्ते ॥ Mr. Pandit construes निभृतैः with दयितानुनयैः, and understands the word निभृतं (which *always* means "Secret, concealed") in the sense of "Open, manifest". According to him, the idea is : "Women who have spurned the svpplications of their beloveds, although later on they might be stung with remorse, are ashamed of openly conciliating them". He says : "निभृत = नितरां भृत. भृत = filled, full. निभृत is therefore="Very full", i.e. "Complete, not half and half, and hence *open*". But such a distortion of the sense of a word to make it yield a meaning which it never has elsewhere, is, in our opinion, scarcely warrantable. We get indeed a very good sense from the stanza by taking निभृतैः as an instrumental adverb (like उच्चैः, नीचैः, शनैः, पराचैः etc.) meaning "Silently, secretly, in their hearts". "Women, though stung with bitter remorse are in their hearts ashamed of conciliating their beloved ones." For adverbs taking instrumental endings see Whitney's Grammar sec. 1112. It must however be confessed that the use of निभृतैः as an adverb in the sense of निभृतम् is unprecedented and that one is, therefore, tempted to change निभृतैः to निभृतम् ।

III. 5. 4-5. गंगातरंगसश्रीकेष "Beautiful like the waves of the Ganges", being made of crystal-steps rising one above another. सश्रीक–श्रिया सहित: सश्रीक: । We may also take the expression to mean "Beautiful with the waves of the Ganges", supposing that the मणिहर्म्य stood quite on the bank of the Ganges.

III. 5. 12. आलोकसुभग "Charming to look at".

III. 6. हरिवाहनदिङ्मुखम् = इन्द्रदिङ्मुखम् = प्राचीनमुखम् " The face of the East" because हरिवाहन "Having yellow, tawny ruddy horses" is an epithet of Indra and he is the lord guardian of the East. उदय here stands for उदयाचल "The rising mountain" i.e. the mountain in the East from behind which the Moon appears to rise. अलकसंयमनादिव "As if by the tying up of the hair or tresses". The idea is :—So long as the Moon had not risen, the face of the eastern quarter (imagined here to be a woman), was shrouded with dismal darkness. Now this darkness is fancied to be the loosely hanging tresses of the lady in the form of the East. The Moon is thought of as the lord of the East, and so long as he was away, the East like a faithful wife did not dress her hair, but allowed them to hang loosely about her face. (Cf. क्रीडां शरीरसंस्कारं समाजोत्सवदर्शनम् । हास्यं परगृहे यानं त्यजेत्प्रोषितभर्तृका ॥). With the arrival of her lord—the Moon—she tied up hair and her face brightened up.

III. 6.2, खण्डमोदकसश्रीक "Appearing like a broken मोदक." Dissolve : खण्डमोदकेन सदृशी श्रीःयस्य ।. The Moon has risen some time after it has grown dark. So the orb cannot be full and complete. The विदूषक therefore compares it to a मोदक which is white in colour, and whose apex is broken off. The मोदक is spherical in size with a small suddenly tapering apex, or मोदक may mean a लाडु or a ball of sugar. राजा द्विजातीनाम् । "The Moon the Lord or King of the twice-born." Cf. अमरः—द्विजराजः शशधरो नक्षत्रेशः क्षपाकरः । We get a variant, राजा ओषधीनाम्, which also would mean "The Moon, the Lord or King of the vegetable kingdom." But in the mouth of the Vidushaka who is a Brahmin proud of his own caste, the words राजा द्विजातीनाम् have a peculiar appropriateness and so this reading is to be preferred to the other.

III. 6. 4. औदरिक "A glutton, a gourmand, an epicure, a lover of delicate fare".

III. 7. रविमाविशते सतां क्रियायै । This refers to the अमावास्या day, when, it is believed, the Moon enters into the Sun. Cf. ऐतरेय ब्राह्मणः—चन्द्रमा वा अमावास्यायाम् आदित्यमनुप्रविशति ॥ On the अमावास्या day, certain Vedic rites and sacrifices are performed by pious, religiously-minded people. So it is said here, that the Moon promotes the religious acts of pious people by his entering into the Sun on the अमावास्या day. सुधया तर्पयते सुरान् पितॄंश्च । It is a common-place of Indian mythology, that the Gods and the spirits of departed ancestors (पितरः "The Fathers") derive their sustenance from the Moon, who is supposed to be a repository of ambrosia (सुधा or अमृत). निशि मूर्छताम् "Prevailing or waxing strong at night", हरचूडानिहितात्मने । It is well-known that the crescent Moon forms the crest-ornament of Shiva.

III. 7. 2. ते पितामहेन–" By your grandfather." See I. 3. 28. and note *ad loc.* Cf. also IV. 19, and V 21. ब्राह्मणसंक्रामिताक्षरेण "Who has conveyed his message to you

(अक्षर "Letters, syllables") through a Brahmin (i.e. myself). The moon is राजा द्विजातीनाम् (III. 6. 2.) so it is in the fitness of things that he should convey his message to the King through the विदूषक, who is a Brahmin (i. e. a द्विजाति *par excellence*.). Dissolve : ब्राह्मणे संक्रामितानि अक्षराणि येन ।

III. 7. 7. Mark the skill of the poet in making the maid-servants retire from a scene where they are no longer required. दीपिकापौनरुक्त्य–" Superfluousness of lights or lamps" i. e. "The superfluous lamps."

III. 7-14. ननु दृश्यत एवं सा । "Why, it is only too apparent or manifest", "That of course is perceptible to the eye." सा refers to अवस्था–the condition of the King's health. The Vidushaka means to say, that the King does already appear so pulled down that no comments are required from him to give an idea of his state of health.

III. 7. 17. एवम् एतत् "That is true." मनसोऽभितापः "Anguish, mental agony or suffering," as contrasted with the physical suffering referred to by the Vidushaka above in ननु दृश्यत एव सा ।

III. 8, विषमशिलासंकटस्खलितवेगः । विषमशिलाः एव संकटं, तेन स्खलितः वेगः यस्य । संकट (n) "An obstacle, obstruction, impediment," Or विषमशिलाभिः संकटः, अत एव स्खलितवेगः । Here संकट would be an adjective meaning "Crowded with, hemmed in, full of." विघ्नितसमागमसुखः "Thwarted in the enjoyment of the pleasure of her union or company."

III. 8. I. परिहीयमान "Drooping, wasting, languishing." The Vidushaka means that since the King appears to him just then lively and cheerful (अधिकं शोभसे) in spite of his physical and mental sufferings, the fulfilment of his desires cannot be far off. This has reference to a belief that approaching good luck produces, mysteriously enough, a sudden cheerfulness in a person, although he is for the time being plunged in great sorrow.

III. 8. 4. निमित्तं सूचयित्वा Cf. II. 8. 9. above.

III. 9. आशाजननैः वचोभिः "With hope-inspiring words", "With hopeful speech." This refers to III. 7. 15. and 8. 3. above. गुरुव्यथम् "Whose suffering is intense." आश्वासयति "Comforts, fills with hope, consoles, reassures." Cf. II. 9. above. Ranganatha thinks that the word दक्षिणः also means here " Clever. He remarks दक्षिणश्चतुरो हि दुःखितमाश्वासयति ।

III. 9. 3. प्रत्याशा means the same as आशा "Hope." अभिसारिकावेषा ; अभिसारिकाया वेषः इव वेषः यस्याः । अभिसारिका is a woman who goes to meet her lover of her own accord being impelled by her passion. Cf. मदेन मदनेनापि प्रेरिता शिथिलत्रपा । योत्सुकाभिसरेत् कान्तं सा भवेदभिसारिका ॥ Quoted by Katayavema.

III. 9. 8. नीलांशुकपरिग्रहः । नीलांशुकस्य परिग्रहः (स्वीकारः) यस्मिन् । "Consisting of a blue robe or silken garment."

III. 9. 11-12. अपि नाम अहं पुरूरवाः भवेयम् इति । "I wish, I were Pururavas", "Would that I were Pururavas".

III. 9. 16. सुभगस्य " Of that blessed one". i. e. of Pururavas.

III. 9. 17. परिवर्तितम् इव—रूपान्तरेण परिणतमिव (Katayavema) "Transformed as it were."

III. 9. 21. हृदयचोरः "The robber of my heart."

III. 9. 25. क्रीडिष्यामि तावत् "I shall trifle with her for a while." मनोरथलब्धप्रियासमागमसुखम् अनुभवन् । This expression is intended to bear two meanings. (i) "Enjoying the pleasure of the company (or union) of his beloved (some sweet-heart of his), whom he has obtained according to his wishes." मनोरथानुरूप लब्धा या प्रिया तस्याः समागमस्य सुखम्। (ii) Enjoying the pleasure of the company of his dear one (i.e. Urvashi), whom he has conjured up in his mind or by his imagination." मनोरथे, मनोरथेन वा (न तु वस्तुतः) लब्धा या प्रिया etc. Or मनोरथेन लब्धं यत् प्रियासमागमसुखम्। The first meaning provokes a passing shadow of jealousy in Urvashi's mind as already calculated by चित्रलेखा.

III. 9. 29. मुग्धे का पुनः etc. "But, child (or simpleton), why do you entertain such a strange thought about the company of the beloved' (which I have spoken of just now)?" अन्या–" Strange unworthy, unreasonable." She means to say "Why do you understand the word प्रिया to mean any other person than yourself?"

III. 9. 31 अदक्षिणम् " Illiberal, unkind, ungenerous, lacking breadth or generosity of out-look."

III, 9. 40. अनिर्भिन्नार्थेन "Whose meaning is not clear," "Of doubtful meaning." आकम्पितम् "Is alarmed," "Is perplexed." Urvashi's mind is full of apprehension, because from the King's words it is not clear whether she herself or some other girl is the object of his longing. स्वैरालापम् "His unrestrained, unreserved utterances."

III. 9. 46. अनुपक्रम्यः- Incurable. आतङ्कः "Malady, disease, एवमादिभिः i. e. उपायैः।

III. 10. सर्वांगीणम्। सर्वमंगं व्याप्नोतीति। "Pervading, or applied to, the whole of the body." मणियष्टयः। "Strings or necklaces of gems." अपोहितुम् to allay, to set at rest, to dispel. लघयेत्–(denominative from लघु " Light, ") " Might lesson or mitigate," तदाश्रयिणी कथा "Some talk bearing upon her."

III. 10. 1. इदानीम् "Now that all your doubts are dispelled." इतः = अस्मिन् राजनि ।

III. 10. 6. मिष्टहरिणीमांसभोजनम् । "A dinner of dainty or delicious venison (हरिणीमांस)." Katayavema and also Ranganatha read " शिखरिणीं रसालं च etc." Ranganatha explains शिखरिणी as follows: एलालवंगकर्पूरादिसुरभिद्रव्यमिश्रितं दुग्धेन सह गालितं सितासंगतं दधि शिखरिणीति उच्यते । दध्यतिरिक्तपूर्वोक्तद्रव्यमिश्रितः पक्वकदलीफलान्तःसारोऽपि तत्त्वइवाच्यः ॥ शिखरिणी is thus a very high-class preparation corresponding to our श्रीखंड or शिखरण, in Maharastra. रसाल = रसालफल i. e. "Mango-fruit". Of the eight Mss. collcted by Mr. Pandit, two alone contain the former reading, while all the six remaining ones contain the latter. The latter reading appears evidently to have owed its origin to some late puritanic Brahmins whose religious susceptibilities were rudely shocked to find a member of their own caste showing such a zest for meat. But if we refer to शाकुन्तल Act II. we find the विदूषक in that play also taking meat. Cf. अनियतवेलं शूलमांसभूयिष्ठ आहारो भुज्यते । We therefore think that ' मिष्टहरिणीमांसभोजनम् ' was the original reading and so have adopted it in the text following Mr. Pandit. प्रार्थयमान. "Yearning for it." संकीर्तयन्—"Talking about it." आश्वसिमि । "I comfort myself," "I take cheer."

III. 10. 8. इदम् = मिष्टहरिणीमांसभोजनम् । संपद्यते "Is easily obtained."

III. 10. 11. एवम्– refers to what the King is going to say below in Stanza 11. "I think that", "I say."

III. 10. 12. असंतुष्टे । "Oh discontented one." Urvashi is not satisfied about the sincerity of the King's love for her even after his passionate declarations in stanza 10.

She wants further proof of his love, before she casts aside the veil and shows herself to the King. चित्रलेखा therefore reproaches her by addressing her as the discontented one.

III. 10. 13. कथम् इव "What is it that you think."

III. 11. निपीडितः "Pressed," "Struck against." कृती— "Blessed, fortunate, lucky" भुवो भरः—"A burden to the earth" i. e. existing to no purpose, in vain.

III. 11. 3. गतायाः। As Katayavema points out the Genitive case is used here with the sense of "Disrespect": षष्ठी चानादरे। Panini II. 3. 38. उदासीन इव "Appears to be indifferent to me; does not notice or mark me; does not deign to regard me."

III. 11, 6. अतित्वरिते "Oh you impatient or hasty one," अनुत्क्षिप्त "Not cast aside," तिरस्करिणी—"Magic veil of invisibility."

III. 11. 9. वाचंयमः "One who has taken the vow of silence." The अनुस्वार in this word is prescribed by Panini VI. 3. 69 वाचंयमपुरंदरौ च।

III. 11, 11. संवृताकारम् adv. "On your guard, collected." आकार is the outward expression of the face serving as an index to the inward thoughts and feelings.

III. 11. 15. अलम् आवेगेन "No cause for anxiety", "do not be worried at all." उपवासनियमवेषा "Wearing a dress suited to the observance of a fast."

औपहारिकम्–उपहाराणां समूहः औपहारिकम्। "Materials of worship." पूजासामग्री–Ranganatha.

III. 11. 23. ननु "Why"—It is an interrogative particle meaning किं न "Is it not that etc."

III. 11. 27. स्वस्तिवाचनम्, or स्वस्तिवायनम् as Mr. Pandit has it, means "A present of sweetmeats given to a Brahmin in order to receive his good wishes and blessing." Vide Note on II. 13. 7. above शुभदर्शना—"Cheerful, pleased in her appearance."

III. 11. 30. उभयमपि घटते "Both (causes) are quite possible." मां प्रति भाति "Appears probable to me."

III. 12. मंगलमात्रभूषणा "Having only the auspicious marks (such as the कुंकुमतिलक, the मंगलसूत्र etc.) as her ornaments." लांछित "Chequered, marked with". वपुषैव प्रसन्ना दृश्यते—"Appears well-pleased towards me, even by her very person." i. e. her bodily appearance itself bears testimony to her change of heart. व्रतापदेशोज्झितगर्ववृत्तिना (qualifying वपुषा) "Which has given up its haughty deportment under the pretext of a vow." A person who is observing a vow has to give up all the passions that trouble the human mind, such as anger, greed, pride, jealousy etc.

III. 12. 8. स्थाने "Deservedly," "It is but proper or in the fitness of things that etc." देवीशब्देन उपचर्यते "Is honoured or greeted by the title देवी." "Is addressed as देवी." The word देवी means both "A queen" and "A Goddess." The King uses it in the first sense; Urvashi, however, understands it in the second sense. न परिहीयते "Does not lag behind," "Is not at all inferior to," "Does not fall short of." ओजस्वितया "In regard to splendour."

III. 12. 9. असूयापराङ्मुखम् adv. "Without the least shadow of jealousy," "In a manner averse to jealousy or free from jealousy." साधु मन्त्रितम् "You have spoken well." "That is well said."

III. 12. 12. पुरस्कृत्य "With reference to," "In regard

to" with the help of मुहूर्तम् उपरोधः "A moment's obstruction or inconvenience."

III. 12. 17. स्वस्तिवाचनवान् "Accompanied by presents of sweetmeats" (given to a Brahmin to receive his blessings.)

III. 12. 20. प्रियानुप्रसादनम्। "Propitiation or conciliation of the beloved one (husband)."

III. 13. अकारणम् "Needlessly." मृणालकोमलं गात्रम् "Your person delicate or tender like a lotus-stem." ग्लपयसि "You waste (your body)." ग्लपय् is the causal form from the root ग्लै to be wasted, to languish, to wither. The form ग्लापय् is also met with. प्रसादम् etc. Construe: य उत्सुकः (सन्) तव प्रसादम् आकांक्षति स दासजनस्त्वया किं प्रसाद्यते। Cf. शाकुंतल

III. लभेत वा प्रार्थयिता न वा श्रियम्।
श्रिया दुरापः कथमीप्सितो भवेत्॥

and कुमार V. न रत्नमन्विष्यति मृग्यते हि तत्॥

III. 13. 2. इमस्सिं = एतस्याम् Although the form इमस्सिं is not sanctioned by Prakrit Grammarians for the feminine gender (the correct form according to them being इमीए or इमाए), still Kalidasa uses it here and elsewhere also (in मालविकाग्निमित्र), as Mr. Pandit points out. बहुमानः "Regard, respect, esteem." This remark of Urvashi shows that her mind is apprehensive that she may fail to win the King's love permanently. For although she is sure, the King has fallen desperately in love with her just now, who knows, his respect and love for the Queen may not assert themselves in the long run? Cf. III. 14. 11, below.

III. 13. 5. नागरिकाः = दक्षिणाः कामिनः। "Gallants." She means to say that cunning lovers show exaggerated attention to their first mistresses or wives, while courting others. दक्षिणाः " Solicitous to please, generous, indulgent." अन्यसंक्रान्तप्रेमाणः-अन्यासु संक्रान्तं प्रेम येषाम् ।

III. 13. 8. एतावत् " So much, this much" *i. e.* "Thus." It thus refers to the quality rather than the quantity of the King's words in stanza 13 above. मन्त्रित is the causal past pass. part. meaning " Has been made to say."

III. 13. 10. सुभाषितम् " Auspicious or good words." प्रति + आचर् "To act against, to oppose." सुभाषितम् refers to the words of the Queen in III. 13. 8, where she says that her vow has already begun to bear its fruit.

III. 13. 13. मणिहर्म्यगतान् = मणिहर्म्यपृष्ठगतान् " Touching or kissing the terrace of मणिहर्म्य."

III. 13. 14. गन्ध " Scent" or " Sandal ointment."

III. 13. 18, औपहारिकमोदकान् " Sweet balls or sweets forming part of the materials of worship."

III. 13. 22. बहुफलः " Attended with immense success." उपवासः " Fast." The fast, in fact, forms only a subordinate part of the vow the Queen is observing.

III. 13. 31. साक्षीकृत्य " In the presence of." अनुप्रसादयामि " I seek to propitiate, please or win the favour of." प्रार्थयते " Wooes." प्रीतिबन्धेन " With affection or friendship." वर्त्तितव्यम् = अवश्यं वर्तिष्ये । " The potential partic. shows *futurity* with *certainty*." Pandit.

III. 13. 35. किंपरम् = किंतात्पर्यम्. " Of what import." Urvashi means to say that she does not know whether the Queen is sincere and means what she says or is only reproachful and sarcastic. विश्वासविशद " At ease with confidence." विशद " Clear, calm, untroubled." *i. e.* delighted, relieved of its tension.

III. 13. 39. महानुभावया " Exalted, noble." पतिव्रतया "Dutiful, single-minded in her devotion to her husband."

III. 13. 43. छिन्नहस्त: "Foiled in his efforts to catch," "Baffled in his attempts to catch." हस्त = हस्तकौशल "Skill of hand" in catching the fish. तादृश: "To that extent, in that manner, so much." The Vidushaka means to say that the King cannot be so dear to the Queen, since she is giving him away to other ladies of her own accord.

III. 13. 48. आत्मन: सुखावसानेन "At the cost or sacrifice of my happiness (or pleasure)." निर्वृतशरीरम् "At ease or happy in his body," "Physically happy."

III. 14. कर्तुमेव वा दासम् । "Or to make me your slave." Katayavema has हर्तुमेव for कर्तुमेव । In this case the sense would be "Or to take me back, your slave."

III. 14. 3. यथानिर्दिष्टम् "As prescribed or laid down" in works dealing with vows and observances. This speech as well as that appearing below, III. 14. 7, shows the self-respect and loftiness of manner possessed by the Queen.

III. 14. 8. अलंघितपूर्व: "Never violated before." नियमः "A rule or restriction in connection with a vow."

III. 14. 11. निवर्तय् "To reclaim, tc turn away, to withdraw."

III. 14. 13. किं पुन: त्वया निराशया निवर्त्यते । Supply the object हृदयं from the preceding speech. "But say, why do you withdraw your heart in despair?

III. 14. 18. विश्रब्धम् "Safely, confidently, securely." स्वैरम् "Of her own accord."

III. 14. 20. अपि नाम "May it be that; shall I hope that; would that; how I wish that etc."

III. 14. 21. कृतार्था भवेत् "May be happy or blessed, or may accomplish her object."

III. 15. कान्तम् "Charming, agreeable" We have preferred this reading of Ranganatha to Mr. Pandit's कान्ता (beloved), which is rather inconveniently separated from the word उर्वशी with which it is syntactically connected as its adjective. साध्वसवसात् मन्दायमाना "Moving slowly or slackening her pace, through fear." पदात् पदम्—"Step after step, step by step." बलादानीयेत "Would be dragged towards me (by her friend)," "Would be brought or led up to me by force."

III. 15. 2. तावत् "At once, forthwith."

III. 15. 3. संज्ञापयति–"Makes a sign or beckons to," in order to acquaint him with the fact.

III. 15. 4. नारायणोरुसंभवा वरोरू: "The fair off-spring of the thigh of Narayana."

III. 15. 7. किमत्र ज्ञेयम् । "What is there to be known?" i. e. it is as plain or evident as anything can be. Mr. Pandit has किमत्राज्ञेयम् "What is there that cannot be known?" The sense of both the expressions is ultimately the same.

III. 16. अनंगक्लिष्टम् "Tormented, afflicted by love." The कुमुद is a species of the lotus that blooms in moonlight only—such is the convention of poets. We read चन्द्रस्यैवांशुभि: instead of चंद्रस्येवांशुभि: as Mr. Pandit does. With our reading the contrast between तपनकिरणै: and चंद्रस्य अंशुभि: becomes emphasized as it ought to be

III. 16. 3. एकासने–"On the same seat as he himself occupies." So that his body comes into contact with that of Urvashi. Cf. III. 16. 9, below (शरीरसंपर्कं गतास्मि ।)

III. 16. 5. एतत् does not refer to सुखम्, but is to be connected with उपपन्नम् in the sense of "Just now."

उपपन्नम् "Attained, obtained." The King means to

say "I was not happy before I met उर्वशी but now that उर्वशी has come to me, I may say that I am really happy."

III. 16. 9. अस्य प्रणयवतीव "Like his beloved or loving wife." पुरोभागिनीम् "Officious, obtrusive, meddlesome, forward." पुरोभागिन् means "One who takes the first share or more than his proper share," hence "One who meddles in another's affairs, obtrusive, presmptuous. meddlesome."

III. 16. 11. कथम् इहव युवयोः अस्तमितः सूर्यः । Mr. Pandit translates "What, have you been here since evening?" According to him this remark of the विदूषक is called forth by Urvashi's words: हला देव्या दत्तो महाराजः । The Vidushaka thinks that Urvashi and Chitralekha must have heard the words of the Queen in III. 13. 26. and must have been there all the evening though remaining invisible all along. But we think that this is not at all a satisfactory explanation. From III. 16. 3 and 16, 7, we see that Urvashi and Pururavas were sitting quite close to each other. And we may presume even that Pururavas began to toy with Urvashi by way of fondling and caressing her and that she too returned in her own way his fondlings and caressings, cf. III. 17 below. Now this appears rather shocking to the Vidushaka and he says in his usual light-hearted vein; "I wonder, how the Sun has set to you even here i. e. even in the presence of myself and Chitralekha." "How the Sun has set to you" means "How do you openly carry on these fondlings and caressings, which ought to be done in *strict privacy, after the Sun has set?*" In the present case of course the Sun has already set. Vidushaka's point, however, is that they must not do these things openly.

III. 17. व्यापारं व्रजसि । (Ranganatha explains व्यापार as

आलिंगनादि–आरम्भ) "Take loving liberties with my person." कस्यानुमते "By whose consent."

III. 17. 2. विज्ञाप्यम् "Request," "Prayer."

III. 17. 6. वसन्तानन्तरे "Following the vernal season or spring." उपचरितव्यः=सेवितव्यः, उपस्थातव्यः। उप+चर् "To wait upon, to attend upon, to worship."

III. 17. 12. अनिमिषैः नयनैः मीनाः विडम्ब्यन्ते। "Fishes are mocked with winkless eyes." It is believed that the denizens of heaven never close their eyes, even for a moment in winking.

III. 18. अनिर्देश्यसुखः। "The happiness in which is indescribable." अनिर्देश्यं = वक्तुमशक्यम्।

III. 18. 2. अकातरा भूत्वा "Banishing all fear or apprehension from your mind."

III. 18. 10. वृद्धिः "Good fortune."

III 19. सामन्तमौलि etc. Dissolve : सामन्तानां मौलिषु ये मणयः तैः रंजितं शासनम् (आज्ञापत्रम्) एव अंकः (वैशिष्ट्यापादकं चिह्नं) यस्य। "Having the distinguishing mark viz. that the royal edicts (mandates or commands) are tinged with the gems in the coronets of the feudatory princes." i. e. are humbly borne on their heads by feudatory princes, and are implicitly obeyed. सामन्त—"A borderchief, a tributary prince," who obeys the commands of the universal soveriegn. एकातपत्रम् अवनेः प्रभुत्वम्। (Cf. एकातपत्रं जगतः प्रभुत्वम्। Raghu. II. 47.) "Sovereignty of the whole world, characterized by one single umbrella." A universal monarch alone possesses the privilege of using the आतपत्र or छत्र. कान्तम् आज्ञाकरत्वम् "Charming servitude."

III. 19. 2. नास्ति मे विभवः etc. Urvashi means to say that she ought, really speaking, to return the compliment of the King by saying something more beautiful in admiration of the King. But she cannot excel the King in this matter-so exquisitely fine is the sentiment expressed by the King.

III. 19. 3. विरुद्धसंवर्धनः "Giving rise to contraries or paradoxes."

III. 20. ते एव "Those very i. e. those that used to pain or torment me." मनोऽनुकूलाः "Pleasant or agreeable to the mind." This reading appears to us better than ममानुकूलाः adopted by Mr. Pandit, because it stands in clear contrast to सुखयंति गात्रम् in line l. "The rays of the Moon delight the *body*: the shafts of cupid please the *mind*." संरंभरूक्षम् रोषदारुणम्। "Harsh (as if) through anger or malice." अनुनीतम् इव–कृतसान्त्वनमिव "Is pacified or appeased as it were."

III. 20.2. चिरकारिका–"Delaying, tarrying."

III. 21. उपनतम्=अधिगतम्–"Obtained." Literally "Which comes to one's share." रसवत्तरम् "More agreeable." निर्वाणम् "Complete or supreme happiness, satisfaction, gratification." तप्त "Scorched by the heat of the Sun." Cf. मृच्छकटिक I. सुखं हि दुःखान्यनुभूय शोभते। घनांधकारेष्विव दीपदर्शनम्।

III. 21.3. वासगृहम् "Inner apartment," "Bedchamber."

III. 21.7. अभ्यर्थना–"Earnest wish," "Eager desire." शतगुणिता इव "As if it were drawn out in length or extended a hundredfold, "As long as a hundred nights." Katayavema reads शतगुणितामिव मे गता त्रियामा। and explains: एकरात्रिः शतरात्रितुल्यकालतां गता। "Attained as it were to hundred-fold-ness."

सुभ्रु Vocative sing. According to पाणिनि, the form ought to be सुभ्रूः. But Sanskrit poets often use the form सुभ्रु. Cf. भट्टिकाव्य VI. 11. कुमारसंभव V.43. मालतीमाधव III. 8; Mallinatha sets forth the pros and cons of the case in his comment on कुमारसंभव V.43.

ACT IV.

[The fourth Act opens with an Introductory Scene (technically called प्रवेशक) which serves the purpose of narrating the events that have transpired since the union of Pururavas with Urvashi as described towards the conclusion of the third Act, and of introducing the reader to the main scene of the Act.

Introductory Scene:—(LOCALITY NOT INDICATED.)

The introductory scene contains a dialogue between two Apsarases, सहजन्या and चित्रलेखा—friends of Urvashi. From their conversation we learn that Urvashi and Pururavas had gone to the Gandhamadana Grove for their honey-moon. But before they had passed many days there, a strange mishap took place resulting in their separation. Pururavas once came across a beautiful Vidyadhara damsel sporting on the sands of the Mandakini, and was so fascinated by her charms, that he at once began to devour her beauty with his eyes. When Urvashi saw this, she was so enraged that she spurned all his apologies and prostrations, and, in the frenzy of her jealous rage, rushed into the charmed and forbidden Grove of Kumara and was immediately transformed into a creeper. Pururavas has gone mad with grief at her disappearance and has been searching for his lost beloved day and night, in every nook and corner of the Grove. The Apsarases hope and pray that the King be restored to his beloved before long.

The main scene of Act IV is for the most part, a soliloquy of Pururavas gone mad over the loss of Urvashi.

In the words of Prof. Ryder it is a long lyrical monologue addressed to the various creatures and objects of the forest and inspired by despairing passion. Kalidasa was perhaps the first to introduce such a lyrical melodrama in the ancient Indian Theatre. It is a song play within the drama. Later dramatists like भवभूत (मालतीमाधव, Act 9), राजशेखर (बालरामायण, Act 5), जयदेव (प्रसन्नराघव, Act 6), हनुमत् (महानाटक, Act 4), and भास्करभट्ट (उन्मत्तराघव) have tried to imitate it with some degree of success. Its pre-eminently musical character has been perhaps respnosible for the insertion of Apabhramsha stanzas and the stage-directions for their recitation. (Vide Introduction, p. XII-XIII.).

The main scene of Act IV contains very little of dramatic action. The locality appears to be somewhere in the neighbourhood of the Gandhamadana Grove. It is a rainy day in summer. The King is presented in a frenzied and woe-begone state—almost on the verge of madness and raving—addressing the various objects he comes across—animate, sensible or insensible—birds and beasts, trees and rivers, rocks and mountains, clouds and lightnings—and beseeches them to assist him in his search of Urvashi. He indulges in all sorts of speculations and fancies about the sights and sounds he comes across, but is cruelly disappointed by them one and all. At last he lights upon a very bright precious stone which is announced by an invisible voice to be the famous संगमनीय gem, which, when worn on the body, is capable of restoring a person to his lost beloved. The King holds it in his hand and embraces a creeper which is immediately changed into Urvashi. The King is overjoyed by the incident. Urvashi greets him with happiness and victory, and relates to him how she had been transformed into a creeper, and how as a creeper she had witnessed his sad plight all along. Pururavas shows her the संगमनीय gem which she wears on her head. Urvashi reminds Pururavas of their long absence from their capital and requests him to return. Pururavas agrees and both of them depart for प्रतिष्ठान in an aerial car improvised by Urvashi from out of a cloud at his request.

It should be noted by the reader that although Pururavas is represented as having gone mad, there is a certain method in his madness—a certain coherency and reasonableness about his utterances. It is much more of a poetic madness than a real one in the strict sense of the term. The King behaves like a madman only in so far as he seeks information in all seriousness about his beloved from sources which are least of all ever likely to give any such information. In all other respects he appears to be quite normal in respect of the powers and functionings of his mind and brain. A similar type of madness is to be found also in the case of the Yaksha in the Meghaduta.]

IV. o. 1. विमनस्का "Sad, uneasy at heart".

IV. o. 5. छाया "Complexion, appearance". म्लायमान is irregular, since the root म्लै is Parasmaipadi and not Atmanepadi. We should better have म्लायत्. निर्वेद "Distress, anxiety". समदुःखा भवितुमिच्छामि "I wish to participate in your sorrow".

IV. o. 10. अप्सरोवारपर्यायेण "In the course of the rotation or coming round, of the turn for the Apsarases".

वार: "The time or turn of doing anything". पर्याय: "Rotation, coming round". सूर्यस्य पादमूलोपस्थानम् = सूर्यस्य उपस्थानम्। "Reverent service of or attendance upon the feet of the Sun". We are told in the भागवत and कौर्म Puranas, that the ऋषिs, गन्धर्वs, यक्षs and Apsarases have to attend upon the Sun by rotation. The reason why चित्रलेखा feels sore anxiety and yearning for Urvashi is that she misses her very much while attending upon the Sun, alone, and further that on account of her continuous engagement for two months in the sphere of the Sun, she is prevented from paying occasional visits to Urvashi.

IV. o. 15. इमानि दिवसानि "During these days". This is accusative of time, according Panini II. 3. 4, कालाध्वनोरत्यन्तसंयोगे। प्रणिधानस्थितया "While I stood in meditation, put myself in contemplation". अत्याहितम् "A great danger, misfortune, calamity". Strictly speaking the word ought to be अत्यहितम्. The second अ seems to be lengthened on the analogy of the word विश्वामित्र (which is really equal to विश्वमित्र). उपलब्धम् "I preceived, or learnt".

IV. o. 21. किल "It would seem or appear that etc." रतिसहाय "Companion in love-sport (रति)". गन्धमादनवनम्–गन्धमादन (m.) is the name of a suburban grove of ओषधिप्रस्थ, the capital of हिमालय. Cf. कुमारसंभव VI. 46, यस्य (ओषधिप्रस्थस्य) चोपवनं बाह्यं सुगन्धिर्गन्धमादनः।

IV. o. 24. स नाम संभोग: "That indeed is an ideal enjoyment".

IV. o. 28. मन्दाकिनी "The celestial Ganges". पुलिनम् "Sandy bank". निध्याता "Was gazed at", "Was looked at intently".

IV. o. 31. दूरारूढः खलु प्रणयः असहनः । Cf. रत्नावली III. 15 प्रकृष्टस्य प्रेम्णः स्खलितमविषह्यं हि भवति ।

IV. o. 36. गुरुशापसंमूढहृदया । "With her heart bewildered by the curse of her preceptor sage भरत." Urvashi being a nymph ought to have known by her supernatural power that the grove of कुमार that she was about to enter was forbidden to women. But on account of the curse of भरत her memory was so stupefied, that she could not know the prohibition in regard to the grove of कुमार. Cf. IV. 40. 14-25. below. काननोपान्त...etc. Katayavema reads कारणान्तरनिवर्तिना, while seven of Mr. Pandit's eight Mss. read कारणान्तरपरिवर्तिना, The meaning is: "Which would cease to be (निवर्तिना) or would undergo restoration (परिवर्तिना), through some unknown cause". But if we adopt this reading, the remark of सहजन्या (अवश्यं किमपि...समागमकारणं भविष्यति।) in IV. o. 52. becomes redundant.

IV. o. 40. अलंघनीयम् "Beyond the reach of." Cf. मालतीमाधव I. 23. सर्वंकषा भगवती भवितव्यतैव । एकपदे "All of a sudden." अनर्थः "Dire calamity, misfortune".

IV. o. 45. अहोरात्रान् । अहश्च रात्रिश्च अहोरात्रः । Acc. of Panini V. 4. 87. अहःसर्वैकदेशसंख्यातपुण्याच्च रात्रेः । निर्वृतानामपि उत्कण्ठाकारिणा मेघोदयेन । Cf. मेघदूत I. 3 मेघालोके भवति सुखिनोऽप्यन्यथावृत्ति चेतः । Also IV. 3 below.

IV. o. 52. आकृतिविशेषाः "Noble, excellent forms *i. e.* persons". आकृतीनां विशेषाः आकृतिविशेषाः । अनुग्रहनिमित्तं समागमकारणम् । The word अनुग्रहनिमित्तम् could be taken either as a तत्पुरुष or as a बहुव्रीहि compound. In the former case the sense would be: "Some cause of reunion, which would bring about the termination of the curse." In the latter case the meaning would be: "Some cause of reunion brought about by the termination of the curse" "अनुग्रह (lit. favour, kindness) is the same as उच्छाप or प्रतिशाप i. e. "The termination of a curse." The curse in this case is the विधि or समय (i. e. prohibitive condition) referred to in IV. 40. 23 below. काटयवेम reads अनुग्रहीतृकम् । उदयोन्मुख "About to rise."

IV. o. 58. आः इति कोपे निपातः । आः is an exclamation of anger. हन्त "Alas."

IV. 1. संनद्धः (i) "Fully equipped" for showering down, ready to shower, (ii) fully armed or accoutred" for battle. दूराकृष्टम् (i) extending far and wide" (ii) "stretched to its utmost." न नाम "Not indeed as I imagined". पटुः "Violent, quickly descending, pelting." कनकनिकषस्निग्धा। कनकस्य निकषः कषणरेखा तद्वत् स्निग्धा । "Glistening like a Streak of gold on a touch-stone." Cf. सौदामन्या कनकनिकषस्निग्धया दर्शयोर्वीम् । मेघदूत I. 39.

IV. 1. 1. रम्भोरू: "Whose thighs are (full, round and fair) like (the inner part of) the plantain tree."

IV. 2. पिहिता = अपिहिता "Concealed, hidden." स्वर्गाय = स्वर्गं गन्तुम् । The dative acc. to Panini II .14. क्रियार्थोपपदस्य च स्थानिनः ॥ भावार्द्रम् "Dripping with affection, saturated with love." कोऽयं विधिः "What a .(queer) fate is this" "What an act of fate is this!"

IV. 2. 1. परावृत्तभागधेयानाम् । परावृत्तं भागधेयं येषां or येभ्यः ते परावृत्तभागधेयाः । "From whom fortune has turned its back" अनुबन्धि "Closely following upon."

IV. 3. For the construction with two चs, see Apte's Guide Sec. 273. अहोभिः भवितव्यम् "The days are sure to be" निरातपत्वरम्यैः "Pleasant on account of the passing away (diminution or lessening) of heat.' काट्यवेम reads निरातपर्द्धिरम्यैः । निर्गता आतपस्य ऋद्धिः सामग्री येषां तानि निरातपर्द्धीनि । तानि च तानि रम्याणिच्व, निरातपर्द्धिरम्याणि । तैः । "Pleasant on account of the intensity of heat having passed away," We have, however, rejected this reading because it is cumbrous as compared with निरातपत्वरम्यैः ।

IV. 3. 1. मनसः परितापवृद्धिः "The growing distress of my mind." मुनयोऽपि व्याहरन्ति etc. Cf. महाभारत V. 132. 16. कालो वा कारणं राज्ञो राजा वा कालकारणम् । इति ते संशयो मा भूद् राजा कालस्य कारणम् ॥ प्रत्यादिश् "To order back, to countermand or counter-order." अथवा etc.....supply संपद्यते after संप्रति. "My royal paraphernalia consist of or are constituted by the signs (tokens) or accompaniments of the rainy season." प्रावृषि भवानि प्रावृषेण्यानि तैः ।

IV. 4. श्रीवितानम् "A beautiful, splendid canopy." निचुलः "A kind of reed." घर्मच्छेदात्–घर्मस्य उष्णकालस्य नाशात्, गमनात् । "On account of the passing away of summer." पटु "Shrill sharp-sounding." बंदिन् m. "A bard, panegyrist, minstrel." The peacocks are well-known as being overjoyed at the advent of the rainy season, which they welcome with loud shrieking and gay dancing. धारासारोपनयनपराः—This applies to the clouds as also to the merchants (नैगमाः). (i) धारासारस्य उपनयने तत्पराः । "Bringing down showers (आसार) of rain (धारा)." (ii) धारारूपं सारं (धनम्) तस्य उपनयने तत्पराः । "Presenting streams of wealth" (by way of the payment of taxes). We read चाम्बुवाहाः for सानुमन्तः This latter reading does not harmonize with धारासार, which means "Showers of rain." Moreover in adopting it we fail to get the conjunctive particle च, which is badly wanted to make the sense complete.

IV. 4. 1. परिच्छद "Paraphernalia, external appendages of royalty, royal insignia." व्यवसितस्य मे "As I make up my mind to search her out." सन्दीपनम् "Aggravation, intensification."

IV. 5. कन्दली is what is called कर्दळ in Marathi. The yellow variety of this plant has red lines upon the petals of its flowers. राजि "A streak or line." सलिलगर्भैः "Surcharged with water. अन्तर्बाष्पे "Suffused with tears." मां स्मरयति "Makes me remember painfully; reminds me painfully of." Cf. for a similar idea रघुवंश XIII. 29.

IV. 5. 1. सूचय् "To trace out, to ascertain."

IV. 6. स्पृशेत् "If she were to touch." वनस्थली "Forest-ground," "Forest-site." पश्चान्नता "Sunk or depressed towards the heels." गुरुनितम्बतया "On account of the heaviness or stoutness of her hips." Cf. शाकुन्तल III. 7. अभ्युन्नता पुरस्ताद् अवगाढा जघनगौरवात् पश्चात्। etc. चारुपदपंक्तिः "Line of beautiful foot-prints." अलक्तकांका "Tinged with red lac (अलक्तक)." He means to say that if Urvashi were to touch the ground with her feet, it would be possible to have some trace of her. But she being a nymph—a celestial being, capable of moving unsupported in the air—there is very little possibility of her walking so close to the ground as to leave behind her foot-prints.

IV. 6. 1 उपलक्षणम् "Mark, sign, vestige."

IV. 7. Construe : इदं (यद् दृश्यते तद्) असंशयं निमग्ननाभेः (तस्या उर्वश्याः) निपतद्भिः (अत एव) हृतोष्ठरागैः नयनोदबिन्दुभिः अंकितं, रुषा भिन्नगतेः च्युतं शुकोदरश्यामं स्तनांशुकं (भवति)। ओष्ठराग "Lip-rouge." निमग्ननाभि "Having a deep navel." Depth of the navel is regarded by Sanskrit poets as a sign of beauty in women. रुषा भिन्नगतेः "Moving with faltering

steps through rage." श्याम "Dark-green" स्तनांशुकम् "Breast-garment" or "Breast-scarf."

IV. 7. 1. नवशाद्वलम् "A fresh green sward or lawn." इन्द्रगोप m. a kind of red insect. प्रवृत्ति "News." अवगमयितव्या= अवगन्तव्या. निर्जन "Lonely, desolate." शैलेयस्थली "Rocky soil." आसारोच्छ्वसित "Emitting or sending forth vapour on account of rain-showers," Cf. रघुवंश XIII. 29. आरूढ "Perched or mounted upon."

IV. 8. प्रबलपुरोवात "Violent frontal wind." नर्तित "Set a-dance." Mr. Pandit reads ताडित "Struck, beaten." शिखण्ड: "Crest." दूरोन्नमितेन "Out-stretched; elongated" केकागर्भेण "Full of shrieking notes." कण्ठेन "With his neck etc." The Instrumental is according to Panini II. 3. 21. इत्थंभूतलक्षणे । (उपलक्षणे तृतीया ।)

IV. 9. उत्कण्ठा उद्गत: कण्ठो यस्या: सा । "With a prominent." दीर्घापाङ्गा "Having far stretched eye-corners" i. e. "Having long and large eyes." सितापांग "Having white eye-corners." दृष्टिक्षमा–दृष्टे: दर्शनस्य क्षमा योग्या "Worthy of being seen." त्वया दृष्टा भवेत् । "May I hope that you have seen?" Mark the alliteration in this stanza.

IV. 10. मृदुपवनविभिन्न: "Dishevelled or ruffled by the gentle breeze" विनाश "Disappearance". काटयवेम reads मत्प्रियाविप्रणाशात् ॥ घनरुचिरकलाप: "His thick and charming plumage." नि:सपत्न: "Without a rival, rivalless". केशहस्त: "Excellent hair". The words पाश, हस्त, पक्ष and कलाप when combined with केश convey the idea of excellence and abundance. रतिविगलितबन्धे "Become loose in the course of amorous sport". This corresponds to मृदुपवनविभिन्न: ॥ कुसुमसनाथे "pecked with dowers". सति "If it were cresent or existing here"; i.e. "In the presence of, by the side of, in comparison with ". किं करोति एष बर्हीं । " What would this peacock have to boast of then ? " Cf. रघुवंश IX. 67.

IV. 10. 2. आतपान्त " The termination or close of the summer season ". संधुक्षित " Inflamed ". मद " Passion "

IV. 11. मदनदूतिम् " The messenger of Cupid ". The impassioned notes of the cuckoo bring estranged lovers together as they cannot hold out any longer and therefore the cuckoo is called Cupid's messenger. Strictly speaking the word दूती ends in long ई. But Kalidasa uses it often with short इ, evidently *metri causa.* Cf. रघुवंश XVII. 53; XIX. 18, 23; कुमारसंभव IV. 16. मानावभंगनिपुणम् " Skilled or dexterous in breaking down or taming the pride of women ". अमोघम् अस्त्रम् " Unfailing weapon. " Cf, रघुवंश IX. 47 and कुमारसंभव III. 32.

IV. 11. 1. किमाह भवती etc. This is what is technically called आकाशभाषित " Speaking in the air to some one and answering his imagined questions ".

IV. 12. आत्मगतम् " Existing in me ", " Arising on my side ", " So far as I am concerned ". प्रभुता " Ascendancy, tyranny, dominion ". भावस्खलितानि " Deviation from faithful love ". काटयवेम remarks : नायिकान्तरदर्शनादीनि । न अपेक्षते "Does not wait for, does not stand in need of ".

IV. 12. 1. कथाच्छेदकारिणी " Cutting short or interrupting our talk (conversation) ".

IV. 13. सम्यग् आहुः " It is well said that ". शीतलम् " Cool " i.e. not painful. आपद्गत " Distressed, in misery ". राजजम्बूद्रुम " The royal (i. e. best kind of) Jambu tree ". अभिमुखपाकम् = प्रत्यासन्नपाकम् " About to ripen ".

IV. 13. 1. एवंगतेऽपि " Even though it is so ", " Nevertheless " इतो वयम्–" Hence away we (go) ". प्रियाचरण-

निक्षेपशंसी "Indicating the tread of my beloved". दक्षिणेन "To my right" or "Towards the south, in the southern direction."

IV. 14. मानसोत्सुकचेतसाम्। Cf. "कालान्तरे मानसस्य हिमदुष्टत्वात्, हिमस्य च हंसानां रोगहेतुत्वात्, अन्यत्र गता हंसाः पुनर्वर्षासु मानसमेव गच्छन्तीति प्रसिद्धिः।" मल्लिनाथ on मेघदूत I. 11.

IV. 15. पाथेयं बिसम् उत्सृज "Lay aside (for a while) the lotus-stalk–your provision for the journey". पाथेय from पथिन्–पथि साधु पाथेयम् "Good for, serviceable on, the way"; hence "Provisions for a journey". Vide Panini IV. 4. 108. तावत् "First, before doing anything else". प्रणयिक्रिया "Service to the suppliant or petitioner"; "Fulfilling the desire of the pretitioner".

IV. 16. नतभ्रूः "Having arching brows". मदखेलपदम् "Consisting of steps graceful through passion". गतम् "gait".

IV. 17. विभावितैकदेशेन etc. The person with whom only a part of the stolen property has been detected is liable to restore the whole of that property.

IV. 17. 1. चोरानुशासी "chastiser or punisher of thieves".

IV. 18. रथांगनामन् = चक्रवाक. रथांगं चक्रं तेन युक्तं नाम यस्य। "Whose name contains the word चक्र which is expressive of a limb or part of a chario".

रथांगश्रोणिबिंबया "Whose hips (श्रोणिबिंब) are round like a chariot-wheel". Cf, I. 11. रथी "An eminent warrior". वृतः "Filled with, overflowing with". Mark again the alliteration.

IV. 18. 1. कः कः इत्याह। The bird cries out कः, कः of its own sweet will and without intending its cries to have any meaning for the King. The King, however, understands कः कः to mean "Who are you? who are you?"

and proceeds to answer this imagined question in stanza 19. बा सामत "That won't do". Cf. Marathi: अशाने नाहीं तें भागणार

IV. 19. सूर्याचन्द्रमसौ etc. The genealogy of पुरूरवस् is as follows: on his father's side he was the son of बुध, who himself was the son of the Moon. On his mother's side he was the son of इळा, the daughter (originally इळ, the son) of मित्र or the Sun. Thus the Sun was his मातामह (मातुः पिता) and the Moon was his पितामह (पितुः पिता). स्वयं वृतः etc..Cf. शाकुंतल III.19. परिग्रहबहुत्वेऽपि द्वे प्रतिष्ठे कुलस्य मे। समुद्ररसना चोर्वी सखी च युवयोरियम्।

IV. 19. 1. उपालप्स्ये "I shall remonstrate with him."

IV. 20. इति च...मयि च etc. "Although..and yet." पृथग्विस्थितिभीरुता "Timidity in regard to separation." भावः "Attitude, disposition." पराङ्मुखः "Averse to." विधुरे "Separated from my beloved." The belief is that the चक्रवाक is so very fond of its mate that it does not brook even the least separation from her. It goes on crying plaintively even though its mate is accidentally screened from its view by a lotus-leaf at night.

IV. 20. 1. भाग्यविपर्ययाणां प्रभावः "The result of the reversal of my fate," We have thought it fit to reject Mr. Pandit's reading: भागधेयानां विपर्ययेण प्रभावप्रकाशः। on account of its clumsiness.

IV. 21. रुणद्धि "Stops, holds back, prevents from going away." ससीत्कारम्। "Murmuring or hissing."

IV. 21. 1. मधुकरं प्रणयिनं करिष्ये "I shall implore or beseech the bee (lit. the honey-gatherer).

IV. 22. यदि अपास्यः "If you had drunk i. e. enjoyed.' We get a variant अवाप्स्यः "If you had obtained."

IV. 22. 1. साधयाम: । "Let us go away." साधय् "To go away." नीपस्कन्धनिषण्णहस्त: "Placing or resting his trunk on a branch of the नीप tree." The नीप blossoms and bears fruit in the rainy season.

IV. 23. अचिरोद्गतपल्लवम् "Newly sprouted," "Bearing fresh shoots." आसवसुरभिरसम् "Full of juice as fragrant as honey (आसव; or liquor)." सल्लकीभंगम् "A twig or branch of the सल्लकी tree", of which elephants are believed to be very fond. अभिलषतु "May he desire (i. e. enjoy, taste)."

IV. 23. 1. आह्निकम् "Meal, daily food."

IV. 24, मदकल "Ruttish, infuriated through rut." This is addressed to the elephant. युवतिशशिकला "The bright lunar digit among the stars of young women." We can also take मदकल...शशिकला as one compound word meaning: "The bright lunar digit in the midst of young women uttering sweet, gentle, inpassioned sound." यूथिका-शबलकेशी "Having her hair bedecked (शबल-chequered) with यूथिका flowers." स्थिरयौवना "Of stable, enduring, abiding youthfulness." सुखालोका Agreeable, pleasant to look at." दूरालोके स्थिता "Has she stood within your distant sight ?" i. e. have you seen her even from afar ? Mark the alliteration.

IV. 24. 1. स्निग्धमन्द्रेण "Sweet and deep." समाश्वासित: "Reassured, comforted." प्रियोपलंभशंसिना "Intimating his having come across my beloved."

IV. 25. नाग "An elephant." दानम् (i) liberality, charity. (ii) The ichor flowing down from the temples of an elephant. अव्युच्छिन्नपृथुप्रवृत्ति (i) Proceeding uninterruptedly and in abundance; (ii) flowing down uninterruptedly and in abundance or profusely. अर्थिषु (i) In regard to suppliants; (ii) in regard to the bees. वशा "A mate." सर्वं माम् अनु ते "Everything belonging to you resembles mine."

IV. 25. 4. उपत्यका–अद्रेः आसन्ना भूमिः "The precincts of a mountain." कथमन्धकारः etc... अवलोकयामि–These words do not appear in Mr. Pandit's text. But their presence is absolutely necessary, as otherwise the words हन्त etc. become quite abrupt. शतह्रदा "Lightning."

IV. 26. अल्पकुचान्तरा–अल्पं कुचयोः अन्तरं यस्याः "Having very little space between the breasts. i. e. with fully developed breasts." The variant अल्पभुजान्तरा does not give a good sense. पर्वसु संनता "Having well-rounded and fleshy joints." इदं वनान्तरम् "This forest-region." अनंगपरिग्रहम्– "Which Cupid has made his residence," "Which is the property of Cupid," and which must therefore be very beautiful. परिग्रह "Property." पृथुनितम्ब "Having extensive sides or slopes."

IV. 27. This stanza contains the question of the King, as also the reply given by the mountain in the form of an echo. In the first case it is to be read with an interrogative intonation. "The question is मया विरहिता रामा त्वया दृष्टा ? The answer is: त्वया विरहिता रामा मया दृष्टा ।

IV. 27. 1. यथाक्रमम् "Just as I said." प्रियतरम् "Something more agreeable." गिरिनदी "Mountain torrent." तरंगवातम् आसेविष्ये "I shall enjoy the breeze passing or blowing over the waves (towards me)." नवाम्बुकलुषाम् "Turbid or muddy with its new waters."

IV.28. भ्रूभंग "Arching of the eyebrows in anger." क्षुभित "Frightened." संरंभशिथिलम् "Loosened or disordered through hurry and confusion." आविद्धम् "With uneven steps, crookedly, tortuously." बहुशः स्खलितमभिसंधाय (i) "Thinking again and again of (brooding over) my offensive conduct." (ii) "With reference to, on account of, the many interruptions (the rocks in the bed)." असहना "Unforgiving, relentless." The last line contains the conclusion proceeding from the considerations given in the first three lines. We should supply तथा "Therefore" before नदीभावेन, to correspond with यथा "Since" in line 3.

IV. 29. प्रणयभंगपराङ्मुखचेतसः "Whose mind is averse to any breach of faithful love." प्रणयभंग = भावस्खलितानि in IV. 12 above.

IV. 29. 2. समुद्राभिसारिणी (i) "Flowing towards the sea," (ii) going up to meet the sea (her lover) like an अभिसारिका." अनिर्वेदप्राप्याणि श्रेयांसि । निर्वेदप्राप्याणि न भवन्ति. "Good fortune or happiness is not be attained by sorrowing or by despendency. Cf. अनिर्वेदः श्रियो मूलम् ।. After the words सुनयना तिरोभूता, the Northern Recension has the stanza अभिनवकुसुमस्तबकित etc. which we have given in full in the Introduction, p. XII.

IV. 30. घर्मान्तशंसि "Indicating the close of the hot season." असमग्रकेसरविषमम् "Uneven owing to the filaments not being fully developed." शिखाभरणम् "Ornaments for the hair (शिखा)." The red कदम्ब blossoms in the rainy season.

IV. 31. कृष्णशारच्छविः "Having a dark, variegated complexion." कटाक्षः "Side-glance."

IV. 31.1. अवधीरयन्निव "As if disdaining to hear my suit."

IV. 32. Cf. Raghu, IX. 55. भुग्न "Turned, bent."

IV. 32.1. हंहो = आमन्त्रणे. Vocative particle.

IV. 33. सुभगं वीक्ष्यते "Looks charming or attractive."

वीक्ष्यते = दृश्यते । With our reading वीक्षते the meaning would be "Looks in a charming manner."

IV. 33. 3. शिलाभेद " The cleft of a rock."

IV. 34. प्रभालेपी " Surrounded with lustre, casting radianee. " आमिषलव: " A piece of flesh." गगनमभिवृष्टम् " The sky has rained down." काटयवेम reads गहनमभिवृष्टम् " This forest-site is drenched on all sides by rain." स्तबक " Bunch, cluster." यमुद्धर्तुम् etc. The gem sent forth its bright rays in every direction and the poet fancies that the sun is eadeavouring to lift up that jewel with his hands (कर-rays).

IV. 35. अधिवासितायाम् " Perfumed or scented with मंदार flowers." अस्रोपहतम् " Soiled with tears."

IV. 36. संगमनीय इति=संगमनीयो नाम । शैलसुताचरणरागयोनि: । शैलसुताया: पार्वत्या: चरणयो: राग: योनि: उत्पत्तिकारणं यस्य । " Produced from the red lac applied to the feet of पार्वती." आवहति " Brings about, effects."

IV. 36. 2. मृगचारी मुनि: भगवान् " Some revered ascetic living the life of a deer " i. e. feeding upon grass and roaming about like a deer. काटयवेम reads मृगचर्मधारी.

IV. 37. विलम्ममध्यया " Having a slender waist." Cf. कुमारसंभव I, 39. मध्येन सा वेदिविलग्नमध्या । Ranganatha reads निमग्नमध्यया. But as निमग्न means " Sunk, depressed " and not " Slender," it cannot be applied to the waist.

IV. 37. 3. मनोरमा " Gladdener of my heart."

IV. 38. धौताधरा " Having her lower lip washed (by tears)." स्वकालविरहात् " On account of the passing away of its season or flowering-time." विश्रान्तपुष्पोद्गमा " Without flowers." चिन्तामौनमास्थिता practising or resorting to silence on account of anxiety." चण्डी "That irascible woman." अवधूय "Having slighted me."

IV. 38. 2. परिष्वङ्गप्रणयी "Desirous of an embrace, longing for an embrace."

तत्स्थाने एव i.e. the creeper vanishes and Urvashi appears in its place.

IV. 38. 5. निर्वृतम् "overjoyed, delighted" विश्वासः न अस्ति "I cannot believe it."

IV. 39. समर्थये "I think or fancy or believe." प्रियां प्रति = प्रियाविषये "In regard to, as having reference to, my beloved." अन्यथा परिवर्तते "Turns out otherwise." This refers to the various disillusionments in regard to Urvashi, that Pururavas has had in his search of her. vide IV. 1. IV.7 IV. 14 etc.–विनिद्रे "Opened." स्पर्शविभावितप्रियः–स्पर्शेन विभाविता निश्चिता प्रिया येन सः। "Who has known definitely that it is his beloved by the (peculiar) touch (of her body)."

IV. 40. तमसि "Darkness, gloom, stupor." गतासुना–गताः असवः (प्राणाः) यस्य सः, तेन। "A dead person.' चेतना "Consciousness, sentiency."

IV. 40, 1. अभ्यन्तरकरणया–अभ्यन्तराणि करणानि यस्याः सा। "Having the senses lying hidden or concealed within." Urvashi means, although her outward form was changed into a creeper, she retained her inner consciousness intact and could preceive all that the King did in her absence.

IV. 40. 7. इदं तावत्प्रसीदतु महाराजः।=इदं तावत् क्षन्तुं प्रसीदतु महाराजः। "May Your Majesty please to pardon me this." The transitive use of प्र + सीद् is remarkable indeed.

IV. 40. 9. प्रसादयितव्यः "To be implored for pardon." सबाह्यान्तःकरणः "Together with the internal and external organs." अन्तरात्मा "My inmost soul." प्रसन्नः "Is overjoyed delighted, pleased."

IV. 40. 15. शाश्वतं कुमारव्रतम् "Perpetual celibacy." कुमारव्रतम् = ब्रह्मचर्यम् ॥ गन्धमादनकच्छः "The bordering region or outskirts of the गन्धमादन grove," विधिः "Rule, restriction prohibitive order." It is the same as the देवतासमय appearing in IV. 40. 25.

IV. 40. 25. देवतासमयम् ', The rule or prohibitive condition laid down by the diety (viz. कुमार कार्तिकेय). अगृहीतानुनया "Not accepting i. e. despising your solicitations."

IV. 41. रतिखेदसुप्तम् "Fallen into sleep on account of the fatigue or exhaustion caused by amorous enjoyment." सहेथाः potential "How could you have borne" that is to say 'If it were not that your separation from me was due to your metamorphosis into a creeper.'

इदं तद् "This thing here," referring to the संगमनीय jewel which he shows to Urvashi. त्वत्संगमनिमित्त मुनेः उपलभ्य = त्वत्संगमनिमित्तत्वेन मुनेः सकाशात् ज्ञात्वा । "Having learnt from the ascetic that this was the means of your union (with me)" यथाकथितम् "As related by you, as said by you." This refers to the words of Urvashi in IV. 40. 25 गौरीचरणसंभवं मणिं विना ततो न मोक्ष्यते ।

IV. 41. 6. प्रकृतिस्था "Restored to my former state."

IV. 41. 7. एवमेव "In this very position of the body."

IV. 42. Construe: ललाटनिहितस्य मणेः स्फुरता रागेण विच्छुरितम् इदं ते मुखं बालातपरक्तकमलस्य श्रियम् उद्वहति । स्फुरता रागेण विच्छुरितम् "Cavered with the gleaming (literally, "vibrating, flashing.") redness. बालातप "Morning sunshine." कमल "a white lotus."

IV. 42. 3. मद्यम् असूयन्ति "Might feel jealous about

me." since I have led you away from your city for such a long time.

IV. 43. अचिरप्रभा "Lightning." विलसितैः "Flashes." सुरकार्मुकम् = सुरधनुः "Rain-bow." सुरकार्मुकम् एव अभिनवचित्राणि तैः शोभते इति । तादृशेन । विमानतां गमितेन "Transformed into a celestial car (balloon)." खेलगमने "Oh you possessed of graceful gait."

In making Pururavas request Urvashi in this manner the poet evidently wishes to impress upon the reader's mind that although Urvashi has behaved herself so long just like a mortal, she is after all a nymph—a divine being—capable of working any miracles; that in other words, she is too much of a nymph to be a woman, as Prof. Ryder remarks.

ACT V.

[Unlike the preceding three Acts, the fifth Act has no introductory scene. Nor are there any sub-scenes. The whole of the act forms one continuous scene in the King's palace.

From a brief soliloquy of विदूषक at the beginning we learn that King Pururavas has come back to his capital with his beloved Urvashi after a rather prolonged honey-moon, and that he is quite happy now all these many years in every respect, except that he has no issue. Just then a great commotion is set afoot in the palace in as much as the much-valued संगमनीय gem has been snatched off by a vulture. The vulture is still seen whirling round in the sky with the gem in its mouth.

and the King is almost on the point of shooting it down when it flies away beyond the range of sight. The King is greatly worried by the loss of the gem. At this juncture the Chamberlain brings the report that the vulture in question was found dead transfixed with an arrow, and hands over to the King the gem and the arrow. The King reads the owner's name inscribed on the arrow and is extremely surprised to find that the arrow belongs to one Ayus—son of King Pururâvas and Urvashi. The King is much perplexed to know when and how Urvashi could possibly have given birth to a son without his knowledge, seeing that he has never been away from her all these many years except on the occasion of the नैमिषीय sacrifice long ago. He is also at a loss to know, why on earth Urvashi should have concealed from him the fact of her having given birth to a son as well as the son himself. Just then a Tapasi (called Satyavati), belonging to the hermitage of the sage च्यवन, is introduced along with a boy. The Tapasi tells the King that the boy accompanying her is none else but the King's son Ayus, who was responsible for shooting down the vulture. She further tells the King, how it was Urvashi herself who, for some unknown reason, had entrusted her son Ayus to her care immediately after his birth and how Ayus was brought up with paternal care and affection and educated in all the civil and military sciences and arts by the sage Chyavana. She says in continuation that on that particular day Ayus violated the discipline of the hermitage by shooting down a vulture and that therefore, the sage च्यवन, no longer wishes to retain him with himself. She has therefore come there to hand over the boy Ayus to Urvashi and wants to see her in that very connection. Urvashi is accordingly sent for and comes in a short time. She is greatly surprised and no less delighted to find her child, now grown up into a fine boy, sitting by the side of Pururavas. The King, Urvashi and Ayus greet one another. The Tapasi now explains to Urvashi the reason why she has deemed it fit to return the boy Ayus to her and then takes her leave. Urvashi then explains in detail to the King why she has so long concealed her son from him. Her only object in doing so was to prolong as much as possible the period of her stay with the King, for, as she tells him now, Indra had allowed her to stay with Pururavas only until the latter should behold the face of his son born of Urvashi. As this has happened now she must leave the King immediately and return to heaven. The King is extremely grieved at the prospect of his separation from Urvashi and makes up his mind to resign his throne to his son Ayus and retire to forest-life, though much against the latter's wish. He forthwith issues orders for the coronation of Ayus as King. Just then, however, Narada comes down from the sky with a message from Indra that Pururavas should not resign his sceptre and sword as his assistance is likely to be required in the near future by the Gods in connection with an impending war with the demons, and that further in consideration of these likely services, Indra is pleased to ordain that Urvashi might stay with Pururavas for life. Both Pururavas and Urvashi are extremely delighted to hear this message from Indra. Narada then performs, at the wish of Indra, as he says, the ceremony of installing Prince Ayus into the position of heir-apparent (युवराज). All shower their blessings upon the young prince and the play is rounded off with a prayer for compatibility and reconciliation between wealth and learning.]

V. o. 9. नन्दनवनप्रमुखेषु देवतारण्येषु. In IV. o. 22, we were told that Pururavas and Urvashi passed there honey-moon in the गन्धमादन grove. The scene of the fourth Act is the Gandhamadana grove. So one should expect to get here गन्धमादनप्रमुखेषु instead of नन्दनवनप्रमुखेषु. ससत्कारोपचाराभिः प्रकृतिभिः अनुरज्यमानः "Highly pleased with his subjects who are honouring him with respectful homage (उपचार)." प्रकृति f. plural. "The subjects of a state." तिथिविशेषः "A special day, a peculiarly sacred day." देवीभिः सह Ranganatha has the singular देव्या। उपकार्या f. "A tent." Cf. रघुवंश XVI. 73. अनुलेपनमाल्ये अग्रभागी "The first sharer in the perfumed pastes and flowers." अनुलेपन means any perfume like sandal, yellow pigment, saffron etc. reduced to the form of a thick paste. माल्य "A flower" "Flowers collectively." अनुपलेपनं च माल्यं च अनुपलेपनमाल्यम् (a समाहारद्वन्द्व compound). The विदूषक is a Brahmin and a personal friend of the King. He, therefore, rightly claims to have a share in the scents and flowers used by the King, and further, to receive it, not after the King has finished his toilet, but while he is still doing it.

V. o. 10. तालवृन्ताधारे निक्षिप्य "Having placed it upon a fan or basket made of palm-leaves" तालवृन्त (n) means a fan made of palm-leaves. दुकूलोत्तरच्छदे। "Covered with a piece of white silk" दुकूलम् उत्तरच्छदः (covering) यस्य। अभ्यन्तरविलासिनी "Dearest wife" i. e. उर्वशी. अभ्यन्तर "Intimate, dearest." मौलिरत्नयोग्यः "Fit to be worn as the jewel in the crown (मौलि)," i. e. " Which was used as the jewel in the crown." आमिषशंकिना The vulture mistook the jewel for a bit of bloody meat, because it appeared unusually red against the back-ground of the white silken cloth.

V. o. 25. अत्याहितम् " Misfortune, mishap." " What a mishap !" परं बहुमतः " Highly prized or valued." असमाप्तनेपथ्यः । असमाप्तं नेपथ्यं प्रसाधनं यस्य । " Who has not finished his toilet," i. e. " Without finishing his toilet."

सावेगपरिजनः " With his attendants in a hurry, or in a confused state of mind, or agitated."

V. 1. आत्मनो वधम् आहर्ता " Bringing on i. e. courting his own death." It would seem from this as also from the प्रवेशक in Shakuntala Act VI, that theft of costly things was capitally punished in the days of कालिदास. विहगतस्करः । विहगः एव तस्करः । " The thief of a bird," " The winged. thief." तदेव प्रथमं, तत्प्रथमं, स्तेयम् । " The first theft." गोप्तुः गृहे " In the house of the protector (of mankind i. e. the King)."

V. 1. 3. मुखकोटिलग्नहेमसूत्रेण-मुखकोट्यां लग्नं हेमसूत्रं यस्य । " Whose golden thread or chain is caught in the point of his beak (मुखकोटि lit. " The point of the mouth " i. e. the beak). आकाशम् आलिखन्निव " As if drawing or tracing lines in the sky." The gem, as it was being carried by the bird swiftly in the sky, cast about its red light in the form of shooting rays and so the bird appeared to draw, as it were, red lines on the surface of the sky.

V. 2. आलंबित "Held. caught." मण्डलचारशीघ्रः । मण्डलाकारेण यः चारः (संचारः) तत्र शीघ्रः । "Moving or flying rapidly in circles." Ranganatha reads "मण्डलशीघ्रचारः"

तद्रागरेखावलयं तनोति "Draws or describes a circle of the red lustre of the jewel." अलातचक्रप्रतिमम् "Resembling the circle described by a fire-brand (अलातम्) which is rapidly turned round."

धनुर्ग्राहिणी यवनी—Ionian Greek girls were employed as servants in the courts of kings in ancient India. In the Shakuntala also (Act II) we find that King Dushyanta's retinue consists of several Ionian Greek girls and in the sixth Act of the same drama we have an Ionian maiden whose duty is to carry the bow of the King wherever he goes.

V. 2. 7. दक्षिणान्तेन "In the southern direction," "Towards the south." शासनीयः "Fit to be punished," "A culprit." कुणपभोजनः "Corpse-eater, carrion-eater." कुणपः or कुणपम् "A corpse."

V. 3. प्रभापल्लवितेन (प्रभया पल्लवितः (संजातपल्लवः) प्रभापल्लवितः तेन)=प्रभया विस्तृतेन। "Increased in size by its effulgence." The idea is that the gem appeared swollen as it were on account of the rays it emitted in all directions. दिङ्मुखस्य अवतंसकम् "An ornament for (the face of) the quarter of the sky in which the bird is flying." अशोकस्तबक "A bunch or cluster of अशोक flowers," which are red in colour.

V. 3. 3. हस्तावापः "An arm-guard." It is a leather band for protecting the arm against the strokes of the bow-string.

V. 3. 4. बाणपथः "The range of an arrow, bow-shot." क्रव्यभाजनः-कुणपभोजनः in V. 2. 7. above. क्रव्यम् "Raw flesh, carrion."

V. 4. मणिविशेषः "The excellent gem." लोहितांशः "The

planet Mars." It is so called because of its reddish appearance. परुष "Thick dark." घनच्छेद "A piece or patch of a cloud." संयुक्त "Closely attached to i. e. concealed behind." मद्वचनात् "By my order, at my command," "In my name." नागरिक: "Chief police officer of the city, the Kotwal." निवासवृक्षाश्रयी "Sitting upon its perching tree." विचीयताम् "Let him be searched out."

V. 1. 7. कुत्र गतः भवतः शासनात् मोक्ष्यते "Going where can he escape from your chastisement ?" i. e. where can he go so as to escape your punishment ?

V. 5. प्रियया supply सह. संगमितः = संयोजितः

V. 5. 1. परिगतार्थं कृ "To inform a person of something," "To acquaint one with something."

V. 6. वध्यः "Doomed or condemned to death." मार्गणतां गतेन "Transformed into an arrow." प्राप्यापराधोचितम् "Having received or met with the punishment which he deserved for his crime." The word शासनम् must be supplied after अपराधोचितम । समौलिरत्नः "Together with the crest jewel,"

V. 6. 3. पेटक (m. n.) "A safe."

V. 6. 7. नामांकितः "Bearing a name upon it." वर्णविचारक्षमा "Able to decipher or recognize or make out the letters." We know from III. 1, that the कञ्चुकिन् is an old man.

V. 6. 10. अनुवाच्य "Reading to himself." सापत्यतां रूपयति This is a very strange direction. One fails to see how this piece of acting was done so as to convey to the audience an idea of the King's fatherhood !

V. 11. नियोगम् अशून्यं कृ "To go about or attend to one's business." This is a clever device to withdraw a character from the stage, when its presence is no longer necessary.

V. 6. 14. प्रहर्तुः "Of the striker."

V. 7. ऐलसूनोः पुरूरवसः पुत्रस्य । ऐल=पुरूरवस् who was the son of इला by बुध. धनुर्भृत् "An archer, bowman." प्रहर्तुः द्विषदायुषाम् "The destroyer of the lives of his enemies."

V. 7. 2. संतान (m. n.) "Progeny, offspring."

V. 7. 3. अन्यत्र नैमिषेयसत्त्रात् "Except on the occasion of a sacrifice in the नैमिष forest." सत्त्र is a sacrifice lasting from 13 to 100 days. नैमिषम् is the name of a sacred forest in which sacrifices used to be performed in ancient times and in which सौति narrated the महाभारत and the पुराण्s to the holy sages. The name is thus derived यतस्तु निमिषेणेदं निहतं दानवं बलम् । अरण्येऽस्मिंस्ततस्तेन नैमिषारण्यसञ्ज्ञितम् ॥ गर्भव्यक्तिः "Sign or revelation of pregnancy." आलक्षिता "Marked, noticed." प्रसूतिः "Offspring, progeny, issue." This refers to संतानेन occurring in V. 7. 1. Pururavas means to say that in the first place he knows of only one occasion when he was separated from Urvashi, viz. when he performed a sacrifice in the नैमिष forest. How could then Urvashi have given birth to a child without his knowledge? In the second place, even supposing that Urvashi was delivered of a child just when Pururavas was staying away from her in connection with the नैमिषीयसत्त्र, how could he have failed to notice any decided signs of pregnancy before that?

V. 8. आविल "Dark" (मलिन). पयोधराग्रम् "Nipple." Ranganatha also records the variant "आनीलचूचुकाग्रम्", which means the same as our reading. लवलीदलपाण्डुराननच्छायम्—लवलीदलमिव पाण्डुरा आननच्छाया यस्मिन् तत् ॥ आननच्छाया "Complexion of the face." लवली is a kind of tree with pale-green and whitish leaves. तानि दिनानि "During those days." This is Accusative of time. We get a variant कतिचिद् अहानि "For a few days." अलसेक्षणम् "With dull, languid eyes." The words किं तु show that Pururavas regards these signs as only superficial and not decided or certain.

V. 8. 3. Vidushaka means to say that the Apsarases are mysterious in their ways and habits and that they cannot be judged by human standards. It is therefore wrong for the King to wonder why he could not see any definite sign of pregnancy in her.

V. 8. 6. कः देवतारहस्यानि तर्कयिष्यति । "Who can unravel the mysteries of divine beings?"

V. 8. 10. तापसी "A female ascetic."

V. 8. 18. तत्रभवान् क्षत्रियकुमारकः "The venerable prince of the warrior-class." गृध्रलक्ष्यवेधी "Which pierced its mark viz. the vulture." अर्धनाराचः "A crescent-shaped arrow" i. e. "An arrow having a semi-circular edge."

V. 9. बाष्पायते "Sheds or emits tears." This is a denominative from the word बाष्प, which means "Tears," according to पाणिनि III. 1. 16. बाष्पोष्मभ्यामुद्वमने ॥ दृष्टिः "Eye." वात्सल्यबन्धि-वात्सल्यं बध्नातीति । "Full of affection." मनसः प्रसादः (जायते) "My mind becomes calm or tranquil; becomes gratified." प्रसादः "Calmness, composure, serenity of mind."

काटयवेम reads "वहति प्रसादम् ।" for "मनसः प्रसादः" संजातवेपथुभिः "Seized with tremor." उज्झितधैर्यवृत्तिः "Giving up all patience, firmness of mind or self-control." अदयम् "In a cruel merciless manner" i. e. "forcibly or powerfully."

V. 9. 1. एवम् "Thus" i. e. "Here, in this place."

V. 9. 6. विस्तारयिता "Lengthener," "extender," "increaser." औरस: संबन्ध: "Paternal relation."

V. 10. हार्दम् "Affection, love." इदम् (to be construed with हार्दम्) "Such, so great." उत्संगवर्धितानाम् "Brought up on the lap," "Grown up on the lap."

V. 10. 7. जातमात्र: "As soon as born." मम हस्ते न्यासीकृत: "Was entrusted to me, was committed to my care." जातकर्मादि विधानम् "Sacred rites such as the birth ceremony." गृहीतविद्य: "Having mastered all the learning." अभिविनीत: "Was instructed or trained in." धनुर्वेद "The science of archery."

V. 10. 10. सनाथ: "Furnished or equipped or provided with a protector."

V. 10. 13. आश्रमविरुद्धम् "Contrary to (the rules or discipline of) the hermitage."

V. 10. 17. किल "As they say " for the तापसी had not actually seen it herself. गृहीतामिष: "Holding flesh in its mouth." This flesh was in fact the संगमनीय jewel as we saw above in V. o. 26. लक्ष्यीकृत: बाणस्य "Was made the target of his arrow" i. e. was shot down with an arrow.

V. 10. 23. निर्यातय "Return, make over." हस्तन्यासम् "The thing placed in your hands i. e. entrusted to your charge."

V 10. 25. आसनम् अनुग्रह् "To favour a seat, to oblige a seat i. e. to be pleased to take a seat."

V. 11. सर्वांगीण: "Pervading the whole of the body with a thrilling ecstasy of joy," किल, "I have heard it said." तेन "Therefore." उपगतेन "By coming near me." The past, pass. partic. उपगत is used here as a noun in the sense of "Approaching." माम् is to be construed with आह्लादयस्व ।

V. 11.4. अशंकित: "Without any fear.

V. 11. 6, The विदूषक means to say that there is no reason why his sight should frighten Ayus, since he looks neither better nor worse than a monkey (शाखामृग) with which Ayus is already familiar in the course of his forest residence.

V. 11. 16. शिखण्डक: means "The tuft of hair on the crown of the head." सत्यवतीसूचित: "Indicated by (the presence of) सत्यवती (the तापसी)."

V. 12. त्वदालोकनतत्परा "Eager or impatient to see you" or "Fixing her gaze upon you." स्नेहप्रस्रवनिर्भिन्नम् "Saturated or wetted through and through with the flow of affection," i. e. with the milk oozing from her breasts owing to her affection for her son. निर्भिन्न literally means "Broken, pierced through." स्तनांशुकम् "Breast-garment."

V. 12. 2. प्रत्युद्गच्छ "Rise up to receive."

V. 12. 5. बहुमता "Highly esteemed."

V. 12. 10. पितरम् आराधयिता "The gladdener or delighter of thy father." The genitive is prohibited by Panini II. 3. 69. न लोकाव्ययनिष्ठाखलर्थतृनाम् ।

V. 12, 11. पुत्रवत्यै "To the blessed mother of the son." There is a peculiar appropriateness in the King's addressing उर्वशी in this manner now.

V. 12. 16. कवचहर: " Of an age fit for bearing the heavy armour upon the body." Vide पाणिनि III.2.10. वयसि च । The form would be कवचहार: if age is not meant. विसर्जयितुम् used in a passive sense "To be dismissed." उपरुध्यते "Is interfered with."

V. 12. 21. अवितृष्णा = सतृष्णा "Desirous." उपरोद्धुम् "To come in your way and cause you inconvenience," "To detain you." पुनर्दर्शनाय Cf. I. 15. 15. above.

V. 12. 24. मां प्रणिपातय "Convey or present my salutations."

V. 12. 18. पूर्वस्मिन्नाश्रमे = ब्रह्मचर्ये । द्वितीयम् = गृहस्थाश्रमम् । अध्यासितुम् "To enter upon, to step into."

V. 13. यः सुप्तवान् who used to sleep. कण्डूयन "Scratching." जातकलापम् "Who has grown his plumage." मणिकण्ठक-the name of the peacock.

V. 14. पौलोमी=शची She was the daughter of the demon पुलोम. पुरन्दरः=इन्द्रः "The destroyer of the enemies' forts" पुरं शत्रूणां नगराणि दारयतीति पुरंदरः । Cf. रघुवंश III. 23.

V. 14. 1. रोदिति–"Weeps" i. e. silently and inaudibly. Hence it is that विदूषक speaks of her as अश्रुमुखी "Shedding tears, having her face suffused with tears."

V. 15. Construe: हे सुन्दरि वंशस्थितेरधिगमात् यम महति प्रमोदे उपपन्ने (सति) पीनोन्नतस्तनविसर्पिभिः अस्रैः मुक्तावलीविरचनापुनरुक्तिम् आनयन्ती किं प्ररुदिता असि । वंशस्थितेः अधिगमात् "On account of the attainment of the stability of the family" वंशस्थिति means "Stability of the family," hence "What brings about or leads to the stablity of the family i. e. a son who perpetuates the family." मुक्तावलीविरचनापुनरुक्तिम् आनयन्ती "Bringing about the superfluousness or repetition of the pearl-necklace" i. e. causing another necklace by means of the continuously flowing tears and thus making the pearl necklace superfluous. Cf. III. 7. 7. above: अभिव्यक्तायां चन्द्रिकायां किं दीपिकापौनरुक्त्येन । प्ररुदिता = रोदितुम् आरब्धा "Begun to weep."

V. 15. 5. विस्मृतास्मि that is to say the समय or condition referred to in the following sentence and in V. 15. 17. below. महेन्द्रसंकीर्तनेन "By the mention of Indra's name;" this refers to V. 14, where जयन्त, शची and इन्द्र are mentioned. आयासयति "Pains or torments me."

V. 15. 7. गृहीत "Captivated, borne away."

V. 15. 18. वंशकरस्य "Of a son, the perpetuator of the family." महाराजवियोगभीरुतया–this was the real reason why Urvashi kept away her son in the आश्रम. विद्यागमनिमित्तम् this is the pretext under which she entrusted her son to the care of सत्यवती, the तापसी. अप्रकाशम् "Secretly." एतावान् "This much," "Thus far and no farther." संवासः "Residence, dwelling with."

V. 15. 24. सुखप्रत्यर्थिता "Hostility or adverseness to the happiness of human beings."

V. 16. आश्वासितस्य "Comforted, gratified." Mark the force of the particle नाम which here means "Just, no sooner than."

व्यावर्तितातपरुजः । व्यावर्तिता आतपेन (=आतपकृता) रुक् यस्य । "Whose suffering caused by the summer-heart has been removed or allayed." वैद्युतः अग्निः "Lightning-fire."

V. 16. 2. अर्थः "Good fortune" viz. सुतोपलब्धि. अनर्थानुबन्धः "Followed by a series or succession of mishaps or misfortunes." अनुबन्धः "A series or a chain or a succession." This refers to the loss of Urvashi which the विदूषक thinks, is sure to be followed by the King's retirement to the forest as a recluse. गन्तव्यम् the potential pass. partic. is used here in the sense of the Future, = तत्रभवान् गमिष्यति ।

V. 16. 6. मामपि etc. Urvashi means to say, that this is another link in the chain of misfortunes alluded to by the विदूषक in V. 16. 2. that the King is likely to misunderstand her in that he will think that Urvașhi left him the moment that her son was well-educated and was restored to the King, as if her selfish object was fulfilled, and as if it was no longer necessary for her to remain with him.

V. 17. सुलभवियोगा परवत्ता "Dependence or servitude in which separation from one's beloved is only too easy or natural and to be expected at any time." परवत्त ("Dependent") तस्य भावः परवत्ता । आयुषि न्यस्तराज्यः । "Entrusting the government of the kingdom, delivering the charge of administration, to Ayus." विचरितमृगयूथानि "Inhabited by herds of deer," "Wherein herds of deer roam about. "The King assures Urvashi in this stanza that he will not at all misunderstand or think unkindly of her as she fears he will, for he is only too painfully aware of the wrechedness of the state of servitude.

V. 17. 1. पुंगवधारितायां धुरि "To the yoke drawn by a mighty bull or steer." दम्यः "A young bullock who is unbroken to the yoke and who requires a good deal of training and experience before he can be safely harnessed to a carriage."

V. 18. गन्धद्विपः "Scent-elephant." गन्धप्रधानो द्विपः । His ichor or rut emits such a strong odour that other elephants run away at its smell, being afraid of encountering him. Cf. यस्य गन्धं समाघ्राय न तिष्ठन्ति प्रतिद्विपाः । स वै गन्धगजो नाम नृपतेर्विजयावहः ॥ शमयति "Subdues, puts down." कलभः "A young cub." वेगोदग्रम् । वेगेन उदग्रम् "Deadly or virulent bv its circulation; वेगः means the circulation or taking effect of poison." स्वकार्यसहो भरः "pre-eminence which enables one to discharge one's duty or task howsoever difficult." जात्यैव "By one's very birth" जन्मनैव "Rooted in ones very blood, not in one's age." Cf. Raghuvamsha XI. तेजसां हि न वयः समीक्ष्यते। अमात्यपरिषद् "The council of ministers." संभ्रियताम् "Let preparations be made for." सं+भृ "To bring things together."

V. 18, 4. दृष्टिप्रविघातं रूपयन्ति "Show as if their eyes were dazzled."

V. 18. 5. निरभ्रे "In the cloudless sky." विद्युत्संपातः "Flash of lightning, descent of lightning."

V. 19. गोरोचनायाः निकषः गोरोचना निकषः। स इव पिङ्गः जटाकलापः यस्य। गोरोचना is a kind of bright yellow pigment derived from the urine or bile or the head of a cow. निकषः means "A touchstone." It secondarily means a streak or line on a touchstone." Cf. IV. 1 कनकनिकषस्निग्धा etc. शशिकलामलवीतसूत्रः। शशिकला इव अमलं वीतसूत्रं यस्य। वीतसूत्रम्=उपवीतम्=यज्ञोपवीतम् "The sacred thread." मुक्तागुण etc. मुक्तागुणानां ये अतिशयाः (उत्कर्षाः) तै संभृता मण्डनश्रीः यस्य। संभृत "Heightened, enhanced." मुक्तागुणातिशय "Excellent wreaths of pearls." Or अतिशय may be conntected with संभृत, "Extremely heightened or enhanced." This is to be construed with जंगमकल्पवृक्षः हेमप्ररोहः–हेममयाः प्ररोहाः यस्य। Having golden branches." जंगम "In motion." Cf गिरिरिव गतिमान् अपक्षलोपात् III. 3. With this description of the appearance of नारद Cf. शिशुपालवध I. 4–10.

अर्ध्यम् "A respectful offering consisting of water, scents, flowers etc. made to a distinguished guest on his arrival." गंधमाल्यादिसंयुक्तमुदकम् अर्ध्यमुच्यते।

V. 19. 4. अर्हणा "Worship" i.e. "Materials of worship."

V. 19. 5. मध्यमलोक=मर्त्यलोक "The world of mortals."

V. 19. 6. आवर्ज्य "Letting down" scil, the materials of worship." "Offering the materials of worship."

V. 19. 9. अपि नाम एवं स्यात् "Would that it were so."

V. 19. 11. और्वशेयः=उर्वश्याः अपत्यं पुमान् according to पाणिनि IV. 1, 92- तस्यापत्यम्. । Cf. गांगेय, वैनतेय, शाकुन्तलेय etc.

V. 19. 13. विष्टर: "A seat." Cf. V, 10. 25 above.

V. 19. 18. वनगमनाय कृतबुद्धिम् "Resolved to take to the forest." अनुशास्ति "Advises."

V. 19, 21. Construe: त्रिकालदर्शिभिः मुनिभिः भावी सुरासुरसंगरः आदिष्टः। त्रिकालदर्शिभिः "Seeing i. e. able to know the past, the present and the future" भावी "About to take place in the near future." आदिष्ट "Predicted, foretold." सांयुगीनः–संयुगे साधुः "Skilled or well-versed in warfare." See Panini IV. 4. 98. and 92: तत्र साधुः। प्रतिजनादिभ्यः खञ् ।. सहधर्मचारिणी "Partner in the performance of religious duties.

V. 19. 26. अपनीतम् "Removed, extracted." इव is to be construed with शल्यम् "A dart as it were" शल्य here means "the painful thought of the imminent separation."

V. 19. 27. परवान् "Dependent."

V. 20. त्वत्कार्यं कुर्यात् "Should help you." तस्य इष्टम् आचरेः "Should act up to his desire." समेधयति "Causes to blaze," "Supports with splendour." The idea here expressed is that the sun deposits his splendour in the Fire at sun-set. The Fire does the same at sun-rise with reference to the Sun. It is this mutual helpfulness of these two Deities that keeps the world going. Cf. रघुवंश IV. 1; also आदित्यो वा अस्तं यन्नग्निमनु प्रविशति। अग्निं वा आदित्यः सायं प्रविशति। Also मालविकाग्निमित्र I. 13. अतिमात्रभासुरत्वं पुष्यति भानोः परिग्रहादनलः।

संभृत: "Collected, put together." यौवराज्याभिषेक: = यौवराज्याभिषेकसामग्री । "Materials for installation as a crown-prince or heir-apparent."

V. 20. 6. भद्रपीठम् = हेमादिमयपीठम् "A stately seat for auspicious purposes."

V. 20. 8. आवर्ज्य "Pouring down or emptying the contents of the कलशs or jars containing sacred waters." The sprinkling of water (अभिषेक) forms the central and the most important part of the coronation, and it is therefore performed by नारद himself; while Rambha is directed to do the remaining minor ceremony (निर्वर्त्यतां शेषो विधि:)

V. 20. 14. कुलधुरंधर: "Pre-eminent in the family."

V. 21. अमरमुनि: "The immortal or divine sage, the godly sage." बाधन = बुध "Mercury." देव: "His Majesty." गुणै: पितु: अनुरूप: "Worthy of your father by reason of your excellences." अतिशयिनि वंशे "In your exalted family," आशिष: समाप्ता एव "All blessings are indeed already fulfilled, are already attained or realised." Cf. Raghu. V. 34.

V. 22. Construe. उन्नतानां पुरस्तात् स्थिते अस्मिन् तव पितरि, अनाकम्प्यधैर्ये स्थितिमति त्वयि च विभक्ता राजलक्ष्मी: हिमवति जलधौ च व्यस्ततोया गंगा इव इदानीम् अधिकतरं राजते । The expression उन्नतानां पुरस्तात् स्थिते applies to the mountain Himalaya as well as to the King; while स्थितिमति and अनाकम्प्यधैर्ये apply to the Prince आयुम् as also to the Ocean. उन्नतानां पुरस्तात् स्थिते (i) standing at the head of the exalted (ii) standing in the forefront of the lofty. स्थितिमति (i) observing स्थिति or the rules of right conduct (ii) observing i. e, not transgressing the boundary. अनाकम्प्यधैर्ये (i) of unshakable courage (ii) whose calmness is imperturbable. व्यस्ततोया "Having its waters divided or distributed," Cf. Raghuvamsa V 66.

V. 22. 2. पुत्रस्य युवराजश्रिया "The glory of heir-apparentship belonging to your son."

V. 22. 5. साधारण :–" Common. " She means to say that her good fortune was their good fortune also, as the Apsarases were but her sisters. ज्येष्ठमातरम् i. e. the Queen Aushinari.

V. 23. महासेन=कुमार कार्तिकेय who was placed by Indra at the head of the heavenly forces on the occasion of the battle with the demon तारकासुर. सैनापत्ये अभिषिक्तम् " Installed as commander-in-chief " of the army of the Gods. मरुत्वता=इन्द्रेण. सेनापतेः भावः सैनापत्यम् । Vide कुमारसंभव canto XIII.

V. 23. 1. एवम् अनुगृहीतः " Being thus favoured " i. e. by sprinkling upon his head the sacred waters of the coronation ceremony.

V. 23. 2. पाकशासनः । पाकं शास्ति इति । Indra the slayer of a demon called पाक.

भरतवाक्यम्–The final benediction or epilogue at the end of a drama called भरतवाक्य in honour of भरत the founder of Indian Drama.

V. 24. परस्परविरोधिन्योः the hostility between Wealth and Learning is proverbial in Sanskrit Literature. Cf. निसर्गभिन्नास्पदमेकसंस्थमस्मिन् द्वयं श्रीश्च सरस्वती च । रघु० VI. 29. एकसंश्रयदुर्लभम् " Very hard to find in one and the same abode." संगतम् "Union."

After this the Northern Recension has the stanza सर्वस्तरतु दुर्गाणि etc. which we have given in full in the Introduction. p. XII.